THE CARETAKER'S SON
Skip Savage Remembers Old St. Paul

By W. Jack Savage

Printed in the United States of America

ISBN: Softcover   13:978-1986703543
ISBN: E book   10:1986703541

Books by W. Jack Savage

Bumping and Other Stories

More with Cal and Uncle Bill

State Champions

The Petorik Thesis and Tales of the Global West

The Children Shall be Blameless

The High Sky of Winter's Shadows

Imagination: The Art of W. Jack Savage

Forward

_Not every mind can give voice to our memories. In this book, The Caretaker's Son: Skip Savage Remembers Old St Paul", W. Jack Savage (WJS) uses his half-life of 35 years' experience with his on-air writing in broadcasting news. With it, he weaves tales of his Highland Park childhood, so that you can reminisce with him, no matter if you were raised on the East Side or Rice Street or some far off place. His life as actor, educator, broadcaster and Vietnam Vet, gives him a keen sense and perspective of detail, and memory of what it felt like to be a child growing up in St Paul. His memories of the 1950's hearken to streets of kids with their baseball cards, or comic books, of neighbors burning leaves, of paper sales, and his antidotes will bring you home to your own childhood. On a site created by Mark Youngblood, managed by Ron Ciccone and Debra Deutsch Erickson, and full of historically correct information by Jim Sazevich, this Facebook site is filled with memories of Old St. Paul, minn (OSP) children. It is enlightened by Walter Jack Savage's weekly reminiscences compiled in this book. These are poignant and stand out, as does his weekly changing profile artwork that has graced both museum and publications. These create scenes of yesteryear and the future in bright bold colors. Now retired, he fearlessly forges where many of us debate to tread: images of the good and bad of our childhoods. He paints a feverish picture of the best of times with his words, and details the "what-ifs" as well. He and this site have enthralled the St. Paul citizens whose hearts still reside there, whether they now physically do or do not. WJS, as I have referred to him, penned his missives and has invoked for many, their own childhood memories; and his stories sparked recall, sometimes in depth, things we had long forgotten. May his writings collected here, take you on the same journey he has happily allowed many of us to enjoy, over these last few years
.Jean Logajan Day, OSP FB member and friend of WJS.

On a walk through Jack's life and his river city hometown, we meet the people he knew and met on his journey, a look at St. Paul through the eyes of a storyteller who lived it. If you grew up in St. Paul, you won't be able to put it down and it will leave you wanting more.
John Winterhalter

I was the only child of Walter and Barbara Savage and was born late in life to the pair. They were loving and hilarious in good times, and bad. My mother was the best but when my father was laid-off at Union Brass and Metal, my mother went to work and my dad stayed home with me. There were any number of problems that arose from this, but in one sense, I got to know my dad better than a lot of kids my age, well into my teens. One of the ways I got to know him was his lack of exposure to entertainment. He and his brother grew up on lower James and played daily at Palace playgrounds in the late 20's and throughout the depression. There was no TV and those who had money for the movies apparently didn't include my dad. Those films he missed in the theater were on every day and nearly every night in TV re-runs while I was growing up. So over time I was not only his son, I was his TV and movie buddy. In this way, I not only got to know my dad through his strengths (of which he had many), I got to know his sensitivities and proclivity to be brought to tears by films that were made in his formative years that he never saw. Now I am his son, and was reacting to my own emotions at the time as well. *Goodbye Mr. Chips,* the original for which Robert Donet won an Academy Award is a tearjerker certainly, and I remember us both shedding a tear over that one. The worst was when he conceded to knowing a story ahead of time and after a couple of drinks, he would make remarks that let me know what was coming next. My dad was an alcoholic but he was a great guy, a mesmerizing storyteller, and at one time a noted athlete in Old St. Paul both in Cretin High School and in semi-pro sports in football and basketball during the depression. He died while I was on leave from Vietnam after a year and a half of service. His drinking had made his life a nightmare and I was glad his suffering had come to an end. In better days, I had an extraordinary relationship with Walt Savage. For one thing, we were both suckers for violin music in films. I happen to know there are some who would be glad to trade their relationship with their dad, for me with mine.

No matter how small our world was, growing up in St. Paul, if you made that journey as "baby boomers" like we were, the landscape was always changing and as it did, it became a reason to go out of our normal way to investigate. My first such upheaval was the empty lot next to Dave Schreiber's house on Brimhall. We played there a lot and when a new house started to be built, the construction site became a new kind of playground with that great smell of sawdust. When Watson's Appliance store was built on Snelling, Dave and I nearly got picked up by the steam shovel during construction. We used to cut through the orphanage grounds on Randolph on our way to Highland Park or even that field on the south end where we played football. There was also a pond, but when they took down the orphanage, I can't tell you why but I never played there during the demolition. Many of my friends did but not me. Later, I did go down Warwick more often to play in the construction of Derham Hall. That was bittersweet though, because they plowed down the bluff near Warwick and ended the greatest kite-flying site ever known to man. There used to be a big soccer field on Snelling with ice rinks in the winter on the stretch between Highland Parkway and Ford Parkway. They built another reservoir there and the first huge water tower. Taken for all-in-all and in developing the poetic nature of my heart, I suppose I began to look on these changes sadly even as a boy. These were small losses but it was still my neighborhood so I took them personally. The best thing about progress during those years, was the sidewalks. I roller-skated and you couldn't beat the new sidewalks. But we were lucky. We never experienced whole neighborhoods being plowed under like many people did; not in Highland Park anyway.

One of the great things to realize about our childhood is how much fun it could be, even if it wasn't always. Now, take Miller Hospital for example. Over one period it seemed like we went there quite a bit, but kids couldn't go up to the rooms and I stayed out in front. There were two terraces on either side of a broad stairway separated by a cool double chrome handrail in the middle. The terraces were surrounded on three sides by these concrete and brick walls that were fun to crawl over. So if you started at the far end of the one, nearest the top of the stairs, you'd crawl over the wall, drop down on the stairs, run to the chrome handrail, crawl over it, race to the other side and climb back up and crawl over the other wall to the far terrace. Sometimes there were other kids and you'd race from one side to the other. I've written about this before, but it's funny how I can close my eyes and almost feel what it was like to do that, while imagining you were in a war movie or something. When you were a kid it wasn't much fun at the hospital or the beer joint or shopping or waiting for something, anything really, to be over. But it could be, and as antsy as the thought of those things still makes me, it's funny how I can still remember how much fun it was now and then.

While it's true the long cloudy winters of my youth got me down and there was a lot of trouble at home (Mom and Dad separating and all that), there were enough good things going on to keep me on track. At the heart of it though, I remember feeling like I had no choice. When you're a juvenile, you really have no rights and fewer options. That is to say that if you get into trouble, even just a little trouble, you can be kept on probation forever. For me it was being caught riding in a stolen car and basically, from that moment on, all I wanted to do was escape from St. Paul. There were reasons of course why they kept me on probation, excessive absence from school mainly. Once it was clear that until I towed the line I'd never get off probation, my goals changed in a way that did clarify what I had to do; so after a pretty good junior year at Monroe High School, I was all caught up and on track for a senior year on cruise control, so to speak. I also had a job that summer and had saved what I thought was enough money and after three years of seeing him with some regularity, when I came before Judge O'Connell for the final time in the summer of 1965, I was finally ready. I had shown through getting all caught up that I had changed and I said all the right

7

things, so he let me off probation. I went directly from the courthouse that day to the Greyhound Bus station and got on a bus for California. I didn't last long, a few months was all and when I came back home, I enlisted in the Army. That's it really. That's what happened to me in high school and as I've said pretty much ever since, I'd go through Vietnam again before I'd go through the years leading up to it.

On a trip home recently I picked up my four White Castles & fries at the Lexington and University location and parked facing east, just next to the driveway. Where I was sitting, the old Lexington Roller Rink used to be. Ahead of me, I can't remember what was there and this was only last Wednesday. I only remember what was there years ago and it began with the drug store and fountain on the corner; somewhere in the middle, a Best Steak House and adjacent to the alley, that great bowling alley with the lighted bowler rolling his ball down the alley...a sign like none other I'd ever seen. The Dairy Queen is still there I noticed and somewhere behind it, Jose's after hours joint from another era. Around the corner was the Centre Theater where I took the bus to see *Sweet Bird of Youth* for probably the twelfth time that summer. To my right was Sandy's and I can't tell you one thing about what's on any of those spots today, only what they were when Lexington and University was great...to me at least. They're not making movies or writing music aimed at me anymore, but you'd think they'd consult me about the changes to one of the great intersections in St. Paul.

I often forget that world events happened while I was growing up in St. Paul. In October of 1962 the world had its closest brush with nuclear war. I seem to remember hearing something about it on the news but it wasn't until the following Monday that Professor Tigue, our social studies teacher went around the room asking if we realized that the world nearly ended the week before. For the most part, we did not. We were pre-occupied with our lives: teenagers in high school. A year later, President Kennedy was assassinated. That was a shock, but I seem to remember we got over it fairly quickly. In October of 1964 Khrushchev lost his job and, oh yes, Mad Dog Vachon regained the AWA title in wrestling by beating Verne Gagne. The following October, having skipped my senior year in high school, I enlisted in the Army. In October 1966, after having been wounded at Tuy Hoa, I began my last two years in Vietnam being a helicopter door gunner. Four pretty big years in world history, but the weight of my personal world was pretty much all I could bear. If the world wanted to blow up, that was fine with me. Killing President Kennedy was awful but so was high school and sure enough, just when things were looking up, I became a high school dropout just to get into the war. I'd love to say these events shaped me in ways that would have a profound effect on me for the rest of my life, but the truth is they really didn't. I was in high school.

When I was young, if I saw a pretty girl walk by it wasn't unusual for me to find an excuse to go that direction as well. I got busted a couple of times, "why are you following me?" "Oh, ah no, I'm just going over to my friend's house." It was always like that too. I never came out and said, "You're very pretty and I'd like to get a chance to know you." Instead, I was having a fantasy. I was marrying her and raising a family and enjoying all of those things I knew were there to enjoy, even if I wasn't exactly clear on what they were. I followed a girl from Hamline to nearly West 7th Street once. It was just something to do. I mean growing up was in total slow motion. Sometimes it felt like life was never going to happen and all the best stuff was when you grew up...driving around in your own car, women, whatever. When they'd say, "these are the best years of your life" I wanted to say, "are you nuts!" Childhood to me was like doing time. I always wanted to be older. Even the kids on TV were dorks. There was no one under twenty-one I ever wanted to be. That's why I'd dress up in a sport coat and go downtown to a movie or just to walk around. It's why I smoked and later why I drank, to begin with anyway. No, in my day and maybe it was just me, beyond a certain point...twelve or thirteen, all I ever wanted to do was grow up.

Before I ever really did anything in my life, I knew I would fail. I knew the spotlight would be too scary and with everyone looking at me, I'd screw it up. But somewhere in the back of my mind behind all of that, there was a question..."what if I didn't?" It was the sixth inning and my Hilltop Giants Little League baseball team was losing and in the shadow of St. Paul's Highland Tower, the spotlight waited for someone. After saying I didn't want to pitch the first time, coach came out and asked me to. The second time he took the ball from our pitcher's hand and tossed it to me and said, "Skip, pitch", and he walked back into the dugout. There was one out and the bases were loaded with Tigers: THE biggest mouth team in Hilltop Little League and the catcalls began. I threw two balls but somehow threw a strike on the next pitch. I threw five more strikes and struck out the side. That shut the Tigers up real good but they hung on to win. "What if I didn't?" was answered in short order. After that game I went from a good hitting, somewhat quiet second baseman into one of the big mouth Tigers like I had struck out that day. Hilltop Little League taught me a lot about myself and not all of it had to do with baseball.

Counting Randolph and going all the way up to Thomas on Snelling, there used to be ten traffic lights. There may be more now but in the old days, I'm pretty sure it was ten and I have a memory of every one of them. On Jefferson and I've mentioned this before, cars went faster than both Randolph and St. Clair and Porte's was on the corner. St. Clair had the theater, the Broiler, Sorini's, and later Romano's and McGill's Submarine sandwiches. Grand had a barbershop I went to for a while and Macalester College. After Vietnam, I tried to enroll in Macalester twice. The second time they gave me my money back. On Summit, there was Immaculate Heart.

We didn't play them much in Catholic league sports. I don't know why. On Selby was Dewey's, the Park Rec and O'Gara's. There was a pool hall called the Cue and Carom and Towey's Drug Store. Marshal was kind of a mystery intersection with Minneapolis on the left and Central on the right somewhere. Then there was the freeway and then Snelling. If you don't have any history with Snelling and University, I just don't know...Midway Center, The Trend, Wards and the Hamline Theater where I saw *Ben Hur*. I even screwed up my knee playing tennis one time on the courts up by Thomas. After that, I can't say I have many memories until you get to the Fairgrounds and nothing north of it until Uncle John's Pancakes was built. It was before Perkins and since I'm a pancake guy, the coming of Uncle John's was progress for the human race. So let's take a bus ride in your neighborhood. Where were the cool places?

I had a dream early this morning about St. Paul. I grew up in the apartment building on Brimhall and Randolph and over recent years (given my age and everything), I've thought what a kick it would be to live there again. In my dream, my good friend Bill was there and we were sharing the apartment but here's the thing: the place was on the north side of the building, kind of like the "North Pole" side and though we lived together, I evidently wasn't there much and had just come home. Bill had twins for friends, a man and a woman and I was talking to them when I noticed the back lawn had grown to three feet high. I used to mow that lawn and so it immediately occurred to me that this idea of mine wasn't working out too well. Finally, as I couldn't find anything in this kitchen of ours, I asked Bill to make me a cup of coffee. He did and just then I woke up, wondering about the significance of the twins, the overgrown lawn, a back apartment and my inability to make coffee for myself in a place where I lived. So here we go: the twins were nice people but like most people in St. Paul anymore, I didn't know them, Bill did. The significance of the north side apartment was that while it was in my building, it was never on the side of the hallway I would have chosen to live. It just

11

wasn't. The overgrown back lawn is the key. All of the years I'd been away, things undone, untended to and while I was going to cut it, it meant I was not looking forward to hacking through all those years of inattention; and yet Bill's willingness to make me a cup of coffee was a positive and like most cups of coffee, meant that this too could be overcome. It was vivid enough that it was the kind of dream where you wake up taking account: where am I? What's my situation? All I can say is that I'm glad I won't be cutting any grass today.

Growing up in St. Paul I was an optimistic kid. Sure, I didn't have my own room but I had three beds to jump on instead of one, a laundry room to play in in the winter, a big yard to play on in good weather and nobody to tell me I couldn't because my mom and dad were the caretakers. I couldn't have a dog or a cat but I had the best parakeet in the world, no brothers or sisters but "improvisation: thy name is childhood." And while many of us dreamed of an endless summer, my parents loved the four seasons and for a while, so did I. Eventually though, there was an arc to my optimism and my mental health overall. All you needed to do was take a look at my report cards from school to see that I was a bright child whose grades gradually went down during the winter months. Today, it's called "Seasonal Dysfunction Disorder" and I'm sure I had it. I'm certain because during my two and half years in Vietnam, I enjoyed the best mental and emotional health of my life. That would seem to be at odds with my circumstance for being there but I assure you it was true. When I got home again to St. Paul in the fall of 1968, I can't recall a seeing a single sunny day until the following summer and my mood and especially my drinking reflected that change. Today of course, I live in California and come back to St. Paul usually twice a year for a visit. It works for me anyway.

As I can imagine people who were raised near the ocean having a personal relationship in some way with it, I was raised in St. Paul and when it comes to rivers, the Mississippi River takes a back seat to no other. My mother was deathly afraid of me going to the river and so naturally, I went down there as often as I could. The St. Paul side is dredged for the barge traffic and the currant is swift and deadly. The Minneapolis side is not and we played a lot under the Lake Street Bridge, which had a sandy beach. You could walk out in the river to nearly the middle and the water wouldn't be over your head. Having read *Siddhartha* by Hermann Hesse at an early age, the idea that a river is everywhere at once became almost mystical to me and so while I never really enjoyed the river from the St. Paul side (as I might one of our Minnesota lakes), I go back to a single moment when I was about twelve or so. My friend and I went down to the Crosby Lake area and beyond it to the river and I was sitting there just watching the water go by when a barge, huge and silent and so close to the shore I could almost touch it, came by. I can close my eyes and see it again now, and I felt a part of the greater world outside of my St. Paul home for a moment. It was almost as if the barge was everywhere at once as well, and would surely go places I could only imagine. I made plans that day to return to that spot and somehow get aboard that barge in the night and by morning be far, far away. I could tell you I never did that but that's not exactly true because now and then, I still do.

In everyone's experience with their hometown, if it's worth mentioning at all, there comes that one day where things seemed to be looking up in a way that changes you. There was really nothing to compare this to and so after what seemed a lifetime of underachievement, in my mind anyway, I dressed up for my very first news assignment for our short-lived Viking News Network of Brown Institute. There were labor problems at the state level and that took me to the Capitol where a brief news conference with a New York fellow who was called in to arbitrate the matter was taking place. I was there with other real reporters from WCCO and KSTP and others I recognized. I was becoming Jack Savage on the radio but was really still Skip Savage, lately of Dewey's Pit and Paddock on Snelling and Selby and not much else, but I did get a sense of who I could be that day and that was important. I spent nearly ten years on the radio in various places: Thief River Falls, Albert Lea, Mankato, and Cheyenne, Wyoming, and came home with my tail between my legs one time where my good friend, also a Dewey's regular, told me: "No, you're not a part of this anymore. You're a hero to a lot of people here because you went off and made a life for yourself...you're a radio guy now, not a Dewey's guy". In the end, it was a short speech I needed to hear and after that, I got my job back in Cheyenne and eventually wound up in Los Angeles for the last ten of my thirty-five years in broadcasting. But I remember that I was ready to re-embrace my hometown and my old ways without further comment before my friend said what he said that day. I bring it up because we all contribute to each other whether we realize it or not and my friend, though dead for many years now, was thinking of me that day and because he was, the train that was my life got back on the tracks when it might not have otherwise.

Old Fire Station 19 used to be on Highland Parkway right at Snelling, and they had a Coke machine. It was those six ounce Cokes in bottles and they hung by their caps sort of and were on tracks. You'd put in a dime if you had one and pull a bottle along until it got to this buckle and the buckle would open. But if you didn't have a dime, there seemed a way to twist a bottle in a certain way to get it out. I have no idea why the fireman let us play with the thing but we did...often because we played up that way. But we never got a bottle out and it was terrible because on a hot, humid day in the summer, nothing called to you like a cold Coke. We never got upstairs but it seemed like a cool fire station...kind of small and intimate. It's funny...Coke for a dime.

When I think of St. Paul I think of the neighborhoods, and when I think of those neighborhoods I think of the neighborhood theaters.

My mother always claimed my first movie experience was *Peter Pan* down at the Orpheum but I know it was *Island in the Sky,* staring John Wayne at the Randolph Theater at Randolph and Hamline. The Hamline Theater, on the other hand was on Snelling and University and I saw *Ben Hur* there. My neighborhood theater was the St. Clair. If you took the bus and transferred, you could go to the Faust on Dale and University and see a triple feature for 99-cents. I saw *The Bramble Bush, Parrish and Cat On a Hot Tin Roof* there. The Centre on Lexington and University was nice (the White Castle was across the street) and The Midway was way out by the State Fairgrounds. The Highland and Grandview are still there I think, but among those that went away were the Gem, the Dale, the Arcade, the Uptown, and so many others. The neighborhoods were great in St. Paul and everyone having local theaters was part of the reason for that.

There was a time when if you worked in or around Dale and Selby and if you were white, you were considered brave. I bring it up because having been raised in Highland and having gone to Monroe High School, the only blacks I ever saw were at track meets up at Central. By the time I got out of the service, I'd had many good relationships and made good friends with guys who were black, in training and in Vietnam; so when I started driving cab and especially working the short hill as we called it (the Dale and Selby area), I had no problems or fears being a white cab driver in St. Paul. It was summer and a bit humid and I had the window open as I pulled up to Dale going west on Selby. I was high on marijuana most of the time anyway in those days and that day was no different. All of a sudden, I hear footsteps and three of my cab's doors opened at once and four black fellas jumped in. They were breathing hard and very tense for some reason. "Where to?" I asked. "The river," one said. Now before I tell you how this turned out, this is what I thought. For whatever reason these four guys were gonna hurt me real bad and rob me when we got to the river. I wasn't feeling paranoid at all. The fact was four tense individuals who happened to be black got in my cab so fast, my mind just sized up the situation in an instant and over the next few blocks, I actually thought about offering them my money right then and hopefully before the beating started or maybe even jumping out at one of the lights. It turned out that these guys were from St. Louis and worked on one of the steamboats anchored at the river; they had come up to the neighborhood, made eyes at a local girl, were nearly set upon by local guys and were fleeing from that possibility when they got in my cab. They tipped me five bucks too, and that was good money in 1970. So there I was, a twenty-two year old Vietnam Veteran who'd never had a problem with anybody of color in all his life, certain that I was going to be a victim of four strangers who jumped in my cab simply because they were black. That's a true story and I've never written it down like this. Things are better today, but back then there was an imprint in our minds that we had, whether we knew it or not

I could say my wife woke up back home in the Twin Cities today except that she flew in on the "red-eye" and never slept at all, she said. This marks the last of our June travels which have been considerable, beginning with the Veteran's event in New Mexico and now her going home only three days later. She's from Edina and I'm from St. Paul and we met in Sheridan, Wyoming. The Edina she grew up in was basically farmland back then and I don't think they had a television until she was about eleven. She was one of six kids, while over in St. Paul I was having a different time of it, being an only child. Places other than St. Paul seemed strange to me as a boy and I wondered what language they spoke and what they ate. These questions did nothing to endear these people to me, but it is strange to think of us in terms of being the "two ships that pass in the night." For example, I took the Selby-Lake bus to the Minneapolis Institute of Art for a while and later, Brown Institute. At the same time, she was taking the same bus to the School of Associated Arts on Summit Avenue. Years later, I lived in a small apartment in a mansion right next to that school and even posed for the artists there now and then.

We even had Dewey's Pit and Paddock in common as she went to the old one down by the Cathedral a few times, and I hung around the last one on Selby and Snelling for years. I remember taking the Sheridan, WY job (radio country mornings) out of desperation and she and her business was one of our sponsors. That was 1986 and we've pretty much been together ever since. We each usually come home separately because, well, she's from the suburbs and I'm from St. Paul. That's just the way it goes.

I lived on Brimhall and Randolph in St. Paul and growing up in the 50's, for groceries we shopped at Klein's grocery store on Snelling just south of Randolph. The way my mother told it, of all the children that were brought along shopping with their mothers in that store, I was considered the most miraculous because just after my second birthday I said to my mother in the checkout line, "Mom, you forgot the Carnation evaporated milk." "Oh my God," said the lady ringing us up, "your baby must be a genius", this, because I could actually pronounce Carnation evaporated milk. Emboldened by this news and having just told me 'no' when I wanted her to buy the first volume of this grocery store encyclopedia and never mind that I couldn't read, my mother picked up the first volume and wound up buying three more before blowing off the whole deal. You see we had other mix and match volumes at home (never K thru L as I remember) but you know I looked at all the pictures for years and eventually added to them with my crayons. Now I wasn't a good student in school for the most part and the word 'miraculous' never passed the lips of any of my teachers describing me, but I was always a good talker and at least according to my mother, my speaking career (which would eventually encompass 35 years on the radio), began that day at Klein's grocery store on Snelling somewhere during 1950.

I've always admired people, to a degree, who can't remember things. They just grew up; and their Dad yelled now and then, and there was supper and a paper route, and high school, college, the service maybe. They just never captured anything of those little moments that have been with me all of my life...every moment. For example, I grew up in St. Paul and on the site where the parking lot of the apartment building on Randolph between Warwick and Pascal is, there used to be a slopping lawn and on that lawn there was a hole in the ground and a nest of baby rabbits. Nothing much came of it, but on the other side of the alley on that block, there was a lilac bush. I got lilacs for my mother myself once or twice from that bush. There was a wall there and this one kid was pulling off lilacs and fell off the wall backward right on the sidewalk. Some adults saw it and I was there too, and they suggested they give him a ride home. He cried of course but recovered quickly and as he did, he simply said (as we had all been taught),"I can't take rides from strangers." He recovered and was walking home with his friend and I picked up the lilacs and asked him if he wanted them. He didn't. How do you forget the moments of your life? What drive or ambition allows you to blot out the little dramas that take place all around you, even today? One block and here's the last story. I was coming back from somewhere and Bob Weaver was passing me in the opposite direction in winter right near the corner of Pascal. Bob hung around Jake's...the tougher corner of St. Clair and Hamline, but he was a nice guy, kind of quiet. I told someone he pushed me into a snow bank and of course, I didn't do anything because he hung around Jake's and I didn't. He never did push me and I don't know why I said it except to say his name and mine in the same sentence. I never knew Bob but four or five years later my mother would meet his mother and hear the heartbreaking story of the last letter Bob wrote as a Marine in Vietnam while I was there, before he was killed. And so I ask again, how do you forget those little snapshots that brought you to this point? As I said, I admire it but frankly, don't understand. Bob Weaver was the first kid I knew of in our neighborhood to be killed in Vietnam. I never heard about it until I got home. Now it's all these years later and I feel I needed to write his name again.

Many of you had brothers and sisters growing up. I didn't and I can tell with no embarrassment or reservation at all that I couldn't have made it as a child growing up in St. Paul without my best friends. My first best friend was two years older than me and had a brother. My other best friend who was my own age, and had a brother and sisters, happened about fifth grade when the age pecking order took over; and while I stayed friends with my older best friend, everybody just fell into place based on familiar things...age, interests, and school where you saw the same people every day and all went to the same school. I'd like to tell you what it was like to have no siblings. I've tried before but many if not most of you cannot grasp the concept. But I can say that it seemed as much of an advantage as it was a disadvantage. Being born late in life to my parents, who never thought they'd have children to begin with, they weren't exactly on the ball when it came time for this or that and as a result I missed my first year of eligibility for Little League Baseball for example. There were issues with father-son and even mother-son things that got missed; none that were that important, or so I've come to believe. But with my best friends and through them and their parents, (who by having older children knew the drill a little better than some of the others), I managed to fit in a little better than I might have. You know, (and I don't want those of you with brothers and sisters to take this wrong, because I've known enough of you to have heard how you could have done without, let's say, as crowded a household as you had to negotiate), I did in fact have it pretty good and made the best of those things where I didn't. I slept in the same bedroom with my parents for fifteen years, three beds to jump on rather than one, was the position I took. And yet, (not exactly for reasons of my not having to share things), there were people who made me feel as though I was the only, only child in the world. It was the one time I really had nothing to say and yet I might have said something, but I had a strong sense that anyone who would do that did so more out of angry envy than for any other reason and I chose to just let it go.

When I got home from Vietnam, it was the end of my service and another guy from my company was leaving about the same time, so we sort of made a date to have a drink in Seattle before heading off home or wherever. The hotel I took didn't have phones in the rooms and I can't remember how he knew to call me there but he did, and by the time I got to the phone down the hall he had hung up. I knew what that meant and that he was tired and just wanted to get home, you know. So I got dressed and went down to this little peanut bar in the Hungerford Hotel and managed to get served and proceeded to get drunk and wound up in a little diner around the corner around midnight. It was the beginning of the feeling of being lost without the army. Less than a day away from it and six months shy of my twenty-first birthday, nothing looked familiar or even remotely like some place or even some country I wanted to be in. I tried for several months after that but after the money was gone, I went to the recruiter's office and he was going through this routine...all total bullshit about, "Well, we need to get you back in first and then"...so on and so forth. I wanted to get in his face and just say, "Who do you think you're talking to asshole? I'm a twice wounded veteran and you give this line of crap when all I came down here to do was re-enlist?" I left there feeling like that ship had sailed and by then, this idiot recruiter was treating everybody like he was some kind of carnival barker and 'there's a sucker born every minute.' It was like of all the recruiters I could have talked to that day, God sent me to that one to tell me, "No, son...move on, that deal is over."

There was a time I would have been embarrassed to admit this, but that ship has sailed as they say and so I will tell you that from time to time, television instilled in me a feeling that if I dressed and acted like an adult, I might actually be accepted as one. Overall I suppose it was a blessing, but as a child growing up in St. Paul, looking very young most of my life became a handicap I really couldn't overcome. However, I did learn, albeit slowly, that there were women in the world who liked young men who aspired to bigger

20

things and of course that was my dream, if you take my meaning. In fact, I was in the midst of that dream one day in Dayton's, shopping for adventure of any kind, really. I had on a sport-coat with my open shirt collar over the coat collar (not unlike Paul Newman in Sweet Bird of Youth) and stealing looks at a lady of perhaps twenty-five who was gorgeous and wonderfully abrupt as she went from thing to thing. Now remember, my longing for her was all in my mind or so I thought and actually was pretty sure she hadn't noticed my attentions. She finally bought whatever it was and as the girl rang it up, she paid with a charge card and suddenly looked at me, as if I was with her and had been all along. "Would you mind carrying these things for me?" she asked. I was paralyzed but managed to say, "ye, ye, yes of course," looking behind me to be sure she was talking to me. There was parking in Dayton's ramp after a certain point growing up, and while I can't exactly remember, I felt like I was hypnotized or something, I carried this woman's packages to her car, in Dayton's, wearing my Paul Newman look. I think she asked me a thing or two and of course, under questioning, I reverted to a nice young schoolboy at once. But I do remember this: as she put the packages into her car and I stood there awkwardly, trying to understand what was happening, she finally stood up again, smiled beautifully and as I thought she would offer me a gratuity I was resolved to refuse, she leaned towards me and kissed me lightly on the cheek. "Thank you", she said with just the slightest hint she wanted to say more. That's it in its entirety and I have never forgotten her once in all the years. Boy that I was really, it would be a few more years before I knew women, and yet her kindness that day by first noticing me and allowing me to be her "gentleman" even for a few moments, built me up like nothing else in my life at that point.

In my world, the geography of growing up lent itself to all matter of milestones that took place in alleys. I liked to kiss the girls from an early age and alleys were perfect for that and of course my friends tended to treat their back doors, as I did, as the preferred entryway to their houses. I lived on Brimhall and Randolph in the apartment building there and behind the building was a great alley. It was a T-alley, which is to say it ran east and west from Brimhall to Saratoga. Going north it went to Palace and then continued across the street, but coming south it ended at the east-west alley, which brings me around to crying. When you're little and you get hurt you cry. It doesn't matter where you are, crying follows hurt and the venue can be anywhere. But as you grow older and having heard, 'Only babies cry' or 'Don't be a cry baby', you learned to hold off crying, say, on the sidewalk or in someone's yard and if you could make it to the alley before you burst into tears, that was a good thing. For me, that short Brimhall to Saratoga alley was perfect if you had to cry because it was shorter, more intimate. Later of course, when crying was no longer acceptable no matter where you were, most likely you weren't hanging out in alleys as much anyway. Still, I remember taking my early pain and little heart breaking disappointments to that little stretch and as it took less and less time to recover, I knew one day it would just be an alley I used to cry in.

There was a kid in our neighborhood in St. Paul. He was a few years older and was into cars real big, working on them and driving around and stuff. My friends and I got to know him better one summer and started hanging around with him a little. He was a kind of short, tough guy but also strangely charming at a certain level and funny too; but the charming part eventually took a turn into violence. I was almost one of his victims but got out of it before it really happened. A couple of years later and few more episodes of violence finally wound him up in Stillwater prison for several years. By the time he got out, I was back from Vietnam and out of the army and some guys I knew went to see him and that was pretty much the last I heard. There are guys like that in a lot of neighborhoods and I never thought much about what he might have come to after that, but I figured whatever it was, it probably wouldn't be very good. Anyway,

I met a guy recently who knew him and still sees him all the time because of their mutual interest in cars. It turns out, he married not too long after getting out of prison, moved south of the Twin Cities and has been doing great for decades. I found myself sort of happy for him because there are so many guys who once it gets going wrong, it stays that way and multiple incarcerations are not uncommon. When I thought of him at all, the word "crazy" seemed to apply and yet, somehow he got beyond that and had a very settled, productive life. I guess I'll always wonder how he did it.

Purpose is not a built in concept for many of us and there are those who are busy enough in their daily lives to really never consider what it's all about in any meaningful sense. "I think, therefore, I am" is so much nonsense to them, as it should be. They are surrounded, nearly inundated with purpose. They wake up each day at a run, basically. Things and people they are responsible for depend on them and demand that kind of attention. They seldom if ever shake their heads and say, "wait a minute. What the hell is this all about?" They never wanted to do that and so their lives are constructed in such a way as to insulate them from anything resembling the word, "why?" The army did that for me. It kept me busy every second of the day it seemed and eventually, I thrived under that idea. I slept well every night, got up at a run and all day long dedicated myself to one purpose or another. Within, I'd say, a week of getting out of the army, the whole thing fell apart. I intended to bring that energy to the rest of my life but it all went away as fast as it had begun and I had to regain my energy at a speed I was comfortable with. I can't say that concept ever worked either and for years I stumbled from thing to thing and looking back, wonder how any of it happened at all. There are tricks of course, to bring that enthusiasm and energy to our lives. Anyone who went to a good, intensive sales seminar can tell you that, but at the end of the day, they're still just tricks. I'm reacting to a slump I'm in and wondering what I'll do if it turns out to be more than just a slump. I can't use..."something else" as an answer like some others. I wind up looking beyond that question and when I can't see anything there, it doesn't scare me really. It used to but now it's just the unknown, and I have come to know it for what it is and it's just that...unknown. These questions are why we have churches and bars...and the gym, I suppose.

I only imagine I'm a dog when I have my NFL walk-on try-out fantasy with any team. They would look at me and shake their heads and I'd say, "Give me the ball...see if anyone on this field can catch me." Then I take the ball and become...a dog. Not a super hero...just a dog. I'd make child's play of their feeble attempts to tackle me, often going back and giving them a second try. The linemen offer no challenge but the mean linebackers and free safeties along with the fleet cornerbacks don't just want to tackle me. They want to kill me. I run through them and around them and away from the fastest men on the team, looking back as I do. My powers are not from Krypton. They are the powers of the animal shelter. I am a man with the powers of...a dog. And you'd pay any price to have me on your team...oh yes, you would. Canine powers would send me to Canton, Ohio, and the Hall of Fame with a guaranteed place long before my playing days were over. Records that would never be broken would fall weekly as I ran over, under, around and through tacklers and approaching the end zone, fight off the urge to go back and do it again. My speed, my cutting ability, my ability to change directions on a dime, to accelerate, hurdle and otherwise befuddle the best the human race can produce...I can do so, with nothing more than the powers...of a dog. Yes, keep your "tall buildings in a single bound" and give me the gifts of a dog and I'll re-write the record books time and again as the man "with the powers of a dog."

I hung around a corner when I was growing up. About eight or nine blocks north was another corner and guys hung around there too. They were generally two or three years older than we were. Older meant bigger in some cases but more experienced certainly, and they had a lot of fights and won most of them. That's the story that trickled down to us anyway and no one on my corner was in any hurry to want to fight any of those guys. Nor did they mess with us either, gratefully. Anyway, one of them was about five feet tall and wasn't going to get any taller. He was a good looking smaller guy and walked with a perfect, confident posture as well. But in fights, he was known for stomping on guys real bad. Actually, by the time I left high school, of three guys he had stomped on in previous years, two had died (some sort of head trauma for one and the other just never woke up one morning); and one lost an eye and wasn't seeing too good out of the other. These all happened within a year or so of the actual fight so he was never prosecuted. In my life, this had the effect of making me very wary of short guys; not fighting them actually because as I've said before, I'm not much of a fighter and avoid that sort of thing if I can. But the part about what happens when you're on the ground and think it should be over is different when you're fighting a short guy. Your big guy or even a guy of equal height might give you a break. But a little guy, once he has you down, might want to punish you for being taller than he is or will ever be. This theory I developed was proven to be true many times over the years with other smaller guys, so I tried to be extra careful about pissing one off. I found it to be a good policy.

I'm not entirely sure why, but when I was a little boy in St. Paul, I didn't much like being a little boy for several reasons. First of all, my mother insisted I have a crew cut. I didn't like that. I wanted big boy hair, with a part in it. There were also fashion disasters, in my view anyway, that were uniquely meant for us kids. Raincoats were bright yellow and they came with a hat that sort of looked like the Ku Klux Klan, only in yellow, with just a rectangular slit to look out on the world and which prevented completely, any peripheral vision. So being unable to see left or right, you'd turn your head but the hat wouldn't move, so unless you turned your entire body in the direction you wanted to see… you couldn't see at all. You were also talked down to a lot. "So you want that candy bar, do you little boy?" "No," I thought of saying more than once, "I'm just standing here at the cash register holding the candy bar in one hand and the money to pay for it in the other just so I could exchange this bit of commerce with you in order to ascertain the kind of adult I never want to grow up to be under any circumstances, and you're doing a fine job as that role model." The worst of course is when they tell you, "These are the best years of your life." I remember always wanting to say, "Well, if you're any example, I can see your point." It wasn't all bad but looking back, it was kind of marking time until I could walk down Randolph in the rain like Robert Mitchum and not some Russian Cosmonaut. Astronauts hadn't been invented yet.

To choose to live somewhere else (after being raised in St. Paul), there are reasons of course. But there is usually a catalytic agent, a spark where you say, "that's it." I remember mine and while it's somewhat embarrassing let's face it (as I have), I could have seen the inside of a jail cell for other reasons along the way with far less prospect of leaving anytime soon. I never owned a new car and indeed I have owned some turkeys along the way and when winter sets in and it begins to snow, "snow bird tickets" become somewhat inevitable. For those of you who don't know what a snow bird ticket is, they're a lot like savings bonds. The longer you keep them, the more of them mature into arrest warrants. You get them for not moving your car when the snow plows come through. It was spring and just west of Victoria and University where I got pulled over and after checking my license plates, I looked in the rear view mirror to see both officers get back out, unsnap their holsters and approach my car once again and I knew at once I was under arrest. To make a long story short, I was in jail few hours and my Uncle Albert (Big Al Loken) came down and bailed me out and two things became clear in my mind: snow bird tickets of mine had gone to warrant before, but I paid them before I could be arrested, and for certain if I stayed in St. Paul I would continue to get them. That was it and the next job that came along, KFBC in Cheyenne, Wyoming, would mark the beginning of the end of my living in St. Paul. There might have been other reasons but the prospect of spending at the minimum a few hours every spring in jail was good enough for me to make other arrangements.

I am not a good fighter. I never was. In spite of that I hung around some venues where, let's just say there was a lot of testosterone going on: growing up, the war, hanging around the bars, etc. While I wasn't much of a fighter I was always a talker and once in a while was called on to back up my mouth which brings me to this guy named Bob...the best actor I ever saw. Bob was about three years older than the young guys he hung out with so he was the leader and a big talker. I saw him back down a guy who you figured could tear him apart. Actually, I saw him do it more than once. Finally, I ran into this guy who was Bob's age and went to high school with him. I asked him about Bob and the guy looked at me with this astonished expression and said, "Bob???" It was then I realized it was all an act and that to really sell it, you almost had to believe it yourself. So anyway one day, in one of these venues I was running my mouth and sure enough this guy gets up to challenge me. Saying this guy could have kicked my ass wasn't much really because like I said, I wasn't much of a fighter. But I remembered this Bob and decided that since I was gonna get my ass kicked anyway, I'd give his act a try. What I learned was this...ya don't have to scare the guy...ya just have to create a little uncertainty. He knows he can probably take you but he's not entirely sure and since he's the one who made the challenge, he has the most to lose. I avoided an almost certain beating that day but was never sure enough it would work again, so I started watching my mouth and managed to avoid most of it in the future.

If there was anything to be gained apart from our training and what we had been told and what we told ourselves about serving our country, when I got to Vietnam it came to me at least with the understanding that we might be all in it together; but as far as our feelings for each other, we couldn't have been farther apart. In the infantry in particular, the new guys were treated badly. The guys who had been there awhile had their own clique and those who were "short" or about to go home were either quiet or cautious or they acted like superior assholes. This may be hard to comprehend because nobody talks about it, but not long after I got there, we lost a guy. He was living when they put him on the helicopter but we heard he died later. He only had three weeks left. He was the biggest prick in the platoon and while it was never said out loud, (there were those of us, especially those who'd been abused by this guy, made the brunt of laughter whenever he got the chance and so forth), who couldn't have cared less when he got killed. There would be no heartfelt letters to his folks' back home saying what a great guy he was and that was a shame he was killed so close to going home. In the infantry, there was heat like you wouldn't believe and the humidity and the chance you might become wounded, maimed or killed. But there was also an awful pecking order that resulted from the 'Tour of Duty' concept we all fought under...new guys scum, old guys great. Like I said, nobody talks about that part of Vietnam but I assure you, it was there.

After inadvertently finishing a broadcasting course at Brown Institute in Minneapolis, I took a split- shift DJ position at KTRF, Thief River Falls, Minnesota. I did 9 AM to 12:30 PM and 3 PM to 6:30 PM every day and ended both with an on-camera newscast for the local cable TV hook-up. I did color commentary of high school football with Clark 'Big Red in the Morning' Hendrickson from the back of a pickup truck. I made less than six hundred dollars a month, so with a wife and daughter and my son on the way, I enrolled in Northland Community College and carried a full load to get me GI Bill money. I played Roger Whitaker 'The Last Farewell' and polkas every day at 11:30 AM. I hosted 'The Bible in Your Hand' with Pastor Phil Young of the Thief River Falls Seventh Day Adventist

Church, got my associate's degree and made the dean's list. It amounted to the best year and a half of my adult life and I cried at the end of my last shift on the air. If they had offered me eight hundred a month I'd still be there.

I was going through my high school yearbook for my junior year and realized something that kind of bothers me. If you were to have asked me how many kids I went to grade school with that also went to my high school, I'd have guess maybe five...six on the outside. There were twelve. Twelve kids I spent eight years sitting next to that somehow attained the status of invisibility at the next level. None of these people ever hurt me or did anything that would cause me to just...color them gone. Some of these guys I still hung out with but the rest, where did they go? In a couple of cases I can't remember ever seeing them in the halls in high school at all. It's almost as if these people were like someone I'd done time with and that the memory of it and subsequently them became so unpleasant I just blacked them out. Now, even today, I'll be thinking of someone, maybe someone I worked with or even were friends with and think to myself, "I should give them a call." Then I pause for a moment and think, "Geez...what's wrong with you? Of course you should give them a call." But here's the other side. They're not giving me a call either. The phone works both ways. And for every ex-classmate I walked by in high school, they never reached out to me either. But I mean its Wednesday after all, and we all need some introspection on Wednesday.

This is a St. Paul story but I have a feeling there is a universal quality here that we all share. I remember my heart breaking and I can't remember why. While we were growing up, getting used to broken hearts, as the job of being human demands, I can still remember moments that took me out of my broken heart that were not welcome. I was having a broken heart dammit! You have no business making me laugh or taking me out of that in any way! Well, decades pass, as they do if you're lucky, and I'm having one of those parent moments..."Where's my daughter? Is she close? What's going on?" and I walk to the front window to see a little drama being played out. My daughter Lisa picks up Sylvester, a neighbor's cat, and Sylvester has other ideas and scratches my daughter. She drops Sylvester and heads home. But on the way, she sings a little song and starts to pick up something interesting in the street as she heads to our front door. I watch the whole process and as she comes within earshot, fifteen feet or so, she breaks into tears and I meet her at the front door. "What's wrong, dear?" I ask, taking her in my arms. "Sylvester scratched me," she says. "Oh, I'm sure he didn't mean to. Here..." I said, "let's get that washed off," and we go and do what fathers and daughters do when mother isn't home. I clean and dress my daughter's little scratch and as I write this, my wife Kathy is in the next room telling me I have to come and see all the stars watching an Andrea Botticelli concert on PBS and I go and say, "That's great" because that's what we do. We balance the 'here and now' with our memories that made life the gift that if we're lucky, makes it all worthwhile. Sylvester and Lisa on a fall day on Blair between Snelling and Fairview somewhere.... in the 70's and we had a fireplace we never used...I wasn't sure about things like that.

In Catholic grade school in the 50's, art was not seen as any kind of a priority. It was rather given as a treat of a Friday afternoon where, in the lower grades (say 1st through 4th) we were given mimeographed line drawings of the baby Jesus or the Virgin Mary or some Saint and were then instructed to take our crayons and color these offerings. I was always good at art and often my coloring of these line drawings was held up as an example of good work. This particular day I learned a lesson that has stayed with me for more than fifty years. Nearly everyone in class had the same Crayola Crayons with your basic colors in a small, straight-line box of one row, but on that day everyone that is except Linda Hassett. She had the five-tier large box of crayons with exotic colors like Burnt

Sienna and Lime Green. As usual, after twenty minutes of coloring a picture of the baby Jesus, I was asked to walk up and show the rest of the class my work. Actually, I remember it well: a rather subdued interpretation well shaded in blues and browns for the most part. However even as I did, students near Linda Hassett's offering were frantically trying to get Sister whatever-her-name-was attention (actually I think it was Sister Demerice and that would make it third grade) for Linda to show her picture. It was quite beautiful really and why not? She had every damn crayon in the universe to work with but her choices, shading and the reddish brown hair of Our Savior blew mine away in a heartbeat. Being an only child who only brought home A's in art, after hearing my story, my mother and father saw that this shit would never happen again...and it didn't. The lesson: if they're just better than you, fine; if they have more to work with, fix it. Do it now!

We used to play a version of soccer in the spring inside the boards of the hockey rink at Cretin High School in St. Paul. There'd be a lot of checking and pushing and grabbing and it was a lot of fun. We had a couple of bullies in our group: one somewhat affable if he liked you and the other, nobody really liked but it was better to stay on his good side. Anyway, the bad bully put a nasty check on the okay bully and you could just see that it was a matter of time before he got his revenge. So the game went on and sure enough, the offending bully got close to the boards with the ball and the other one lined him up and put a devastating block on him, sending him into the boards with such force they collapsed that section. But I must say he took it well because he knew he had it coming and it wasn't fun if it wasn't rough. There was a begrudging respect for these guys because most of the time, they could take it as much as they could dish it out. It depends on the game I suppose, but if you're going to play 'hardball' in any arena you wind up running into these types. Everybody has their place I guess.

I admire winners. I think we all do to some degree. I'm talking about the people that do it the right way to begin with and stay on that path. Still, there's just nothing like being an abject failure and six months later, catching your reflection in a window maybe...looking good, confident, doing an important job and thinking, "How in the hell did I ever get here after being down there?" In general, we're underachievers. God has given us a lot more than we usually feel like using with any regularity, and compounding that good fortune with something like hard work is rarely considered either. We'd rather pull a rabbit out of a hat from time to time just to show ourselves and others we can do it. I say "ourselves" because it is the kind of thing we are never quite sure we can pull off. But when we do, we wink and sort of act like we had it in our shirt pocket all the time and just stumbled around to make people think we didn't. We do realize how lucky we are however, and are usually very generous in supporting others through tough times. We should be...we find ourselves going through them ourselves with some consistency. The real winners look at us and smile but rarely hang out with us and with good reason...they're winners. We mostly pretend that sort of thing is not important but we know the truth. Being an up and downer does have an upside though. In general, we have a lot more fun and people don't tend to put too much faith in us to 'stay the course' for very long and that's a wise policy. In important things, we bore easily and often quickly too, but the world would be less fun without us. That part is true also.

I'm a sports fan and yes, I know what I'm talking about. I should, I've been watching it for sixty years. So now and then, when I think about betting based on my expertise.... I lose my ass...not just sometimes but almost every time. Why? It is because I know too much and that clouds the judgment. I bring it up because some years ago I had a few bucks and on an expert's advice (I heard it on the radio), I thought I'd invest in a stock. I did pretty good so I invested some more. Again, I did pretty good. Since then and understand this...I don't know anything about stocks or investing, I've done pretty good. Then I made one mistake. Say you have five thousand to invest. They let you buy ten thousand in a stock. It's called buying on margin, so just don't do it, ever. Since that mistake, I'm almost back up to where I was before I started. Again...I know nothing about investing. Sure, I watch it a little but I really don't learn anything...I'm just guessing and like I said, I do pretty good. It's kind of fun and one thing I know.... if the sky is falling...for some reason, Wall Street doesn't listen and if they do, they don't care. You see...the "sky is falling" is a message for the morons. That's what they think anyway and because they do, I have more money than I would have otherwise. Well, that's the way I felt anyway and over time I continued to be lucky until one day I reached twenty thousand dollars. Right then I should have diversified, but I got to thinking how sweet doubling the twenty would be and I found a stock I liked and went all in. I lost it all. Of course what I really lost was about the forty-five hundred I started with and I've been deducting the loss on taxes for the allowable sum each year for a while now. This past year I got in the market again. It's fun. I'm up about fifteen hundred but one thing I'm pretty sure of. I'd have done no better betting on ball games.

When I first got out to Los Angeles, I was an actor. I could do other things of course and knew that I'd have to do those things, but I had years and years of stage experience and I had a pretty good 'bad guy' look; and so I went about trying to make it happen...pictures and resume of course and in those days, a copy of *Dramalogue* with ads in it for non-paying acting work in student films and other similar projects. These were all you needed to get started. But I kept seeing ads for something I didn't have. It was an SASE. I didn't know what a SASE was only that I didn't have one, so I just skipped over those ads and only applied to people who didn't insist on a SASE. Now, as I think back, I remember some cryptic smiles on the faces of the people I'd tell this to, "Yeah, as soon as I get my SASE I'll be all set." It didn't seem to matter to me that I didn't know what a SASE was and could just simply ask someone. I just acted like I did and that it was on my agenda that 'someday' I'd be getting my SASE and then I'd really be in business. I'm pretty sure as long as a month went by before I finally heard someone say..."Self-Addressed Stamped Envelope" and put it together with SASE. I'm not sure how many people I ran into who got a kick out of my confusion but I'm pretty sure there were a few.

If you forget about the war part for a second, the Vietnam experience was like nothing we'd ever gone through in some very basic ways. For one thing, for those of us who were there, there was no TV. I know that seems obvious but in the quiet moments it forced us to talk to each other. You'd be on guard or something, maybe on a detail or even just getting ready for sleep and there was nothing to do but talk to one another. It was called bullshitting with each other because of course, a lot of the stories we told were gross exaggerations if not outright lies: things about how tough we were in high school or how many women we had, and the best bull-shitters were like the top TV shows. They were our entertainment. America or wherever you were from in America was called "The World." "Hey man, where're you from in the world?" someone might say. Some of us would just bullshit with anyone but in general, guys liked to bullshit with the people they felt most comfortable with: blacks from big cities, Hispanics and country boys or someone from your home town or region. After I was wounded, I came down with malaria right away and was moved to a tent city hospital in Nah Trang. A guy I went through training with came in with his wounds and we got very close. My malaria wasn't getting any better and I seemed to be getting sicker and sicker. My friend wound up bringing me my meals from the mess hall for a while. Finally, they figured out I had dengue fever and after that passed we spent another good week just bullshitting all day, every day. But we did open up to each other about how scary it had been and how we really felt about things. He and I agreed that the big thing was to hold our own out in the field. Anyway, I got shipped off to Cameron Bay for a few weeks and finally back to my unit. After a month or so my transfer was approved to be a door gunner on air gunships and that ended my infantry time. I saw my friend one more time at LZ Pony. His platoon had gotten into it with some NVA but he had come through with a sense of accomplishment. I could tell he was more at peace with who he was and what he had to do. I can't tell you why but I just knew I'd never see him alive again. He was killed about a week later, they said.

Many years ago now, my friend's wife began telling a story about the first time they ever heard 'Hey Jude' by the Beatles. They loved the Beatles as most of us did and she was smiling and you could tell it was sweetly nostalgic for her to recall the event. "We were driving in New York City at the time," she said, and my friend interrupted his wife with a remark about all the trash in the streets. She continued with her story but as I thought about it later, I knew the answer. That's who my friend was and he would always see any environmental blemish before anything else, even a sweet remembrance by his wife. Years later, I was telling a joke I'd heard about Hubert Humphrey and his terrific memory. This co-worker couldn't let the name Hubert Humphrey go by without making a snide remark. Generally normal people, regardless of their politics, would at least wait until the joke was over or in the first instance, let his wife tell her story. But the people who suffer from this affliction cannot, and moreover, never see as 'insufferable' how lame they sound when they do this. Their position on the issue supersedes anything else. It's much the same with people who hate America. Never mind that money from America keeps this individual and his family alive each and every day and without it they would die within a month. To them, everything and everyone in America is bad and American news, in particular is all lies. It's the same with people who are the lovers of America who contend, whether you asked them for their opinion or not, that America is always right and never wrong. I hosted a call- in talk show in Cheyenne, Wyoming, years ago and there was this one guy. It didn't matter what the topic was: city issues, sports or parking spaces downtown, this guy would call in and point out that it was the Israelis' fault and then proceed to tell you just how awful they were. It almost goes without saying that if you have an ax to grind AND you believe in God, you're always right. I'll confess to not paying all that much attention while being taught about God and religion while I was growing up; but for the part about belief in God and always being right, I must have been home with the flu the day they taught us that. These people (and again, nobody has a corner on the market), come in all shapes and sizes and are beloved of talk-show hosts and coffee house owners, because there's just nothing like a good caffeine buzz to give legs to their assertions and conclusions. Fortunately we are not all like them while unfortunately we all know a few. They're not all that bad as long as you keep the topic away from that which causes their mouths to salivate and that ever so slight tremor in their hands. To hate that much, to love that much and to be that certain all the time must be a difficult albatross to carry around their necks every day. But even as they read this, if they do, they know clearly that I am the one to be pitied because it is I who lack the clarity of their inner vision…rock on people, rock on.

As a kid growing up, through TV and commercials in particular, I could visualize and appreciate my entire life long before I ever got started living it. I remember this Arrow shirt commercial, for example. The scene was in a trophy room at some university and here were five or six guys, let's say, after a banquet or something, all with their suit coats off, throwing around a football. The sense you got was that they were alumni and former players, now with gray hair in these great looking white, Arrow shirts. And there I was, a child imagining how great it would be to live that scene to be with former teammates late in life, enjoying that time. Now that I'm old I can tell you it never happened. I never did play college ball of any kind nor attend any alumni function either. What I have instead is what has become a yearly reunion of my flight platoon in Vietnam: door gunners like myself, crew chiefs and pilots and our wives in a beautiful setting in North Carolina for a week. I can't tell you how great it's been or how much it means to me to be a part of that group but I can say it meets and surpasses all my childhood expectations of joining with other men in a shared experience in what seems a lifetime ago. Strangely, the war doesn't come up very often at all anymore and it's not the big drinking affair it was years ago either. We're just seven couples or so and a few singles now and then who at a glance could have been top ten sales men and women from some company back in the day. The longer I live, I think that those commercials I watched as a kid were like crystal balls where, if you dreamed hard enough, if you were lucky, you could see your future.

If my life ended today, I would be one of the most educated people in the history of my family, served my country in battle, had a career in radio, been married for two months shy of twenty years, still had contact with friends I met in first grade, saw my Twins win two World Championships and my Gophers win a Rose Bowl, finally learned to zero out my credit cards each month, ran seven marathons, wrote six books, never had a new car (nor particularly wanted one), saw the Miracle on Ice, the Grand Canyon, Frank Sinatra, Ella Fitzgerald, Maui and my children all grow up to be fine people. If don't die today, I still have plenty of time to do better, do more and screw up worse than I ever have; choices...that's why God threw us out of Paradise and I for one, can't thank Him enough for doing so.

I was asked recently what was the best job I ever had that didn't pay anything. The answer is easy but does need some qualification because it wasn't the kind of job just anyone could do. That is, because I was a radio announcer I could do the job. It was a daily broadcast for the station I worked for and it had to be done. Even so, if you were not enough of a sports fan to do the job with some authority, that is not mispronouncing common sports names and generally sounding like you knew what you were talking about, you'd only get to do the job once. I had no problem in those areas but I did wonder why anyone would do this kind of remote broadcast for no compensation at all. I didn't wonder for long. The Minnesota Vikings opened their summer camp at Mankato State University yearly and after a day's work out, coach Bud Grant would come back to Gage Center and update the press on the latest developments: "Yes, Chuck Foreman's ankle is better but we thought it best to keep him out for another day just to be sure and oh yeah, we picked up so and so and so and so and let so and so go". Usually, it didn't amount to much and was just about that brief. Then, the reporters, mostly from the Twin Cities, were allowed to ask few questions of the coach. This was a little tricky because while Bud Grant was a great couch, he was a very dry kind of fellow and not given to having a lot of fun with the press. For this reason, if you were going to ask a question you needed to be sure it was not too stupid because Bud didn't suffer fools easily. The day I write of was my first time covering this daily event for the local radio station for which I was news director. It happened to be the day after the baseball All-Star game which was played at the Seattle Kingdome that year. During the game one of the announcers mentioned how dark it was in the Kingdome. Coincidentally, the Vikings were going to play their first pre-season game in the Kingdome against the Seahawks that coming weekend. So I asked about it and did any of the players ever mention they had trouble picking up the ball, say…on punt returns, when it sailed into the dark before coming down. Bud said, "It is dark but of course the football is bigger and there is no problem." I nodded and after another question, it was over. I then had to hurry down the hall to the only phone on the floor and call in my report. But before I did, one of the reporters said to me, "Good question about the Kingdome…see ya in the cafeteria."

As I finished my report, I wondered what he meant about the cafeteria so went looking for it and soon realized why there was no pay for the Vikings Report. We got to eat with the Vikings: steak smothered in mushroom, chicken, ham, Baron of Beef, sometimes prime rib. It was a cafeteria setting with any number of side dishes and a dessert area with Coach Grant's favorite ice cream as well. It was a dream job, no money but the perks were terrific. Now the writers, like the coaches and players generally ate together. During dinner I was wondering how I could somehow be designated regular Viking Report guy, but soon learned it was a revolving position and we usually got to cover it once a week. A look around the table at the overweight regular sportswriters told me that was probably a good thing.

Holidays are interesting for a lot of reasons, for what they celebrate of course but also the time of year they're celebrated. For me and many in the Twin Cities of Minneapolis and St. Paul, Labor Day always marked the last day of the Minnesota State Fair. Halloween was also fun but usually came around about the time it was starting to get colder. By Thanksgiving, winter was starting to set in and by Christmas it had, and after New Year's, for us at least, it was a kind of waiting for winter to be over. Somewhere in there was Valentine's Day and then Easter. Pretty soon came Memorial Day and then the 4th of July. Now with my best childlike remembrance of these holidays, I can tell you that it was the last chance to go to the Fair but involved no days off because school hadn't started yet...so no big deal. Halloween involved no days off from school but did come with costumes and candy. Thanksgiving meant a couple of days off, turkey and football on TV on a Thursday, usually from Detroit. Christmas meant a whole week off from school and getting presents and having a Christmas tree and stuff. New Year's ended the Christmas holiday and meant a lot of football, which was great. Valentine's Day didn't get you out of school, but the exchange of Valentines was kind of cool. Easter meant some time off from school, Easter bunnies and stuff and whereas you might get out of church for Thanksgiving or even Christmas, you had to go on Easter. Memorial Day was very close to being out of school. At one time or another, some serious adult would sit you down and tell you what the holiday meant. I already knew what it meant. You either got out of school or you didn't. That was all that was important to me as a kid. That didn't make me a bad kid...those were just my priorities. Remember that when you start bad mouthing young people for not holding our holidays with the necessary reverence.

I'm not sure but that love for one's pet or pets maybe the purest form of love we will ever know. For example, if anything happens to me, I want them with someone who will not only care for them but love them as well: speak nicely to them, tell them they're good girls and that they are loved and that they deserve the treats you're giving them every bit as much as you enjoy providing them. If they forget me and respond to that love with their love for their new friends, that's fine. All I need and want in the world is that they are loved and cared for every minute of every day and if they are, I'll be happy. I can never return what their love means to me...never. I only hope that when I'm gone, someone steps up and loves them as I did. It's the greatest job I could wish on anyone and the rewards are considerable indeed.

I never thought much about it when I was younger but it occurs to me that if you're the luckiest of all your peers, there'll be no one to say goodbye to you when your life is over. My father died at a relatively young age, while I was on leave from the army, and his visitation lasted a whole day. By the time my dear mother left us, all her friends had passed. My friends and I, whom I have been lucky enough to meet with this week in the Twin Cities, are pretty lucky. Yesterday, Tom said: "now we're all in our sixties...how did that happen?" These are guys I played street football with and went to the same grade school with. I suppose you have to come to a moment like that to truly recognize it. I suppose it's no harder to figure out than surviving the war or anything else...we were lucky. Only a couple of guys from our neighborhood were killed in Vietnam and there were many of us who served. One was wounded badly and later took his own life. Stories like that were common back then. But after all that came life: drugs and marriage and divorce and children, and all the while trying to find focus to make it through another year. When reflecting on these questions one can't help but ask: "If no one will be left to say goodbye...will there be anyone there to say hello when you cross over?" I've said it before...to me it doesn't matter. Seeing them all now is blessing enough.

You may or may not know that the Twin Cities of Minneapolis and St. Paul has in recent years been a re-settling point for thousands of Somalis and other people from Africa. On a recent trip home we woke up to about seven inches of new snow, but I had appointments anyway and I managed to drive slowly and carefully and make my rounds. Each place I stopped I heard warnings from people that the "Africans" are not used to driving in the snow and so "watch out." And yet, unless Africans look exactly like the usual predominantly white drivers of SUV's I have always encountered when driving in slippery conditions in the Twin Cities, I saw no evidence of this. I mean, everyone enjoys seeing a four wheel drive SUV buried in some snowdrift because the driver was going too fast in slippery weather and I'm no different. Yet few, if any of these vehicles I find are driven by Somalis or even blacks of any cut of cloth. In fairness, many drivers of SUV's just love helping people who are NOT driving four-wheel drive vehicles, so I don't want to bad mouth them...I may need them someday.

So here's what happened: my wife and I got on the plane for Minneapolis an hour late while being assured the problem that held us up had been taken care of. A half hour later we're told it has not been taken care of and would we disembark. On the way out, I see this older black fella wearing a Twins hat and an anniversary leather jacket of the black baseball leagues and we get to talking and it turns out to be Jim "Mudcat" Grant, the 1965 20-game winning pitcher for my Minnesota Twins and winner of game one of the 1965 World Series. So over the next hour we talk about everybody he played with and teams he played for, and after a while Kathy joins us and soon the airline says the problem is still not fixed so they buy us lunch and Jim and Kathy and I continue at the Burger King in the airport. Talk came around to the old neighborhood around Dale and Selby and the Celebrity lounge came up. The Celebrity on Selby was started by Earl Battey, our All-Star catcher and Sandy Stevens, our Gopher National Champion Quarterback after his playing days. Jim told a story about one of those "little black jockey" lawn ornaments on Summit near Selby and how Earl conspired with Jim to get rid of it. The first attempt was after hours when they tied a rope to it and then tied the other end to the handle of Earl's truck on the passenger side and took off. It tore the door right off Earl's truck. Over a three-month period he said, there were two more attempts and finally they were sure the anchor of the ornament must have been buried ten feet deep because they never did pull it out. He did say however that they had pulled it over so far that the jockey's hand and face were touching the ground. Sometime after that it was removed. Jim's stories continued and finally it was three o'clock (we were due to leave at 10 AM) and the airline announced our flight was cancelled. Now I try, but things like that piss me off; however running into Mudcat Grant and sharing all those stories made the whole day worth it. It was a thrill spending the day with him.

I was watching the selection show for the NCAA Basketball Tournament a little while ago and I flashed on a Ray Christenson broadcast I remember of a Gopher game sometime in the 50's. There were high hopes that year I remember and two brothers were in the starting lineup: Ron and Whitey Johnson. Ron was a forward and a fairly legitimate All-Big Ten candidate and Whitey was a co-captain and point guard. I can't remember who they were playing but all of a sudden I heard Ray say: "Whitey Johnson brings the ball into the forecourt, barking instructions in Norwegian." Now of course there's nothing strange about Norwegian in Minnesota (provided you don't ask a Swede), but the idea of basketball plays being called out in Norwegian and being understood in Norwegian by not just his brother, but the three other guys on the court at Williams Arena, has remained in my formidable memory for at least sixty years. I do remember that particular team being disappointing but I'm sure Norwegian had anything to do with it.

I'm not sure how to feel about this but I have lived to become very grateful for my education. That is, the education provided for me by my parents and through public high school. It amounted to eight years of Catholic grade school and three years of high school. I didn't return for my senior year and joined the Army instead. During those years I had some very good teachers. Even the two who were very unfair were good teachers…at least to other students and of course they both taught me that they would not be the last of their kind I'd be encountering in life, and that was a valuable lesson too. Later in college, I only encountered one blatantly unfair professor. She thought she taught very well and so did most of us until it came time for her tests. She gave very poor instructions for taking them and then of course blamed us for not studying. This happens in life all the time in the work place so to that extent her incompetence in that area was a form of preparation for the real world I suppose. But think of it, those first eleven years and then later, six years of college (to include graduate school) and I encountered only three losers. Hell, you don't get that good of a ratio in nearly any endeavor and as I said, their failings were lessons for life I for one was surely going to need. No, the truth is too many things went right with my education to continue to hold grudges on the three that didn't. And yet all these years later, I still need to remind myself not to be bitter. Sometimes it works.

Some guys are just Joe or Joey or even Joseph. But some of us have several names and it occurred to me that names #3 and #4 in my case began with a book I read in Vietnam. My name is Walter Jon Savage Jr. My nickname, the main one anyway, was Skip and many people back home in St. Paul still call me that. But my cousin's wife sent me a book when I was overseas called The Arrangement by Elia Kazan. In it, the main character's real name was Elijah...something Greek which I can't remember. After college and times being what they were ethnically speaking, he changed his name to Eddie Anderson and got a job as an advertising executive. But on the side, he was a writer and called himself Evans Arness. Soon after that and not realizing its influence, some guys and I went on R&R and decided to call each other by our first names. So I was free to choose and decided on the shortened version of my middle name, Jack. Then I was Jack Savage for more than thirty years on the radio. When I registered with SAG during my acting days I had to add W. to the Jack and kept that when I started writing. It all makes sense in a certain way but I do wonder if that book influenced me.

My dear mother saw two men go off to war in her lifetime, one at the St. Paul train station and one in Minneapolis. Both my dad and I came home. My great uncle Willie Patton went off to World War I and was killed in action. The biographer of the Savage family, Zoe Lapin, wanted more information of how Uncle Willie died. The records office in Washington, whatever it was, sent her back a one sentence reply: "Going over the top." That meant crawling out of your trench and walking into gunfire for the most part. Anyway, evidently my grandmother Annabelle was very close to her brother Willie and came with my mother to see my dad off to the second World War at the same St. Paul railway station she said goodbye to Willie. That day, she became grief stricken thinking about "poor

Willie, never coming home." Not her son going off to war but her brother not coming back. This angered my mother to no end and according to her they had a big fight about it on the way home. Many years later, Mom saw me off to war and told me that story. Three guys from the same family went off to war and the one who never came home was still being celebrated in story as the last one left. There is symmetry there of course that is, to me at least...justice somehow.

I painted a picture of my hometown, St. Paul, Minnesota, not long ago. The vantage point I chose was from an area we call Harriet Island, looking up across the Mississippi River toward the downtown loop. Naturally I took a bit of license with the buildings and what have you, because I was working from memory only and chose the 1st National Bank Building for my center of interest. Actually, the 1st National Bank isn't that close to the Mississippi River which separates Minneapolis from St. Paul but it's an important landmark to me. From where Children's Hospital used to be, below the Summit Avenue bluff, you could see the 1st National Bank sign on top of the building. I was a patient there as a little boy. There was nothing really wrong with me and I knew that. My mother used hospitals to get some space between her and difficult situations. I was being a difficult child because I wouldn't eat and so they put me in the one place I for sure wouldn't eat...Children's Hospital. I knew Mom and Dad were just getting some space from me and it made me very sad. I used to look at that sign every night feeling more and more like my life, as I knew it, was over. After five days or so I was taken home but I never forgot that week or that landmark. We all moved on from there but much of my childhood was never the same after that. However, I did start eating more after that. I suppose that's something.

If I tried to pinpoint the view of it, what it looked like, it was the difference between fluorescent and regular light. That's what my childhood depression was like. Not the cold but the wind, and even then only in gusts. It was an endless cloudiness and a darkness that seemed to begin moments before leaving for school and came again moments after getting home. I fought that darkness with light, with every lamp in the apartment on. One spring, we raked the dead grass around the apartment building, Rick and I. It was slow going but was warm enough to take our T-shirts off. I was as white as a piece of paper evidently and I remember the guys at the gas station across the street staring. I was very thin too, and must not have looked well. After we finished, Rick commented that I: "didn't look like a ghost anymore." But the winter had taken its toll and it wouldn't be the last. There were problems at home but there was a problem with winter too. It seemed to get worse as I grew up.

It was the saddest look I'd ever seen. My mother didn't believe in babysitters and she took me downtown shopping a lot. My reward for being "good" was either hamburgers at the White Castle or a hamburger at Eddie Weber's. They were good in both places and I remember my mother would refuse to call a hamburger a hamburger at Eddie Weber's. A ground beef sandwich is what she would order. They usually came back with a hamburger anyway but once, sure enough, they came back with a ground beef sandwich, cut in half on white bread. She sent it back and I got my bun but it was a source of aggravation to me. Eddie Weber's was also a bar and had a mural behind it with various dogs depicted standing at a bar. The place was somewhat dark as was the style of bars then, and there were booths and tables and chairs. I think we were leaving when someone commented on something to do with me. I say that because they were all looking at me and smiling after it was said. I must have been embarrassed because I got a little ahead of my mother just then moving toward the door. And then I saw her. She had a glass goblet of beer and sat all alone in a booth. She looked at me and smiled so sad a smile it nearly made me cry. I remember I stopped and looked back, asking my mom to "come along" in my sudden haste to escape. I didn't look back at the woman, I couldn't. But it was a snapshot I've never forgotten. I told my mother about it and she supposed the woman had perhaps remembered something in her past that I reminded her of. I agreed but though I hadn't done anything wrong, I remember feeling very bad that I could be the cause of such a sad, heartbroken smile.

It was the field beneath the Highland Park Library. I had somehow missed my first eligible season to play Little League baseball. The second year I had hoped to be picked by one of the major league teams during tryouts but I wasn't. Instead I was picked by the Millers, a minor league team and had gotten over the disappointment by the time this day of practice had come around. I was a pitcher and utility infielder as I recall and when this black Cadillac pulled up I barely noticed. The man inside got out and came over to Mr. Segal our coach, and soon three or four of us were playing catch in front of this guy. Moments later I was being asked if I wanted to move up to the Giants in the major league. Naturally I said yes and was then instructed to ride down to another field to join their practice. It was up a long big hill of some five blocks and then down another long hill alongside the golf course. I had a flat tire. I didn't know what to do and so I walked my bike as far as I could, rode it with the flat down the big hill and walked it as fast as I could the rest of the way. If I didn't make it, I was sure they'd give up on me and choose someone else. I'm pretty sure I cried on the way but by the time I got there, practice was ending although everyone was still there. I was introduced to my new teammates as though nothing had happened and when Mr. Rosenberg saw I had a flat, he drove me and my bike home. When I got there my parents knew all about it because they had stopped by the other practice site and the coach had told them. The difference between the major and minor leagues on the playground at school was a thing of status about the hat you wore and school was just ending for the year. Within a week, I got my Giants hat and asked my mother if I could wear it to school. She smiled and reminded me school was out. I swear I was almost disappointed.

I had waited more than twenty years and my moment was at hand. Then, I don't know what happened. I knew the day would come but I suppose I'd been smiling at the prospect for so long, I just couldn't help give myself away. Back in 1975, the power went out on my three to six-thirty shift on KTRF in Thief River Falls. I was new to the job, but the show had been going well that day and then this happened. I came out of the control room in a panic and said: "We're off the air!" With the lights out and the speakers silent this came as no surprise to anyone there. Don Howe came over and said: "Just settle down. Go back in there and explain that we're off the air and we'll be back on shortly". It seemed reasonable. And a moment later there I was, sitting in the dark control room explaining to a dead microphone why we were not broadcasting. Somewhere in the middle I must have noticed them laughing because it suddenly occurred to me. Then, nearly twenty-five years later, all those years between events and it was my turn to pass on the joke. I looked at the young announcer seriously and began to calmly explain what he should do. And then, I just blew it and started laughing. I couldn't help it. I've wondered about it ever since. I think I enjoyed the story and the fact that it happened to me, perhaps too much to relinquish the role of being my own punch line.

I'm not sure where in the scheme of things I placed myself just then. I seem to remember not feeling very accomplished, being between jobs and maybe feeling a bit old. I was new to shooting baskets again and so naturally my game was a little weak as well. So here he comes. You couldn't help but like him, a nice looking, clear-eyed soccer dad of I'd say thirty, wearing a Princeton tee-shirt, wondering if he could shoot a few baskets with me? "Of course", I said and we did. It turns out he was a civil engineer or something and he did graduate from Princeton. I was somewhere in my late forties I'm guessing, but in any case I wasn't thirty and never went to Princeton. In fact, I was several credits short of my bachelor's degree, a condition I stayed in for more years than I like to remember. Now I can't remember how long I had been there, or where in the interest of 'getting a little exercise' my workout was that day, but I remembered he seemed fresh and I did not. We talked a little while we played but soon I just wanted to go home. It was nothing in particular and I'm sure I took my ball and left while he could have kept playing. I'm sure he'd never remember me and yet I've never forgotten him. In fact, I've become quite a bit more accomplished in the time since we met. I finished my degree, went on to get my master's and have since taught at the college. I wonder if he had anything to do with that.

I've been thinking about the futility (in general anyway), of not accepting the status quo even though you're happy. Then it becomes about goals and things like that. Which is fine, but now in my retirement it doesn't seem to make the sense it once did. It was a useful carrot to chase in a lot of ways but in fact, once you realize you're in the home stretch of your life, so to speak anyway, the 'hard and fast' rules just seem less.... hard and fast. I'll give you an example. Some years ago, knowing I had been ignoring certain skills in certain areas and feeling my age I suppose, I said to myself: "Hey...you will produce, in some way, shape or form, ten books." After all, that's really a small number for a career communicator (radio, news, etc.) who never fell into the 'local phenomenon' category, broadcast wise. What with divorce and searching for the meaning of life, I did in fact manage to make it to the second biggest radio market in the U.S. long enough to receive a small pension; and believe me when I say that's a rare achievement in radio overall and especially these days. Anyway, yesterday my seventh book Imagination: The Art of W. Jack Savage was published and it was time for this. I'm not in a writing mode and haven't finished a novel that should have been done two years ago. It's been so long in fact, that I have nearly enough short stories for a new collection. But my art production is enjoying a remarkable resurgence period with some real quality there and that's something, surely. The rest will come back when it and I feel the time is right. It seems simple now, without a job to factor in. See what you have to look forward to?

I was flying home to Minnesota last year to visit friends and family. It was winter and I thought going home to the snow and cold might be fun in the short term. That was the plan anyway. The flight was a red-eye leaving LAX around midnight and getting in to Minneapolis/St. Paul about 5 AM. I mention it because I think if I had flown out at 5 AM and got to Minnesota around noon their time, this might not have happened. I had all day to think about it you see, and about an hour before we were to leave for the airport, my anxiety was getting worse and worse until finally I was having a real panic attack. I have no fear of flying. I don't like flying only because it's become so uncomfortable in the last few years. I just could not go and so my wife said, "then don't go" and I started feeling better right away. This trip had been postponed once for another reason but I was (or at least thought I was) looking forward to going home. I'd never cancelled like that; not really. The last panic attack I had was a few years ago or so and a friend, a Vietnam Veteran I served with up north finally lost his battle with cancer and I planned on driving north to the wake and funeral. I became filled with anxiety and foreboding but I felt I needed to go so I did. The experience was terrible and after the visitation I went back to the motel and got very drunk. When I woke up, my wife called to say there were very high winds and we lost some shingles and had no power. As a result, I just came home and missed the funeral. I don't know, maybe I'm getting older and feeling my mortality. Naturally, I thought about this latest panic attack for a while. Overall, I've had maybe three or four panic episodes in my lifetime but at least there was some hint as to what might have brought it on. That time I couldn't go to the airport there was no hint. Although gradually, leading up to the trip,

I was beginning to work on an itinerary of the people I wanted to see and what days they might be available and so forth. Since I've retired my world has gotten very small and I've probably gotten together with old friends fewer than ten times since I stopped working. The idea of seeing and socializing with eight or nine people in six days at five or six different venues would represent a whirlwind of activity for me. I'm sure, the more I thought about these things and how much time each stop would take to get to the other place later…it just got too much. You spend time waiting and waiting for something to happen and wind up wishing it was over before you even do it. So I won't be doing that anymore. I'm just going to get on the plane and when I get there, drop in on people and hope for the best. The strange part is, I'm very happy in my little world here. It's just gotten smaller and quieter and that's okay until you begin thinking you can just visit and party for five days in a row like the old days without regard for the status quo. Anyway, that's what I've come up with. It doesn't worry me. It just makes me feel dumb and I've felt that a lot more than I've felt panic.

I have wished and even prayed for a variety of outcomes in my life. I prayed for things of course, probably starting with Christmas. As an only child I can say I was rarely disappointed. Because of that I was able (in receiving that for which I had yearned for so much) to realize early on that the yearning and even the planning was often more satisfying then the outcome or the object. I learned from this but it never gave me a clear picture of what the ramifications of my decisions would be. One morning in Vietnam I got a clear message, and I've always felt the important decisions and my ability to make them as a man began that day with someone telling me how stupid I was to be doing what I had done. After being wounded and sick with malaria and Dengue Fever, I heard they needed door gunners in helicopter units and I put in for a transfer. Time passed, I got better and went back out in the field. There were leeches in certain parts of the jungle that didn't seem to need water and when you'd spend a night near them they got on you and that's just the way it was. In the morning we'd strip down sort of and check each other out and burn the leeches off with cigarettes before starting our day. A guy across from me had heard that my orders transferring to this helicopter company had come through, and he kept telling me how crazy I was and that door gunners got shot at a hundred times more than infantrymen and so forth and as he did, he burned a leech off his eyebrow and I knew at that moment my decision was right. I hated living in the jungle more than I hated being shot at and it's a trade-off I'd make again anytime. Sometimes it's about your environment and not your purpose.

Growing up, there was only one hero for me and that was Tarzan. Then one day many years later, I surprised myself by being able to instantly express why it was Tarzan. After all, I hadn't thought about it or Tarzan in many years, but the question of why Tarzan over all the other possible heroes of my life was an easy question to answer. Tarzan was athletic and handsome yes, but he had complete mastery over everything I feared as a child and everything I feared lived in the jungle: lions, snakes, spiders, crocodiles and natives who when they caught you, tied you between two trees that were bent over and when they cut the ropes you would be pulled apart. There were other things. Tarzan got along with all the good animals: chimpanzees, elephants, etc. and they all loved him too. And let's not forget about Jane. Maureen O'Sullivan was so great in the part that I fell in love with her right away, as well. I remember one line from "Tarzan and His Mate" in particular. That's kind of strange because they gave Johnny Weissmuller very few lines because he had kind of a high voice. Anyway, Jane had spent time with Tarzan and fell in love with him and as she was being rescued, her father said of Tarzan, "He belongs to the jungle." To which she replied, "No, he belongs to me!" I remember thinking, who wouldn't want to be loved like that?

I was supposed to meet a friend today and our signals got crossed, and he went one place and I another. While I was sitting there, for no particular reason I got thinking about doing things for people, helping them out, you know? There are some people who everyone depends on to do that. Often they're expected to do it so much, people just forget to even say thank you. I had an uncle like that. You could depend on that guy like the sun coming up. I came home on leave once during my army days and asked Uncle Al if I could borrow twenty bucks. He said: "Sure", and after I left, I went back to the fort and when I got paid, I went to the post office and got a postal money order for twenty and sent it to him. My mother said he was so touched that I paid him back, she said he'd probably loan me any amount of money in the future. Maybe for that very reason, I never asked. However, one time I had a bunch of winter parking tickets (snow bird tickets, we called them) and a couple turned into warrants before I could get them paid. Then when I got pulled over, I got arrested. The girl I was with went over to my uncle's and he came down and bailed me out. Years later he wound up in a nursing home and I visited every time I went home. I thought how sad it was that the one guy who visited everybody should wind up in a nursing home. The last time I saw him he looked at me and said: "I've been here a year today, Skip." It had really been a little over eight years and while he wasn't happy about being there a year, at least it didn't feel to him like eight. Not long after that he died and when they buried him out at the National Cemetery, one of the veterans at the graveside told me they were burying a World War II Veteran every twenty minutes. Uncle Al was the best guy. I was lucky to have him for an uncle.

I look back at several turning points in my life and the one I keep coming back to is running a marathon. Actually, I ran seven and one-half marathons. My best time was a pretty decent one for a guy in his forties and I've always said that had I not dealt with some stomach problems in the first part of the race, I'd have broken four hours that day. The point is this: once you've taught yourself to run twenty-six miles and change, what is there you can't do? I was working at this radio station and we did pretty well for a new format they were trying, but I knew from many years of experience that in spite of our numbers, they probably weren't going to be good enough to keep us going and sadly, I was right. Though I was hoping for the best, I did prepare for the worst and when the plug was pulled, I had a plan in place. Now without going into too much detail (this was during the time I was running), since that day I finished up the bachelor's degree I'd been telling everybody for many years that I had, I got a master's degree, taught college film studies part time for six years, wrote seven books, had individual stories published seventy times, worked ten years on the radio in L.A. (also part time), and retired with a pension at 62. Now for a guy who started the day with the longest roach in the ashtray for upwards of thirty years, the truth is I shouldn't be this accomplished and I know it. So it wasn't long after I finished running twenty-six miles and change for the first time that the impediments to achievement started going away, while achievement itself began to happen. Now I'm not stupid. I could have made these changes earlier in my life but everybody has their own benchmark for doing something and for me, it seems to have been running that first marathon.

You have to be of a certain age to remember but those of us who grew up with the first television shows were imbued with a New York sensibility we wouldn't have had otherwise. Dave Garroway was the host of the Today Show and nearly everything on television in those early days originated in New York. So in a sense, we were all from New York and when you're a child, at least a child living in St. Paul, we just felt like St. Paul was a small version of New York. We had a downtown and to me, that looked very much like the New York we were seeing on our black and white Muntz television. There were guys like John Q. Lewis and Arthur Godfrey of course and later, Steve Allen and Jack Paar, and everyone whether they were from New York or not, were broadcasting from there and it rubbed off on many of us in a lot of ways. There was also the idea that we too could one day go to New York and make it big. Randy Merriman from Minneapolis was the host of the game show The Big Payoff with Bess Myerson, former Miss America modeling a mink coat as one of the prizes. The point is if you watched TV in the 50's, you too were a New Yorker for a while. Actually, I've never been to New York. It's still on my bucket list of course but if I don't get there, in a way like I said, I'm kind of from there so it won't matter so much.

There is this Bevis and Butthead skit where the two are standing in a 7-11 store and one says," I'm gonna go try to score", whereupon he walks ten feet to a woman selecting something to eat and he says, "Ha, ha...chiliburger, huh?" She looks at him, walks away and he returns to his friend who asks him, "Did you score?" He responds, "Sort of." If you're a man and you don't recognize the brilliant simplicity of that piece, then you don't remember being an awkward boy, trying to solve the mystery that is women. You see, by saying something to this woman and having her not respond at all, he realizes he's somehow getting closer to saying something a woman might like. I'm not saying it's fun remembering that skin crawling awkwardness of youth but it does remind us that there was a lot of trial and error going on before we ever achieved "cool", if only in our own minds. I was with a friend once out at Midway Center and we were on our way to Wards for something and this girl really liked my friend. We didn't know her but she followed us and finally came up and introduced herself and everything about her was saying "This is it, pal! This is what you been waiting for all your life!" I could see it but somehow it seemed like he couldn't. They exchanged numbers and all that and when she left I said:" What's wrong with you? She like... fell in love with you and you acted like it wasn't happening!" To this day, I remember his reply as the most startling honesty I ever heard. That's probably why I never really told anybody about it later.

He said: "She scared me." When I think of that I think… no, it is fun to think of it, but I wouldn't want to live it over for anything.

There's another side to Mother's Day that should from time to time be acknowledged. There were wonderful women that I have known who never married nor wanted children of their own and almost more importantly, never wanted to go to bed with me, yet loved me and saw things in me that needed cultivating and not just because I was a man. Many men saw it in women and girls as well, who became the mothers our mothers couldn't be. For they didn't take any crap at all and saw through our charm like it was nonexistent and told us who we could be if we ever pulled our heads out of our asses and actually strove for a legacy of some kind based on things we were lucky enough to possess: looks, brains, wit, balls, a sense for what was going on. They bent down and whispered in our ears of our potential, the things we could achieve; the people we could be if we only got it together. They were the ones we came back to and said: "Look...you were right." They just looked at us with that look of theirs that they hypnotized us with into believing they could see our futures and smiled. They never said I told you so because in some ways, they were the authors of who we became. Mother's Day for many of us, is the most important remembrance of our lives.... those magical aunts and mentors and ladies down the hallway and at the store. They saw something we couldn't see, and made us believe they did and we took that football and ran with it. On Mother's Day, me, who had the greatest mother in the world, celebrate all those ladies. Without them I have serious doubts...I really do.

When I was a boy our first exposure to the classics was, for most of us, Classic's Comic Books. I remember Moby Dick and The Last of the Mohicans and along with the pictures, they explained the story as best as they could in comic book length. I came away with two impressions because the truth is, I bought them thinking I'd need to know these stories someday and this was a way to start. First, they were all dark people in terrible circumstances somehow, whether they came through it or not. Secondly, in comic book form, even though I read them each several times, it never seemed worth it. Not the Shakespeare nor the Dickens nor James Fenimore Cooper. As an adult, I read many and played several parts in the plays of Shakespeare during my acting days but I never really changed my mind. They were written in shadows and the shadows are on every page and the result seemed to be that those who were most well versed in the classics shrouded their stories in seriousness to the point where many were unreadable. In other words, without the dark tone, no tale they would ever spin had enough foreboding intent to be considered worthwhile. Somehow though, reading them and those who prayed to them was worthwhile, because it showed a path through the darkness where light could not only prevail but completely defeat the intent of those we studied. That is to say, in writing you needed to come to a place where you not only knew the masters were full of shit, you also knew why. It was then that you were capable of writing without the specter of old depressed men and could actually find something to say in your own voice...or not.

I was raised a Roman Catholic, so as soon as it became my decision whether or not to attend church, I quit going. Catholic grade school left a bad taste in my mouth and while I continued calling myself a Catholic for many years, I never really practiced the faith again. Then one day, I saw an ad, disguised as a public service announcement with Pat Boone, telling me not to see "The Last Temptation of Christ". I can't speak for everyone but I have always made a policy of doing anything that Pat Boone didn't think was in my interest as a Christian. It was a Martin Scorsese film, meaning it would be at least a half hour too long and my wife and I expected to be bored at best, but the fundamentalist Christian stamp of disapproval made it a "must see" on that basis alone. Well, I assure you it had the opposite effect Pat Boone and others warned about because our faith in Christian principles came roaring back to life and we wound up joining the Episcopal Church and have been there ever since. My way or the highway religion has driven more than Catholics away from church and while I believe anyone can practice their religion as they see fit, the old time religion crowd still needs to feel and say that their way is the only way and everybody else is just wrong. Indeed, everybody else being wrong seems to have become more important than their assertion that they are right. Naturally my conservative friends and Christian conservatives in particular don't see it that way and that scares me enough about my own faith to keep it just at arm's length. I realize that knowing the absolute answer to everything is not a virus as such but I wouldn't want to catch it anyway.

Growing up in St. Paul, I feel as though I had a pretty good understanding of radio and television. My first experience was in radio WDGY and Bill Diehl in the afternoon after school. This was in the late fifties, early sixties and he'd run down the Top 40, which as I recall changed once a week. Now the Top 40 in those days was all over the place, it was not uncommon to hear Steve Lawrence sing, "My Claire De Lune," "Stranger on the Shore" from Mr. Acker Bilk, Lee Dorsey singing "Ya Ya", Johnny Tillotson's "Poetry in Motion," and on it went. There was no Elvis that I can recall and aside from the occasional gag song like "Alley Oop" by the Coasters, there was really nothing and no one that stood out. However, there was one song that stayed at the top of the charts for just too damn long. It was Bert Kaemfort and his orchestra with "Wonderland by Night", which featured a tuba solo, no less. I grew to hate this song with all my might and one day, after retaining its number one status for yet another week, I shut off the radio and didn't listen at all for several years. It was strange then, that I should have wound up a radio announcer for all the years that I did. I never forgot Bert Kaemfort though, and every time I'd hear my fellow DJ's bitch about having to play Barry Manilow and Lionel Richie every ten minutes or so, I'd recall the true human suffering I experienced at the hands of Bill Diehl playing "Wonderland by Night". I've never admitted this but I worked an oldies format back in the 80's and in addition to what we would play on our own, there were reel-to-reel tapes from the music service and one night I looked at the playlist and there it was..."Wonderland by Night". Naturally I fast forwarded and by-passed the cut. But here's the worst part...after my shift ended, I went in the production room and with a razorblade spliced the damn thing out of the reel. Sure I felt guilty for a while...then I felt great!

I'm just guessing, but we kids who grew up in St. Paul were no strangers to the idea that somebody yells at somebody smaller who then yells at maybe the dog who chases the cat and on down it goes. I'm thinking Paul Tempke was at least a year older than me or even maybe two. He was the better looking of the twin Tempke brothers. Anyway, I could somehow tell he was going through something because he never picked on anyone and for whatever reason one day he decided to pick on me. Holy Spirit playground was going through some changes and there was a roll of fencing there and while being chased by him, I fell over it and tore my leg open on the prickly end of the roll. It was pretty bad although there wasn't much blood and down at Anchor Hospital it took twenty-six stitches in all to close up the two wounds. It was quite an event for me. Anyway it was summer and everybody was at the Highland pool and I limped up there too and Paul Tempke, guilt ridden over what he had done clearly against his nature, never failed to ask how my leg was and say how sorry he was that it happened. I don't know who was leaning on him that he needed to lean on someone smaller, but because he was mostly always a decent kid, I never blamed Paul. I knew it was the fault of whomever it was who started the cycle. I do hope this particular one ended with me. I think it did but perhaps I'm too easy on myself and that kind of thing was sometimes a part of growing up in St. Paul, like everywhere else.

I was an actor for long stretches of my life. I never made much money at it even after I got out here to L.A. to pursue it seriously, but I always loved it and appeared in plays most of my life no matter where my radio career had taken me. But the first lines I had to memorize and recite complete with blocking (movement and actions in a theatrical venue), was as an altar boy at Holy Spirit Catholic Church. This was back before Pope John the 23rd changed everything so the whole Mass was in Latin. But I did okay in spite of the enormous pressure (I'm not kidding) and got to where if I had to, I could do what was necessary all by myself should one of the others not show up. In those days at Holy Spirit, Holy Mass was held at 6:30, 7:30 and 8:15 A.M. (or so), Monday through Friday and maybe Saturday too. Novena was always on Tuesday night and on Sunday, it was 6:00, 7:00, 8:00, 9:00, 10:00 and 11:00 A.M. High Mass (requiring a cadre of altar boys and a director who clapped when we were supposed to move around) and 12:15 P.M.

I was looking for a picture of the old church because it was kind of interesting. The new church was built on top of the old church but I couldn't find one. However, I did run into a schedule of the Holy Mass at Holy Spirit today and things are very, very different. There are only two services on Sunday and one daily Mass on weekdays except for Monday (how Monday got left off I don't know). There is confession twice a week and something called the Eucharistic Adoration. It's called "devotion" and it goes for three hours on Sunday and on Wednesday for six hours. It seems a rather severe reduction in worship times but I'm betting there are more people in the seats because of it. It is quite a change but then the old schedule was more than fifty years ago for me. I'm not sure why, but the fact that they no longer celebrate Novena made me a little sad. We were a rather small but quite regular crowd on Tuesday nights for Novena and the walk home was always nicer because of it. This site and these memories keep reminding me how nice it was for us in St. Paul during those years.

It's a very difficult thing to understand when the comfortable and familiar things about home become oppressive and suffocating. One day you live in a pretty nice town with mostly nice people and the next, the thought of becoming one of them and never going anywhere else becomes the worst thing you can think of. It seems to happen during that time just before adulthood, when you're not ready for a 9 to 5 job but the thought of more school is just too much. Where you can't legally drink so you find someone to "buy for you" on weekends and then find someplace to drink it before staggering home, only to realize you're in the same place and in the same circumstance. In the St. Paul I lived in during the 60's, military recruiters had no problems filling their quotas with young male graduates and dropouts like me, willing to literally do anything and go anywhere, just to do "anything" and go "anywhere." I drank with friends on weekends and one night we all decided to go see Chief Nils down at the old post office and enlist in the Navy. There was something called the "buddy plan" we'd heard where you could go through basic training together. Anyway, I was too hung over and I missed that enlistment party but not the idea that the service was a way out and a few months later, when I should have been involved in my senior year at Monroe High School, I joined the Army and wound up in Vietnam just as my classmates were graduating. I never regretted that decision and yet I do wish I'd have found another way to make more of my opportunities. I remember how I felt, which led to the choices I made. Of all the possibilities though, St. Paul was a wonderful place to come home to. When I did, I was no more of an adult than I was before I left. More mature in ways maybe, but nothing approaching responsible. For many of us, it took a little longer.

The milk store was just a block away from my house and a short block at that. If you needed milk, that was one thing you couldn't get at the drug store and whereas you could get a half pint of ice cream at the drug store in the old days, if you wanted more the milk store was the place. It was also where we got our Popsicles, Fudgsicles, and Dreamsicles. However in doing research, mostly to find the correct spelling, what I found was Creamsicles rather than Dreamsicles. It was the same deal, vanilla ice cream on a stick sort of covered with orange and strawberry sherbet. But I know it was Dreamsicles! Also there were Drumstick cones, Eskimo Pies and Cheerios that were the same but a little cheaper I think. Push-Ups as I remember had orange sherbet and you pushed it up from its cardboard covering. Porte's, down the street on Snelling had a lot of neat stuff but they were the only ones around who had frozen Milky Way Bars on a stick. The milk store started getting these other things that were kind of cool and I can't remember what they were called. They were like almost shot-glass size servings of ice cream in these plastic cups. They had a lot of different flavors too, and you opened them and sort of squeezed from the bottom and it filling came up and you ate it that way. The cup was blue and the top, silver color. The milk store was cool for one other thing. It was right next to Jerry's Liquor Store who would throw out cigar boxes in the back (more people smoked cigars then) and sometimes, if you were lucky you'd get one of the wooden cigar boxes. All in all, a trip to the milk store was fun and the guy in there was always nice. I can't remember his name. Help me out with the Dreamsicle thing, will ya? I know it was Dreamsicle.

My dad always said the same thing when talking about the White Castle. They were 10-cents apiece when I was a kid. Dad would say: "In my day, they were a nickel" (now wait for it)...."and they were better. "I like that memory because as I grew older I realized..."In my day...everything was better." But a few years ago, I came home and hadn't visited in a couple of years. My friend Nick and I went to the White Castle on Rice Street (off Sherburne I think); I took one bite and said: "Wait a minute...something is wrong!" Nick said..."Oh, it's the salt police" When I got up to the counter the young guy handed me packets of salt without being asked. I actually thought Nick was joking, but salt content evidently is regulated in the Twin Cities now and since. That IS a tragic development and I don't mind saying it is one of the things that will make dying less hard to take because when I tell my son Tony, "In my day they were a dime.... and they were BETTER!"

In the film "The New Centurions," a robbery victim identified her assailant as wearing a red shirt. The veteran cop pulled over a guy two blocks later wearing a brown shirt with orange and white stripes who turned out to be the guilty party. "But she said he had on a red shirt", said the rookie cop. His partner said that what was important was that it was red to her: bright, a shirt that would stand out in a crowd and in her mind that word was red. When I first came to California I took care of an elderly woman and her son who was a stroke victim. He could only say a few words that I could understand but within two weeks it had gotten so I could almost read his mind. He could still only say those few words same words, but by paying attention to the intonation of his voice and various other little signs, I knew exactly what he was saying. These experiences tell us how important it is to not just listen to what's being said, but what those words actually mean and they vary a great deal from time to time and situation to situation. I had a little league football coach who always had a stoic look on his face and he would nod his head slowly. It was always the same and yet we knew the difference. Same face, nod, you screwed up or you did a good job. By learning the difference we learned when we did something right or wrong without being told. People in sales and who deal with the public in other ways interpret what people are saying and what they really mean all day long. "Someday, we'll all have chips in our head and we'll communicate without talking." Hell, we do that now.

I lived on South Brimhall as a little boy with east-west Randolph as our main thoroughfare. So as I looked at child-like maps of my world, I knew that I could get to the Pacific Ocean by going west on

Randolph or to the Atlantic by going east. There was even a bus that I was quite sure did this every day from my home in St. Paul, Minnesota. From South Brimhall, however, my path to both the North Pole and the South Pole was a side street with big elm trees on both sides and so one day, I decided to walk to the North Pole. I didn't get very far for a couple of reasons. Whereas I could cross Brimhall during this stage in my life, I was forbidden from crossing Palace, the first street to the north. I reasoned that the North Pole was probably at least a hundred more streets that I was forbidden to cross but as long as I stayed on Brimhall, it would be okay. Three blocks later I ran into an obstacle I couldn't reason away. Brimhall ended at St. Clair, a mere four blocks from my home and without breaking some serious east-west restrictions to my travels, I decided to head home and the next day opted for the South Pole instead. It was a little further I knew but with the North Pole now out-of-play, the South Pole was all that was left. The next day my plan was to walk up to Snelling, cross at the light (and out of sight of my mother), walk back to Brimhall and head for the South Pole. I chickened out and went to the milk store for an Eskimo Pie instead. Later I learned that Brimhall to the south of Randolph only ran three or four blocks as well, so that would have been disappointing too. However, by that time I was planning on a trip to New York City on the Randolph bus where I could wave to my Mom on TV from the street view of Dave Garroway's Today Show. That never happened either but they were great plans in the mind of the child that I was then.

I love St. Paul and one of the things I love about it, is that it's just big enough to leave nearly all of us wanting in some way. That is, places we never went to, things we never did, treats we never tried and on it goes. I'll give you an example. As a boy growing up I was a finicky eater and believe me I could do three chapters on the big deal people made about not eating something that was put in front of you, so let me be real clear on this point: if it came down to 'eat it or die' I'd have taken death in a heartbeat and no, I've never forgiven those who insisted I eat something I didn't want to and I never will. Once we went to the Forum Minneapolis I think it was called and it was my first experience with cafeteria style dining. Specifically, putting exactly what I wanted on my plate and more importantly, keeping things off of my plate that I didn't want to be there, which brings me around to the Quality Cafeteria on Snelling somewhere around Minnehaha. I always wanted to go there and suggested it to my parents more than once. It never happened. Instead, I was taken to things like the Silver Fox Booya where I assure you there was nothing at all for me to eat. I've never been in DeGiddio's either. I must have passed the place five hundred times and never went in and I can't tell you why. I did get to enjoy Tin Cups before it went away and for that and other spots that are now just a memory, I am grateful. My point is that St. Paul is still big enough to not have tried everything. There's still time for some things I suppose.

The truth is, we independent writers know going in that even if we do all the right things to find an audience for the stories we write, we'll be lucky if we get anything over a hundred readers to actually take the time to read what we write. Moreover, if say, even twenty-five or thirty of them wrote reviews that generated, I don't know, five or six more sales, that would be great. We outnumber writers who have traditional publishers and even though we've been shut out by them (in the hope we'll give up and go home), we can read too and know to a certainty that we're better than most of the slugs who have a name but haven't written anything approaching good since they were much younger. However, we take our sunshine where we can find it and one day a friend called me from St. Paul and said: "Hey, I just checked your book out of the Highland Public Library." "I don't have one of my books in any of the libraries back there," I said. "It takes a little more than just sending them one to get on the shelf you know." Anyway, it was my second short story collection which means, somebody somewhere bought a copy of this book by

W. Jack Savage and took the time and the trouble to get my book accepted and on the shelf at the Highland Public Library, a library that cast a shadow on the very field where I played little league baseball, football and within a block or two of where I played little league basketball at Horace Mann School. What a nice thing to do and I have no idea who did it. I even tried to find out. Well inspired by this, I managed to get my third novel in the downtown library and that's the way it goes...inch-by-inch. I wouldn't have it any other way. Oh, did I mention it was W. Jack Savage?

The hills of St. Paul are one of the anomalous features of our capitol city when compared to say Minneapolis, which I always thought was very flat by comparison. At the same time, my bicycle, a 500-pound no speed (or so it seemed at times), made it fun going down the hills but not so great going back up. The result was I would go great distances to avoid going back up the steep hills I had gone down. An example would be the fun of going down Snelling Avenue where it dead-ends at West 7th. It was steep enough to be fun with a winding path through the woods on either side and at the bottom you faced the Clark 100 gas station across West 7th. Then to avoid the worst of it, going west to St. Paul Avenue and up Edgecombe to where it becomes Fairview was your best bet. That way, by the time you get to Randolph you're in pretty good shape. I tried them all at one time or another...Jefferson from Lexington to Monroe High School...Randolph from Griggs all the way down and so forth. Then one day I got all the way over to the University Club on Summit. That's where I found it...THE STEEPEST HILL IN ST. PAUL! Ramsey Hill and it was almost straight down! I remember looking down at it with my friend and thinking: "No way." Now I can't really say why Ramsey Hill was a hill I never went down, but clearly it was for one of two reasons: the fear that my 500 pound bike would get going and become unstoppable and kill me or, finding myself at the bottom... how was I going to get back up? Remember, I lived on Brimhall and Randolph. In my mind, getting that far away from home on my bike for the first time felt like I had achieved enough and from there, getting back home was do-able. I concluded that from the bottom of Ramsey Hill (should I survive), the hills that would face me getting home were simply too much. So I chickened out. Besides, I was already in trouble for being gone that long without checking in and having to cover that same distance getting home would only make it worse. All these things were true of course but what was also true was that Ramsey Hill was by far the steepest hill I ever encountered in St. Paul and I chickened out...and I'd do it again.

When I say I grew up in beer joints, that's overly dramatic for one thing and not really true for another. However, I was a full member in that group of children who would sit at a table and watch a bottle of pop and a bag of potato chips appear in front of us and be replaced several times over an hour and a half or so. It was always my mother and my father together...nearly always anyway, and since they fell into that "hail-couple-well-met" category, naturally their friends were in no hurry to see them go and that meant keeping potato chips and pop in front of me. I was seldom alone. There were usually one or two other kids and some were more acclimated to it than others. We never talked about it but the sense that I got was that what friends we did have, for the most part, we had in bars. I won't tell you I didn't resent being in there. Not at first but as I grew up I sure did, and of course my Aunt Alice and Uncle Albert always had a bar on University Avenue so Sundays...many Sundays, were spent there. But it was a different world in the 50's. Everybody smoked and the bars of St. Paul were fun and I suspect they're still fun today. I don't want this to sound like it was a form of abuse because nothing could be farther from the truth. It was just the inconvenience of having parents who liked to drink and besides, the bribes didn't end there. Sometimes a sack of White Castles on the way home was in my future and frankly, I haven't met too many situations in my life where White Castles didn't make whatever you endured, seem not all that bad. Looking back I can't really complain. For one thing, no one who ever knew my mom and dad would ever let me, and they'd be right.

On Randolph, the main street I lived on in St. Paul, Minnesota, there was a Catholic women's college, a private military high school (one block off Randolph), a public grade school, a Catholic military high school, two Catholic grade schools (with a third, a block and a half off Randolph and West 7th). That's seven schools in about two miles with three other public grade schools within a few blocks of Randolph; that's ten schools of all shapes and sizes and I wouldn't be surprised if I forgot one or two. Then if you go on a bit farther, The Randolph-Payne bus (14A or 14B) ends or begins in Highland Park and after negotiating Randolph, heads east on West 7th, goes through downtown and then out Payne Avenue to the East Side, and all along the way the density of schools (at least when I was growing up in the fifties) was nearly as thick. I dare say that along that route alone, there were more schools then beer joints and that's saying something for St. Paul. More schools than drug stores and even though, being St. Paul, the Randolph-Payne bus went past two excellent breweries and three or four hospitals you were never very far from a school of some kind or another and this was on one bus route. Counting St. Catherine's College as it was known then, a young lady could go to school along Randolph Avenue alone (I just remembered Derham Hall) and never need the bus at all. I'm not entirely sure I must tell you, but I dare say that St. Paul, Minnesota at any one time in the fifties and sixties had more schools of every kind serving the needs of children and teens than any comparable city in America. There...the king of sweeping generalizations, which I have sometimes been called, has done it again; St. Paul, the Capitol of Education!!!!

I remember a time when I stubbornly refused to believe that my world traveling days were going be over after I got out of the Army.

It was a disappointment to me when I realized they really were. There was this poet a friend of mine said I reminded him of. I can't remember the poet's name but his poem had to do with leaving his home and off to adventure and when he'd come back he would be golden...something like that anyway. It's true. We want to show off for the home folks in some way. I know I did. It was the idea of returning from foreign lands to watch them marvel at our pursuit of adventure while they plowed forward with dismal jobs and lives. For some of us and for many that's what we wanted, because we knew we were never going to find it at home. There was a great girl I knew in high school, popular, a leader in everything, but somehow, she was just behind THE girl in our school; the Queen of everything! Anyway, late in her senior year the girl I knew had a chance to shine (in a side by side comparison, too) and shine she did. She left THE girl in the dust on that occasion and it was as if she had climbed the highest mountain. But the idea of starting all over, as a freshman in college was just too much and she got married and started a family. There's nothing wrong with that but I knew she had higher ambitions as I did and I felt sorry for her just the same. My radio career got me out on the road in America and I am grateful for that. But my world-traveler-adventurer-fantasy would remain just a dream. I should probably be more grateful. I could be doing time in some foreign jail.

When I tell someone I meet that I am from St. Paul, if he or she had any geography at all in school, many will immediately pronounce the name of our state, "Minn...e...soooo...ta." Now, we all know that we have people in St. Paul who pronounce Minnesota somewhat differently than some of the rest of us do. The movie "Fargo" did a lot to reinforce the notion that we all talk like that but I had no problem with it because A. It was really an out-state mystery with very little taking place in the Twin Cities and B. It showed a lot of us what it's like to be made fun of for our regional accent. Ask the folks down south how they liked it all these years. Going on from their pronunciation of Minnesota, there are certain assumptions attached to being a Minnesotan people seem willing to embrace, "You like the cold, huh?" I usually smile, shake my head and then think of what I'd like to say, "No more than a prisoner likes being in the joint, you idiot." In the end, they don't mean any harm and aren't very smart either so what I actually say is, "Yeah, I love the cold...I only live in L.A. for the bottled water and the look on the waitresses face when I order a California Hamburger.... that cracks me up, you betcha." Or, there are also the dyslexic listeners who think I said Minneapolis when I actually said St. Paul, "Yeah, I like Minneapolis," they say. They start forming the next sentence by drawing this little map of the United States and noticing we're a northern state. "I suppose you get up to Canada quite a bit?" There's really no hope for most of them and so you just nod and move on. At least until they say something about the Vikings or the Twins, that is.

You really realize what a small world it is when you're sitting around with some actors on the set of one of those "Unsolved Mysteries" spin offs called "Crimes of the Century" up in Hollywood, and you run into a guy who went to your high school in St. Paul and dated this girl you always had a crush on. That was at least twenty-five years ago now and naturally got me thinking about this girl again. I'm not sure how I tracked her down here but it could have been Classmates.com. Anyway we all went to Monroe while in the meantime Highland Park Junior High was getting ready to go senior, but not before the girl graduated in '65 and I left school early. So she grew up and lived no more than eight blocks from Highland Park Senior High, went to the U of M, became an elementary teacher right in the same neighborhood up there, married and settled in with her husband to raise three kids not four blocks from where she grew up and twenty years later we're talking about her in Hollywood. This was a girl and now a woman who, with the exception of going to Monroe High School, lived practically her whole life in St. Paul within a one-mile square area. Now, I don't want to leave the impression that there was no vanity of mine in this because, I mean, this is a passing heart throb's old boyfriend and I looked like a million bucks in those days and let's just say he didn't and leave it at that. Now after a while I kind of remembered the guy because he hung out with another guy from Monroe I did know. Naturally, he didn't remember me and why should he? He was dating her and I was off to the side somewhere. So that day in Hollywood, he was no higher up on the acting food chain than I was and didn't look half as good. I decided that was good enough.

It was no fault of St. Paul that every time I'd come home I wound up falling in the same holes over and over again. Nor was it always necessary to leave to put myself back on track. To me, there always seemed to be two kinds of St. Paulites, albeit for different reasons: those who could never leave and those who had to leave. I'll never know if I'd have found the courage to go off and reinvent myself had I been raised in St. Cloud or Alexandria. But having come up in St. Paul, I felt urbane enough to realize that all things in the world "not St. Paul" were possible; that I lacked nothing to go off to New York or L.A. and play in those larger venues and succeed...or fail, but play nevertheless and that nothing about my background or where I came from would hold me back. Often, when I read back something I wrote about leaving my hometown, you'd imagine I was a shy, quiet sort of a kid just waiting all his life to break out. You'd be wrong and it's never been fair to leave anyone with that impression. I was very outgoing, bright, athletic, not at all bad looking and well spoken. All of the traits necessary to be a success anywhere and even though my freshman and sophomore years in high school were the worst of my life, I still managed to 'right the ship' by my junior year and had I stayed in school, might well have retaken my place as someone possessed of all those gifts. But maybe that's just fanciful and I never looked back having made the choices I did. Now, nearer to the end of my life than the beginning, I know that things pretty much had to work out the way they did and realize that St. Paul was a terrific springboard from which to venture out. It's part of the reason I enjoy coming home once a year...that and the White Castles, of course.

This happened to me but it's also happening everywhere and all the time and is more than just troubling. It can be deadly. I realized exactly what it was and how it can manifest itself when I heard Lance Alworth, Hall of Fame NFL wide receiver speak about his father. Lance had the kind of dad who simply couldn't grasp the notion of excellence and so he minimized any achievement his exceptional son would receive. "Hey Dad, I was just named an All-American." His father would respond, "Well, no matter how good you think you are, there's always somebody better." It was the same with becoming an All-Pro and finally being voted into the Hall of Fame. I know you recognize this kind of thinking and if you had parents like this, I hope you have been able to forgive them. I wasn't sure Lance Alworth ever did. My parents were always encouraging but there came a time when my friends, at least the guys I hung out with, turned all negative for some reason. No matter what would come out of my mouth in terms of "I'm gonna do...this" or "I'm gonna do that", every response was the same..."No, you're not", followed by something or other completely discounting your chances. For others, who might say the same thing, they were not like that..."Yeah sure...why not...you'd be good at that." I decided that it was kind of like a version of getting my ass kicked every time I opened my mouth and so I gradually left that group (because if you leave too abruptly they'll turn on you). Anyway, they stayed together as friends for decades and had reunions up on the corner where we hung out. I'd have never attended but also was never invited either so the whole thing was a good decision on my part. I'd like to tell you that it was because I was going places and they knew they were not and in some cases that could be true. But overall, we all had our lives...nobody achieving anything more than anyone else, really. The lesson at least to me is negativity. I was lucky but some others were not. Negativity can be deadly. Separate yourself from it and especially those who dish it out whenever you can.

It's not there anymore but there was a Dairy Queen (and possibly later was called Tastee-Freeze) about a block from my house. It was on the east side of Snelling south of Randolph and just past the first alley. It's such a nice memory to envision all the Little League kids being treated to cones after their games in the summer. This was especially so of the Hilltop Cubs. There were six major league teams and they all had full uniforms. Three teams had home or white uniforms and three had away or grayish uniforms. Of all the home uniforms, the Cubs were brilliantly white...whiter than the Dodgers and Yankees. I knew one of the older Cubs and he always got a hot-fudge malt. Now I have to tell you that did sound maybe a little more delicious than your regular chocolate malt and yet it didn't make much sense either. Hot fudge after all was great because it was hot and sort of melted some of the ice cream before it cooled and hardened again. It was therefore, a more sophisticated way to get chocolate into your malt or so I supposed at the time. Now I bring this all up because I was out to lunch with an old radio friend last week in Studio City and malts were offered there in addition to milk shakes and before I knew it, I was ordering a hot-fudge malt. The waitress had never heard anything that funny and so naturally, I laughed too and said with a wink, chocolate malt and that was it. So now I ask you, have I lived so long that the concept of a hot-fudge malt is absurd?

It was 1958 and that would make me 10 years old, and baseball cards ruled that summer. My friend Dave and I had good collections with multiple cards (for trading purposes) of good players. Guys like Hank Aaron, Stan Musial, Ted Williams and Warren Spahn could be traded away for someone else you didn't have without penalty, because you had three cards of the guy you traded away. We got our baseball cards at Joe's Drug Store on Randolph and Snelling and with however much money we had, would pick up four or five cards a day looking for that one guy that made the whole enterprise worth doing...Mickey Mantle. Actually I had more cards than Dave did, but it didn't matter. The morning that he got Mickey Mantle, I simply had to have it and I made a bad deal to get it. I probably had upwards of 80 cards but I offered 50 of mine for his Mickey Mantle. It gets worse. Not only 50, but 50 cards he could pick out of my collection himself. He could take one-of-a-kind cards like Bobby Richardson, the Yankee 2nd baseman...and he did. He left me with only one Lew Burdette of the Braves and took my last Wes Covington as well. All I could do was sit there and watch. It was a bed I made for myself and now I had to sleep in it. When it was over, my collection was gutted but I had my prize...Mickey Mantle the Mount Everest of baseball cards! This is a true story and I remember it like it was yesterday. Two days later I got my own Mickey Mantle and of course wanted to make another deal. But Dave wasn't just older, he was wiser too. I didn't get half of what I wanted back, so I did something I'm still not proud of. I spit on the back of the Mickey Mantle card I traded to him so you could hardly read Mantle's statistics. I'd like to say I never made that bad a deal again but there was a '59 Mercury convertible I bought once on Grand Avenue. That should tell you something.

When I was growing up in St. Paul, Minnesota in the 50's and 60's, we had a champion-caliber boxer named Del Flanagan, who defeated Honey-Bear Akins, the Welterweight Champion of the World in a non-title fight on national television. We had a national champion football team with a southern coach and the only black quarterback in division one football history. F. Scott Fitzgerald was still being celebrated as one of the greatest writers of all time and author of the jazz age. What I am saying is we had no shortage of local hero's at a national and even world level. Think about that for a second. St. Paul: a part of the Twin Cities yes, but with its own identity and champions apart from the larger Minneapolis. My father, Walt

Savage Senior, a St. Paul guy through and through, took great pride in these things I assure you and made me, his only child aware of every accolade; and when he'd say to me, "Skip, thank God every night that you were born an American", I did, but there was always a bit of a wink that made me just as glad that I was from St. Paul. My mother was very much the same and being raised in our little corner of Catholic St. Paul, I was left with the feeling that whatever one's qualifications for success were out in the world, they were all being met by growing up in the St. Paul that I knew as a boy. And that is why, at least in part and with all my blemishes, when my family life went south, I still had a kind of sense that I was one of those who would be expected to weather the storm. After all, even then I was never deprived of anything and yet, while it never really did help, one's roots do serve to set a standard that even if lost for a time, should be recovered to a suitable level. I don't know why it never really did with me. I had ample chances for that sort of thing but as I say or someone said, "Selfishness...thy name is privilege." That is one of the reasons I feel so blessed to be able to write down many of my thoughts and experiences here to honestly document how long it took me to appreciate my opportunities. I do not take it for granted.

I don't know how it is when you've lived in St. Paul all your life because I sort of drifted away in the 80's and have lived out here in California for 27 years. But when I go back home, which I always think of St. Paul as, I sometimes take little trips around the city that might remind me of this or that. I remember just driving by my Aunt Duddy and Uncle Bill's place on Selby where they lived for many years. Then maybe I'll head up University and past the two locations of my Uncle Albert's bars. I don't know; call me a romantic I guess, but one time I remember driving past the houses of all the girls I fell in love with when I was growing up. I remember I parked across the street from one and pulled out the map that came with the car rental as if I was just looking for directions. After a minute or two I felt kind of silly and started the car and drove off. Since I lived in

Highland and went to grade school at Holy Spirit, the tour of my broken hearts, so to speak, didn't take very long at all; so not long after that I cruised down Randolph to the old Monroe High School neighborhood. I was more into "loving from afar" during those years but there were a couple of important ones. Of course I'll never know if I broke any hearts along the way, but the ones I endured toughened me up for those that were yet to come. At least that's what I told myself. So here's a wonderful punch line. Through Facebook and this site, I've reconnected and become friends with at least two of those girls I fell in love with. You could never have predicted that back in the day.

You know St. Paul is not just our hometown. It's where we took our first steps, rode our first bicycle, fell in love for the first time and no matter where you're from now, it was the first place where you imagined yourself having adventures somewhere else; but to do that you needed a simulation area. For example, say you wanted to have a jungle adventure. Pretty tough in the winter I know, but in spring and summer you could find lots of places to simulate a jungle. You didn't need much at all just a few trees and some tall grass and bushes. I remember playing jungle in a rough up on Highland Golf Course once or an empty lot was a wonderful place to try out a lot of the things Tarzan used to do. One by one of course, the things Tarzan could do got crossed off the list by trial and error. Running around in bare feet turned out not to be a very good idea and just how Tarzan kept the mosquitoes from eating him alive with just shorts on remained a mystery. Tree climbing was great but swinging from tree to tree turned out not to be as effortless as Tarzan made it look. His ability to marshal the forces of the animal kingdom when necessary did little to protect you from that mean dog that lived down the alley. Soon, this kind of trial and error brought you around to liking Roy Rogers maybe a little better than you did before; or maybe a smaller version of Roy like… Spin and Marty.

I was playing on a construction site on Randolph between Snelling and Macalister when I was a kid. I rarely crossed Snelling to play but a construction site was irresistible. A woman walking by saw me and asked me to come to her whereupon she lectured me on what 'could' happen to me playing in a dangerous construction site. She was right of course but what I couldn't explain was that the danger was the fun. There's a desert park not far from where I live in California and it has paved trails for bikes and runners, but there are also little dirt and sand trails going everywhere, and back when I was running every day I took them all the time. Some were overgrown and it was as if I was daring fate to put a rattlesnake in my path to try and bite me. It never happened but one day I heard a few that I couldn't see and I quit doing that. That's happened all my life...pushing that envelope just enough to add an element of danger and it seems as natural now as it did on that construction site. Not long ago I wrote about Ramsey Hill and how steep it was and how scary it would be to go down it on my bike. I never did go but I've been thinking about it ever since. My mother had a fear of me drowning and so naturally, every chance I got I was in water...the river, lakes, whatever. I didn't always get away with it, of course. Hopefully we learn from those times but not always. At the heart of it, it's just more fun when it's a little dangerous.

Growing up in St. Paul, there came a time to blame people and things for my life not turning out exactly as I had planned. It was kind of fun, actually. I mean, this way it wasn't your fault at all. There was something else too. It was a marvelous excuse to avail ourselves, however frequently, of the finest taverns this side of heaven. Wonderful places where, if they didn't know your name you were in the wrong part of town. The neighborhood beer joints were especially fun and there were wonderful happy hours with snacks and pitchers. I swear I don't know where the money came from to keep the party going but during seventies, at times, as the song said, it seemed as though it would never end. But of course it had to end and the reasons for that were the guys and gals for whom that bar stool had become an appendage to their once attractive appearance, that frighteningly approximated our own when they were our age. I was lucky. I had a radio career that moved me all over the country and I'd come back from time to time and see first-hand what the party can do to you over time. In the end I didn't do too badly and if my life didn't turn out the way I liked it's because it required more preparation than I was willing to invest. I did have fun though and made a late charge accomplishment-wise and now I view my squandered opportunities more philosophically. Like I said, I was lucky.

When I was a boy in Catholic school, you couldn't get me to go see Audrey Hepburn in "The Nun's Story" for anything. It came out somewhere around the sixth grade and I was already becoming rather resentful of Catholic edict and the nuns. It's a pity I never did see it because in addition to being a terrific film, it made some very profound statements about man's inhumanity to man and specifically during World War II when there was a lot of that going on. Without giving away the end let's just say she found a component that allowed her to hate an enemy enough to participate in the process of doing so, a component without which the enemy wins every time and all the time because they are not so encumbered. What I'm saying is the poets and philosophers are all well and good until there are times, and there are, when enemies need to be destroyed. I remember being rather shocked at the tone of the film because I was expecting something like the "Song of Bernadette" about a saint and what I got instead was Audrey Hepburn's best performance and a very human film that exposed many flaws within the church and that order of nuns. It was also a very chilling ending in a lot of ways that mirrored that kind of determination...the reality of it that was necessary. I fought in my war but I always, before and after, admired pacifists at a certain level. Stranger still was the idea that you would never want to serve with anyone who during those terrible moments couldn't do what was necessary. I say strange because those who wouldn't fight were frequently made to be medics, which anyone in combat can tell you represent the bravest men on the field for the most part. So when I think about what needs to be done, now against a relatively new enemy, the same vision comes up again: a vision of Audrey Hepburn, the most delicate and beautiful of all Hollywood stars, looking left and looking right, as if wondering which way to turn and yet solidly knowing what she needed to do in any way that she could. Her character is needed, perhaps more than anyone. See "The Nun's Story" sometime if you never have.

In the 50's and early 60's there was no war but young guys in the various neighborhoods in St. Paul still served in the Armed Forces. It was cool when they came home, usually thinner and with short hair, wearing their uniforms. Maybe it would be somebody's older brother and we'd stand there, maybe across the street or something and if they should happen to turn and wave at us, that was so cool. Uniforms had a lot to do with the service some of us chose. It did with me. The Navy never really got any consideration, don't ask me why. Marines had cool uniforms but the day I saw three paratroopers, wearing their khaki uniforms, garrison hats and spit-shined boots with their slack legs bloused inside, that was it. That's who I wanted to be and there was no getting it turned around. By the time I came home on leave there were no neighborhood kids to see me because my mom had moved. But I did have moments in that uniform that made it worth it. My father was living a few blocks from Rice and University and not having a car, I took the bus from the Highland area to see him: Randolph and Fairview to Snelling, Snelling to University and University to Rice Street. It's funny because by the time I made that trip and back, in the uniform I had imagined so many times growing up, it seemed like someone else was doing it. I had finally become what I beheld all those times as a kid watching servicemen come home in their uniforms. I was still pretty young myself but the imagining had become real and I remembered this poem a friend had read to me once about..."going away and coming back golden." I felt some of that for sure.

It's strange how we associate certain places with certain things. I don't think I was in Shapiro's drug store in Highland Park more than ten or fifteen times. I certainly never hung out there. But for whatever reason, the best malted milk I ever had goes back to that place. They, like many other places put the whipped cream on the top and I'd use the long spoon to eat that. But that day, I just continued eating the malt with the spoon. It was the most delicious thing I can remember and I've never forgotten it in more than fifty years. In a strange way, that kind of put Highland Park in a special place in my mind. A block east of there I played on two Little League football teams and practiced Little League Baseball. No more than six blocks away at Horace Mann School my team practiced basketball and the Highland Public Library has a copy of one of my short story collections (The Petorik Thesis and Tales of the Global West). Just say the word "malt" and my mind goes back to those horseshoe shaped counters and that one chocolate malt at Shapiro's. Today, when you order malt, what you get is a milk shake for the most part. But if you can find a place to get a real malt, buy one and eat it with a long spoon. You'll thank me later.

I wasn't very good at running my own business as a boy. My Minneapolis paper route was a failure and the things you sell to obtain a badminton set proved too much trouble, especially when I knew I could ask my parents for one and before long they would get it for me. However, everyone has their place and I found mine helping the St. Paul paper boys in my neighborhood on their routes. Paul Tambernino was the first, I think Mark Schwartz was the second and Terry Colstalk the third. I just liked going with them and in the course of doing that, I helped. Paul was a big kid, several years older, so the fact that he even let me come along was its own reward. Mark and I had fun and Terry was a good guy and could also buy me cigarettes. It's funny though because I wasn't very good at showing up for the things I had to do, but I was never even late to help those guys. Being an only child I'm sure it had something to do with wanting to hang out with an older brother figure in some way. It was a lot of fun for me just going and on the way walking along while they folded papers and threw them up near the front step. If they went off to the side in the bushes, naturally, I'd go and get them out and if we came to an apartment building sometimes I'd deliver those and then catch up afterwards. But it was such a small nice memory that I've never forgotten it and as I do, I remember how great my parents were. It was never anything like, "You can't handle your own paper route but you can go help everyone else." There was no judgment in how I passed my time. I was allowed to be the kid I was and as long as I was happy, they were too. I came to realize what a big advantage that was growing up.

When many of us were growing up in St. Paul in the 40's, 50's and 60's, there were always a lot of kids to play with. Baby Boomers they called us and our numbers were great. It's not like that today and may never be again but that doesn't mean we didn't have our share of loners. I was more sensitive to these kids because being an only child I knew I could easily have been one of them. But I had things going for me many of them didn't. I was athletic, not all that shy and I just didn't like it that they were always alone, it seemed. So, I at least reached out in some way to see that they at least were invited to be a part of what we were doing. "Hey kid," I might say. "We need another guy...want to play football with us?" or something like that. Often times they'd say no, but the next time I'd see him he'd acknowledge me and we might talk or something and I'd find out something about him. This one kid, Gary, was a classmate of mine at Holy Spirit and kind of quiet but he invited me up to his house to make these molds with this set he had. It was fun. He was also a musician. He took lessons in some brass instrument I can't remember, and I thought that was cool. I found myself wanting to include him in my world too and with little league football try-outs coming up I sort of encouraged him to come along. He was a kind of big kid and linemen were always needed. Anyway, his mother said no and that she wasn't going to let Gary participate in something where he might get hurt. I tried a little more but it was no use and soon, we didn't get together anymore at all. I know that I reached out to a kid I thought might need reaching out to but in the end, he was back in his world and I was back in mine. I don't know why but I always wondered if I might have either done something different or if we should have just continued making molds or whatever. But kids, I learned, can have some harsh parameters with clearl if not fairly defined lines and once they are challenged, things change. I've never felt bad about me and Gary. I continued to like him but we never hung out again and every time I found myself feeling bad about it and wishing I hadn't even tried, I somehow knew that was wrong. Gary wasn't the last kid I tried to do that with because there were so many really, but he is the one I remember. A painting of mine is called "Nearly Always Alone" and reminds me of those days.

I miss St. Paul more this time. Usually, when I'm home I like it but I'm always glad to go back to our home in California. I came home on Monday and knew the kitchen remodeling wasn't done so I knew how things would be. Tuesday was a little better but then, dealing with the VA on Wednesday poisoned the week like nothing else. I understand, as one always does in retrospect that part of the responsibility for how bad things got was on me. But that's like saying..."someone hit me...so I hit him back...then it got worse because he beat me up." And so I began thinking about how I dealt with things when I lived in St. Paul and also what helped and what didn't. Then it kind of hit me because I remember the old streetlights on Randolph. They were soft and wonderful and then one day, and this particular light is the one I always remember, they put up one of the new, bright florescent type streetlights above Randolph right at Pascal. It gave off a lot of light but it was cold. Light is often synonymous with warmth but not that light. That light came to represent in me the idea that things were changing and not for the better; a feeling that the warmth of my youth would give way to a utility that made growing up seem so futile. Then I thought about first grade at Holy Spirit. I was assigned to Sister Michael Ann's classroom on the northeast corner of the school. It was a room that was light and airy with wonderful natural light until the late afternoon and overhead warm globes of light generated from light bulbs and not hatched in test tubes. After a few days it would be over and school would never be something to look forward to again. Overall, our class was too big and so they thinned us out by creating a third class and I was among those chosen to go there. It was directly beneath Sister Michael Ann's classroom in the damp basement with the windows covered with thick burglar-proof steel mesh so you couldn't tell what kind of a day it was at all. In the back, there were lockers instead of neat, wooden cloakrooms and overhead, florescent lighting. Our teacher was a lovely woman named Mrs. Grady but it was no use. Right out of the box I had the feeling that this would never be a positive experience. Naturally, this was my personal reaction to education based on a first impression and Mom and Dad wouldn't hear of it. We were a generation of "Kings and Queens" compared to the "starving children in India" or so our mothers and fathers told us. Some Bengali child would have needed gastric by-pass in his teens after eating all the food I wouldn't and was about as effective in getting us to eat as saying, "it all winds up in your stomach anyway." So for me it was a combination of things that drove me down the negative fork in the road that somewhat ended in a suicide attempt in my teens. After that I simply did my time and when the Vietnam Conflict came along it was like a gift from heaven...to roll the dice on a life tainted with florescent lights and sub-zero temperatures for a shot at ending the madness with a better epitaph. I took it in a flash and so when I say I had a 'cup of coffee' with depression growing up, I wasn't kidding. Over time it made me more sensitive to those who saw life through a basement window and florescent lighting as I did. I love St. Paul because it's the only place where I can go home. But going home often means gratitude that I survived it long enough to truly realize how lucky I was and how little that mattered once it got going the wrong way.

Among the few modest goals that I have for myself until I either die or get too old to participate in them, one was to someday be able to show my artwork in a gallery. To that end, I stopped downtown in our city a couple of months ago and talked to a woman who was running a gallery and gave her one of my new books: Imagination...The Art of W. Jack Savage. She leafed through it and said she liked many of them but was struck by the different mediums and styles of my art and told me it would be very difficult to show my work because of it. She suggested that I concentrate on showing only one style, abstract for example and that by doing so I would make myself more 'showable', as it were. For the first time in many years it got me thinking of my time in San Francisco where I moved to as a teenager after quitting high school and just before enlisting in the Army. I went into the Keane Gallery; I looked around at the very popular pictures of children and others with large expressive eyes and almost at once realized that Walter Keane and his wife were pretty much locked into painting those expressive eyes forever. I loved their work but came away feeling sorry for them in a way because of it. As of this morning I have never had a showing of my artwork. However, two-hundred and seventy of my paintings and drawings have been published in more than fifty different literary magazines and if each of them had only ten readers, more people would have seen my work than nearly any showing at any gallery almost anywhere for a run of say, one week's time. Besides, this way I don't have to deal with any of the administrators of galleries who try politely (and sometimes not), to tell you they deal only with 'credentialed artists' and I'll leave you to fill-in the possible pigeonholes that moniker might entail. No, I may be more centered in my personal life but I'm more than content to have my art remain 'all over the place' until I die. I'm wondering how many galleries will still be open when I do, what with the limited number of "credentialed artists" around.

A very dear friend made an observation about some of my posts and said that remembering in such minute detail as I do marks a desire in me to return to St. Paul to live. This got me thinking about that poem my friend said reminded him of me. Again, he doesn't remember and neither do I as to who the poet was but the substance of it was a sort of musing by the author..."I will go away from this place and when I return I shall be golden and people will see me that way"...or something like that. I've never forgotten it because I'm afraid it had me nailed, if not in the reality we live in as adults, certainly in the spirit that drove those dreams as children. Still, it was my mother who observed after I got out of the army about how so many of my friends came to see me for the short periods when I was on leave, but when I came back home to stay, I quickly became absorbed back into the woodwork of a St. Paul resident. I was no longer someone to come running for, but a day-to-day traveler among all the other travelers. Having left the army I found myself just another high school dropout facing a long, cold winter from which only in my dreams, once again, could I find escape. I may have, indeed I was planning another escape, when I discovered marijuana and like Odysseus and his men who fell upon Circe and thinking only days had passed, came to realize it had been years instead. My point seems to be that I enjoyed leaving St. Paul almost more than living there so that I could come home again...and again and again. But I have a dream that goes even beyond the popular definition of "coming home again." It is to come home and live in the same apartment building where I grew up on Brimhall and Randolph and to throw a football on the front lawn and feel the crunch of snow beneath my feet as I walk again to Holy Spirit and Sunday Mass. In the simplest of terms, it would be to live out the end of my life in the same place and where I began it. I no longer feel embarrassed by the self-serving nature of such thoughts. St. Paul is as much or more, exactly who I am than anything in my makeup and when I dream of adventures and far off lands still, I dream from St. Paul because that's where my dreams began.

I received a rejection email from a literary magazine out east yesterday and while it was a form letter rejection, it did mention receiving over 200 submissions for the issue to be published. Naturally, I receive many more rejections than acceptance emails and so I often take note of how they do it. It usually goes..."Thank you so much for submitting but we won't be publishing your"...whatever (stories, art, etc.). Then they include a little something to keep you from killing yourself because of it...."This doesn't mean your stuff wasn't the bomb...it just means that it wasn't the bomb and please submit again in the future." Then, every now and then there'll be a personalized P.S, "Your art was great Jack but we went with a local guy," was at the end of the one I got yesterday. I send my art/stories to literary magazines literally all over the world but somehow, I enjoyed learning that A, They liked my art anyway and B, That I lost out to a guy with a regional advantage...local guy. It's important to use local people whenever possible and if they're getting 200 submissions for an issue it means they haven't lost sight of that. As I said before, I've been hugely successful sending out my work (more than forty stories and 270 pictures and drawings have been published in a little over a year.) Some of those publications, be they in print or online, have gone under but there's always new ones starting and besides, they're publishing artists and writers who are just good...not credentialed and interested in money only. No, literary magazines, be they high school publications in Georgia, fledgling operations or somewhat prestigious works that have been around for decades, are publishing real stories and art from people who never learned the 'secret handshake' but whose work is more and more frequently superior to that found on the News Stands. The price is right, too.

It's strange and very interesting to realize, for the first time as a child, that you can feel all alone in a crowd. Whether it is on the playground at school or even in the classroom when everybody, including you, raises their hands to answer a question, but it's as if your hand isn't there at all because you never get chosen to answer. After a while you almost start feeling invisible and then, after you've made a little comfortable place in your invisibility, you get caught not paying attention to what's going on in your real world. Often, it comes with some remark by the teacher that's funny and marks you as someone to be ridiculed...at least to the other children. In a way, it's a warning that there's really no place to hide: not even in your invisibility and here's the punch line. Your attempt to find some relief by not being a part of the whole, results from the actions or inattention of the very people who were ignoring you in the first place. It's very hard to be a child and having brothers and sisters doesn't make it any easier and can make it more difficult. But, at least to me, the worst of it was when someone saw what was happening and tried to help. They suddenly knew what you were going through and wanted to help by making you the focus of something, but the light was too bright by then and all eyes being on you made everything worse. When they realized what they had done, while only trying to help, it had the effect of them leaving you even more alone and the downward spiral continued. Then, they all get together and say, "What's wrong with that child?" never once pausing to consider how simple the answer could be. Today, they might put you on drugs and while that seems extreme, in my day they often just gave up on you and chalked it up to just one of those things. It is then when no adult has the ability to come up with an answer, that a classmate or someone near your own age simply includes you in something that's going on and does so with no explanation at all, that the idea that life might be okay sometimes can begin to take hold. Like I said, it's very hard to be a child sometimes.

About ten years ago or so, I was sitting having a cigarette on our front yard patio watching the cars go by and thinking about all the stupid things I'd done when I was a kid back in St. Paul: going where I shouldn't go and doing everything wrong when I got there. We pushed a log out onto the Mississippi River under the Lake Street Bridge on the Minneapolis side once and then rode it down toward the Monument at the end of Summit Avenue on the St. Paul side. We all made it but in my case just barely. Then we had to climb the riverbank and walk back, barefoot, all the way over the bridge again just to get our clothes. It was nice out on the patio and there were a couple of long, full fern branches that leaned over the fence from our neighbors so the shade was great. I yo-yoed in my attempt to quit smoking back then and couldn't smoke in the house, so I lit up another and wondered why my mind insisted on going back to memories of my near demise in such a serene setting as our front yard patio. I suppose it's natural, as one gets older to realize how perilous it was at times just reaching old age. Then I looked up for a moment. On the fern branches above me were maybe a hundred "yellow jackets". I fought off the urge to get up and run because I realized that they were having no problem with me sitting there smoking, while recalling my childhood in St. Paul when I nearly drowned. By the time I finished that cigarette I'd almost forgotten the yellow jackets were there and in the days to come I shared maybe a carton or two more with them before the exterminator showed up next-door one day and destroyed their nest. I don't know how insects like that decide to just live and let live around humans, but I suppose, while wondering how I survived the river more than fifty years before, I could have been stung to death by yellow jackets; or, had I not finally quit smoking, been dead from that by now.

The cool thing about being a little kid is not knowing for certain what lies beyond the next house or in the next block or in this direction or that. One of the most interesting things about going to school for the first time (I'm talking grade school here), are the lines we all had to get into to go home. Holy Spirit Grade School was on the southwest corner of Randolph and Albert. In the St. Paul of 1954 that I remember in 1st grade, the streets might have been safer and the world a simpler place, but leaving school and going home was rather harshly regimented. There was a minimum of two police-boys per line, not counting the ones who acted as crossing guards at Albert and Randolph. There was the Hamline line going east: one long block away, after which you just walked home by yourself or with friends. The Jefferson line took you north, up Albert and after crossing Jefferson, ended there. The Hartford line was interesting because it seemed that those kids were almost going over the horizon to the south, it seemed so far away. The Randolph line to the west was my line and I remember it ending at Warwick. I did something wrong once and the police-boy walked me all the way back to the Principal's office. I was scolded and sent back home with the police-boy, but with line long gone, the police-boy decided his job was done and he crossed and went home at Pascal, leaving me in front of the creepy orphanage. I wasn't sure what to do because I was told to never cross the street without a police-boy but knew I had to cross three streets to get home. My mother was waiting for me a block and a half from Warwick and when she saw the other kids go by and I wasn't with them, she frantically started walking down to Holy Spirit where she found me, alone at the corner of Randolph and Warwick trying to decide what to do and yes, probably crying. Instead of going home we went back down to Holy Spirit where my mother told me to wait outside while she went in to talk to the Principal. I never heard what was said but that kind of thing never happened again.

I want to recommend a book for you to read, Rose by Martin Cruz Smith. It was just one of the favorite reading experiences of my life. Like most people, I came to know Smith through his Arcady Renko series beginning with the terrific Gorky Park. Later, I started reading some of his other novels, which were interesting and different and one, December 6th, very, very good. But Rose did something to me that no other book ever did and I was reminded of a performance of "Camelot" with Richard Harris I saw in Minneapolis nearly thirty years ago now. It was the final performance of the play in Minneapolis; a Sunday matinee and Harris could barely recite his lines for the terrible sore throat he was laboring through. But somehow his vocal discomfort became a part of his suffering in the play and long before the final curtain he had me in tears. Being an actor myself in those days, I made a silent prayer that a performance of mine could just once, move someone to tears, as I was that day. Many years later, while playing Thomas Mendip in Fry's "The Lady's Not For Burning", I saw a young girl crying at our final exit and my prayer was answered. Then I read Rose and after nearly fifty plays over the years, I gave up acting not long after that and began writing. Some of you know that I've written several books under the name W. Jack Savage. My last novel, The Children Shall Be Blameless received several favorable reviews and one reviewer confessed to tears running down her cheeks as she wrote her review. But as I finished reading Rose by Martin Cruz Smith, I put the book down and walked outside. I don't think I cried. I can't remember if I did but felt changed somehow and as I said, not long after that, began writing my own stories. So many of you think and even say, "I wish I could write stories," when so many more of us know that you can and often do while not realizing it. Again, if I would ask you to read one book that's not one of my own, it would be Rose by Martin Cruz Smith. Perhaps we all have a different book that can move us to letters, as they say and if it's not <u>Rose</u>, I still think I can promise you a wonderful experience.

As a boy, I was into movies...big time! My Aunt Duddy lived on Selby near the old bridge over the railroad tracks just west of Hamline. One day a big sign went up on what looked like Marshal and all I could spell out from her apartment was PEP. It must have been 1960 because that's when the film "Pepe" came out. It starred the famous Mexican actor of the time, Cantinflas and a big cast of well-known American stars in cameo roles. So, being twelve, I assumed the sign was "Pepe" and there must be a big movie house over there. Well, "Pepe" ran and ran, evidently because the sign never changed and of course it was Pepsi on Marshal, not "Pepe." I was never made to feel stupid about my mistake nor did I ever see the film "Pepe," but I never forgot thinking the movie was setting all sorts of box office records on Marshal. After all, you can't grow up without making mistakes. That one was just a little more Hollywood-ish than some of the others.

To give you a little idea of how old I am, my first football helmet in little league was made out of leather and I wasn't the only one. That was the Hilltop Little League in St. Paul where the spread of ages was three years meaning as a new little kid of say, 4th or 5th grade you were being asked to tackle 7th or 8th graders and oh by the way, you never got a chance to be tackled by anyone of any grade because you never touched the ball. The Hilltop League had only three teams and unless you really wanted to play as a little kid, it wasn't very much fun. Highland Groveland was a much better run league with more kids closer to your own age but unless your family came to watch you, you didn't get to play much. One time that first year down there, a game was scheduled on a Saturday at the field just east of St. Leo's and one of the older players on the team, who just happened to be walking by while we sat in the rain waiting for the rest of the team, told us the game had been cancelled. We weren't notified and why should we be? We rarely played anyway so after that second season, I went back to Hilltop, which had only gotten worse but I was a year and a half older so tackling the big guys was less painful. Our team wasn't any good and our young coaches were jerks so I never finished that season up there. My next two years were fun, alternating leagues again and by my final year at Hilltop, I was finally an older guy and finally played for a great coach. Football was a different game then and there was almost no passing, but by far the most fun I ever had playing football was in the street with my friends. By high school, the thought of going through all of that again was not appealing in any sense and so as I think back, little league sports taught me an important lesson: that some things were more fun to watch on TV and play in the street then they ever would be in real life. Come to think of it, that's how most things were when I was growing up.

Being an only child, growing up in St. Paul, I depended on my friends a great deal for companionship and going and doing things together. I also did a lot of things by myself and when I think about it, there came a time when I always went to the movies alone. I loved movies and one summer in particular, I had a lot of acne and didn't go up to the Highland Pool nearly at all. I went to the movies instead and in those days, if a movie you liked moved on from your neighborhood theater (in my case the St. Clair), you could usually find that it was being shown in another theater around town and at the most, that was only a bus ride and maybe a transfer away. I was a big fan of Paul Newman and followed "Sweet Bird of Youth" around that summer from the St. Clair to the Uptown, to the Centre and two or three others. Shirley Knight played the female lead Heavenly Finley, and she and nearly everyone in the cast were nominated for an Academy Award. Years later she played in "The Country Girl", a television production with Jason Robards and George Grizzard that just blew me away. Now, fast-forward thirty years or so, to a hot afternoon up in Hollywood behind the Chinese

Theater where, between acting in student films and independent non-union work, I did security for movie shoots from time to time. The film being shot was "Stuart Saves His Family" starring non-other than Al Franken and as his mother, Shirley Knight. The shoot was over and most of us Security guys were milling around back where the cars were parked and who comes walking by but Shirley Knight. I raised my voice and said, "You were the quintessential Country Girl and you should have won an Oscar for "Sweet Bird of Youth." She stopped, smiled and slowly turned around and I said, "I'm sorry but I just got carried away. I've been a fan of yours for years." She was very gracious and I never saw her again. But all the way home I thought about that summer when I hid my face from the light of day and watched "Sweet Bird of Youth" in nearly every theater in St. Paul by night.

Everything begins somewhere. For running and me, it was the track at Cretin High School. It was not like other tracks. It looked square but was probably rectangular and had a surface of cinders, which was common in those days. Whereas I'd have gladly traded in my endurance for more foot speed, the truth is, if you were chasing me and didn't catch me in the first sixty yards or so, you weren't going to catch me at all. Somewhere during grade school perhaps as early as fourth grade I decided once to see how many times I could run around the track at Cretin. After six laps I knew I could have kept going but it was getting dark and so I went home. Now mind you, even though I could run for a long time, I still wasn't say, cross-country runner fast or anything like that. I could just run forever. As an adult I started running again because during the Carter Presidency I couldn't find a job and worked my way up to nine miles or so and was told once, if you can run ten miles without stopping, you could run a marathon. My last long run in St. Paul was Summit Avenue from the Monument at the River to the Cathedral and back and figured that would probably be it. But even though I did work my way past ten miles I certainly had no plans on trying to run 26-miles and change beyond simply embracing the idea that I could if I wanted to. But I was still unemployed so I started taking radio jobs out of town, always moving further and further west until finally I found myself out here in L.A. where you can run all year long. You see running was like acting in theater for me. That is, seemingly at odds with my personality in every other way. Because frankly, in those days if you gave me a cigarette, a drink and a seat at the bar with someone to talk to, I was just about as close to heaven as I knew I'd ever get on earth. Be that as it may, I looked upon acting and running as good things and activities apart from just sitting there drinking and so I got back to serious running again out here. And sure enough, in my forties I ran seven marathons, a half marathon and a trail marathon in my early fifties. Then I quit smoking, gained a lot of weight and couldn't run anymore and what with the cost of sitting at the bar drinking, I found myself with nothing to do. That's how I started writing, so you see you just can't win. That's the way it's set up, but like I said, everything begins somewhere and of course, everything ends somewhere too so until my fingers get too fat for the keyboard, I'm here for the duration.

It's hard to explain to someone who never lived in a climate that can kill you, what that's like. I live in California and it's nearly always perfect out here and by that I mean, real hot at times in the summer but no mosquitoes to speak of, and only occasionally humid. That to someone from St. Paul, Minnesota is perfect. But in the winter, the weather in St. Paul can and usually does kill a few people every year. It gets real, real cold and stories of people who find themselves in dire circumstances are somewhat common. Let's say you get stuck in the snow or your car won't start. You'll hear a story about somebody who left the cold but certain shelter of their car, walk about a hundred yards, realize that was a bad idea and by the time they get back to their car, it's frozen shut and they can't get in. So they break the window to get in and well, you know the rest and it isn't good. Being a runner, I've shared this story with fellow runners

94

out here who can't imagine running in the snow and cold of St. Paul. It's about this guy who only used one glove. He'd put it on one hand and when he no longer could feel his bare hand, he'd put the glove on that hand and repeat the process over the five or even ten miles or so he'd run in below zero temperatures. But let's say he ran at night, took a short cut (as we runners are known to do) fell down and couldn't get up. If he didn't have a cell phone or even if he did, he might be dead by the time help reached him. I never take water when I run and I've gotten into some tough, dehydrated circumstances a time or two, but I came through it. It's not the same in the cold. The cold is very unforgiving and yet we Minnesotans in general are believed to be a very hearty breed. Those of us who are not, moved out here to California with me long ago.

I wonder how many of you remember the name Elmer Caldwell? Elmer had an "after hours" joint: the last one down on Concordia along the freeway, before he was killed in a shootout at the Ebony Lounge at University and Avon back around 1969. Much of what follows is simply stories I heard and the veracity of which I cannot attest to. There were always after-hours places in St. Paul, usually in the inter-city. They were usually in a house and opened after the bars closed so anyone who wanted to continue drinking or even gambling or perhaps meet a lady of the evening, these things were available at an after-hours place. Elmer, whom I only met once, was considered the king of these establishments not only because he'd been in the business so long, but because he had a relationship with the police that, while not exactly cordial, was certainly cooperative. That is, he'd be told ahead of time when a raid was coming so he could turn away any of his regulars and simply wait for the police to come. It was an offense that only came with a fine but during these rare events, Elmer would also tell the police where every other after-hours joint in town was located. Elmer could afford to pay any fine but some of the others could not and the competition got thinned out a bit. Elmer's also had the reputation of being a little safer than some

of the others and white people had no problems in his place...as long
as they had money to spend and behaved, you know? There were
several other stories but Elmer had no shortage of enemies if for no
other reason than that he was as successful as he was. Indeed he was
part owner of the Ebony Lounge when he was killed. It was over a
woman and Elmer got into it with this guy, snatching him up by the
collar and when he put him back down, the guns came out and they
both had it out right there. Elmer carried an automatic and kept the
chamber empty so he had to take the extra second to chamber a
round and the assailant had a revolver. There were three trials. The
first was a deadlocked jury as the DA sought a first-degree murder
conviction (the thought being that maybe the guy was a hired
assassin), and the second found him guilty of voluntary
manslaughter. That was vacated in the third action because it was
brought up at trial that the assailant had a nine year old burglary
conviction on his record. But I don't know the outcome of that trial
and I can't find it online so I was wondering if someone knows?
After Elmer was gone, a fella named Charles took over and ran a
nice house for a few years, but by then I wasn't keeping late hours
anymore and don't know if there are any houses around now...I'm
betting there are but I just don't know. I won't say who laid this out
for us but his version of events goes like this: if you were going to
kill Elmer, you were going to do it with a revolver because Elmer
was known to keep an empty chamber in his automatic and would
even discuss gun safety as his reason for doing so. People who
carried guns in those days, at least in my experience, liked to talk
about them. This was 1969 and if you'll remember, James Bond
movies made automatics more popular than ever and in smaller
calibers so they were less bulky. Now remember, the DA and
everybody thought something was up because they attempted to try
this assailant for first-degree murder. That would be at odds with a
dispute over a woman in a bar. There's one other matter. Elmer had
bodyguards and both were out of town the night of the shooting and
according to one account, the shooter was on the floor in the prone

position. He could have hit the floor as the result of Elmer's snatching him up by the lapels and letting him go, so he fell then pulled his gun and fired up at Elmer. The last point is the suspect himself...he was from Washington...out of town coincidence? Maybe, but he turned himself in when he heard they were looking for him. Doesn't sound like a contract to me and I'm only a writer, but Elmer was a well-known semi-underworld celebrity, so much of this speculation could be depended upon. So let's review: bodyguards out of town, shooter from across the country, carrying a revolver, shoots from the prone position and then gets out of there quickly and, oh yes, Elmer is a part owner of the bar he's shot in; so unless these two are the only armed people in the Ebony Lounge, even without his bodyguards, where's the help? An old St. Paul Mystery. By the way, the one time I met him, I was actually introduced as a Vietnam Veteran. Elmer Caldwell was the first human being to ever thank me for my service and he bought us our first beers.

It's hard to believe I know, but the people who I exchange gifts with at Christmas would rather receive a gift certificate for a hard teeth cleaning than one of my books. I'm used to it and am therefore most grateful to anyone willing to read my books let alone buy one. My children have never read any of my books that I know of, however my daughter is a fan of my art and so that's something. The truth is (and grateful I am to say it) my children are doing quite well and I'm very proud of all of them, but gift giving and getting is just not that important to them, nor is it to me. So I'm going to tell you again what I do to sort of put the Christ aspect back into Christmas that has not only helps me to ward off the Christmas blues(which I get now and then during the season), but actually makes me feel very good as well. I get a twenty dollar bill (last year I made it two twenties but it was a real good year) and I get in my car and drive around looking for someone who could maybe use a little help: panhandlers at freeway exits for example or even a fella celebrating the holiday with a bottle of beer outside the liquor store, and I hand them the folded up twenty, say, "Merry Christmas" and drive off. In the grand scheme of things it's not very much but it makes me feel good and I ask nothing in return so I've never been refused. For me it's just the point of the thing: I'm doing okay and they're not doing as well. Besides, you don't have to look very far in any direction to see two kinds of people in this world: those who could use a little help and those who wouldn't help anybody for any reason. It takes all kinds of course and I don't want to judge them anymore than I want to be judged by them or anybody else. It just makes me feel good to do it and if you occasionally get a little down during the holidays, give it a try. It works for me.

In some ways, going to Holy Spirit Church in Highland Park on Sundays was like living in a foreign country. Monsignor Keefe was our pastor but he was more of a businessman. He took a hard line spiritually and that's why his line was so short at the confessional on Saturday. At the same time, I can't remember one of his sermons...ever. Father Byrnes was our other priest and he was very nice. I was an altar boy and he could be a little gruff when called upon to do 6:30 A.M. Mass during the week if you laid out his vestments wrong, but apart from that, Holy Spirit was very much like an army mess hall. That is, the mean sergeant always outranked the nice sergeant and so it was at Holy Spirit. But Mass with Father Byrnes officiating was very much like a foreign country because when he gave his sermon you couldn't understand a word he said and I tried, believe me I tried. I can't describe what he sounded like exactly but I can tell you this: he meant every word of it. You could tell that there was a wonderful point to all of it if you could only make out what he was saying. It was not a speech impediment exactly, but it was just unclear with a somewhat emphatic throat clearing noise from time to time followed by exactly the same measure of unintelligible rhetoric. It wasn't as sad as you might think though, because while I couldn't understand him, I could tell his faith in what he was saying was steadfast and if you could get by on that, being that there was no other choice, you were fine. I liked Father Byrnes. He was a fine man and a good priest and I especially liked serving as one of his altar boys because strangely, while I couldn't understand his English very well, his Latin was perfect and for we of the "Old Faith", perfect Latin broke a lot of ties.

We all have things that make up large portions of our lives: things like work, marriage, raising a family, divorce, child support, marriage again and divorce and sometimes child support again. Then, because your earnings during your first marriage didn't appreciably go up and by the time love came into your life the second time (what with child support and all), you became literally or financially (which is the same thing really) half the man you used to be. Your second wife begins to look at you (as she should have before she married you in the first place), as someone who before he became half the man he was, a real good deal but under the circumstances only half the deal you used to be and you got that way through no fault of hers. Now follow me closely here because this may soon be you if it's not you already, and you'll need to know what to do. First of all, remember that your first wife and the children you had together aren't going anywhere and whether or not you ever get a raise, they will cost you more, not less as the years go by and before you even think about it, they will not appreciate you more for it. Rather, since you're not there for them 24/7 anymore, they will take the position that they have it coming in the form of the money you don't have that's made you half the man you once were. Now wife number two, after shaking her head a couple of million times and looking skyward, wondering how she could have not seen things for what they were before she married you, will come up with an idea to save the marriage. What "save the marriage" actually means when they think it and when they lay it out for you are two entirely different things. What it really means is money for her when you're gone and there's a couple of ways to get it. Number one is to have a baby with you and number two is: adopt <u>her</u> children from her first marriage as a sort of show of support that you are for them and all that (support being the operative word). Now read this last part very carefully. Move out...fast, and get on with your life because the one you're in now isn't going to get any better and I know you hate to think of failing twice, but I assure you paying for the same failure the second time is much, much worse. Admittedly, some of us got lucky because that's mostly what it is anyway (luck) and let me say, we were no smarter than you are now. Take my advice and I'll say it again so you remember.... paying twice for the same failure is much, much worse than simply walking away from the second mistake even though hard feelings come with the territory, so ask yourself this one question...who cares about your feelings, Pal? If the answer is you, that's the light you see at the end of the tunnel. Walk toward it briskly.

I decided to extend my tour of duty for a final six months because that way I could leave the Army and Vietnam in late August without waiting until October when my three-year enlistment was over. It was called a 90-Day-Early-Out. Besides, this way, being the end of 1967, I could take a leave and go back to St. Paul for Christmas. I had been in-country for nearly two years and I felt myself very much a veteran of the war by that time and the long trip home seemed familiar because I had made it once before. I only really took away one thing from being in Vietnam that lingered for about a year after I got home for the final time...I was a very light sleeper and you couldn't approach me without my eyes coming open. After the long flight over the Pacific, these guys and I were in the Salt Lake City airport waiting for our flight into Minneapolis and since it was gonna be a few hours, one of guys opened a fifth of Fleischman's Whiskey he bought at the duty-free liquor store on Guam and we each had a few pulls in the men's room and then wandered back out to wait. I lay down on the floor in the flight area and I must have dosed off pretty good because when I opened my eyes, this couple was looking down at me and I mean, they were right there over me. God...! I jumped, but it was more that they got that close without my waking up than anything else. They apologized of course, but I'm sure they thought, well, they thought it was worse than it was. It's not like I was having a flashback or anything. I explained that it was no problem but I'm pretty sure they weren't having any of it. I've always remembered that incident because I'm sure if they ever retold the story it was probably more dramatic than it actually was. That's it, you see. You don't know what kind of a war anybody had so you just imagine what it must have been like. I was just startled that I was so tired and a couple of pulls off the bottle could knock me out like that, and that someone could walk right up on me like that. I'm sure they thought it was something else.

I've explained before that being the first generation to grow up with television, baby boomers in Minnesota had significant disadvantages as we sought to be just like our role models. To begin with, these shows were filmed everywhere except Minnesota. Therefore, there were no tough detectives with beautiful secretaries wearing sensible Minnesota winter clothing. Take Lee Marvin in "M-Squad" for example. He wore a hat, sure and even a topcoat but nothing over his ears and no gloves. Richard Diamond was the same and Peter Gunn; so... some of us tended not to wear these things either. In fact, large numbers of us were completely in denial about winter altogether. That brings me around to hitchhiking. We all did it, all the time too. We hitchhiked mostly until the bus came but sometimes because we didn't have bus fare. Now, not picking up, say, four of us hitchhiking together I can understand. However, alone and maybe even carrying books (while trying to look like Mike Hammer when it's -10 below zero), that was tough but here was the worst and if you lived in Minnesota and hitchhiked in St. Paul, you remember this one very well. You're doing everything right, with the books and alone and standing at the traffic light during the day and a car stops at the light; the driver looks at you and reaches over and you think he's going to open the door to let you in and…(now wait for it)… he pushes down the lock on the door. Should I make the interview for heaven when I die, I feel I at least have explanations for a few of my failures in life that may or may not fly; things I maybe made up for the best as I could along the way. However, if the question about the things I wished for the drivers that did that to me on cold days (when I was thirteen in St. Paul) come up, I'm going to be in serious trouble. Hey, I'll be well known in either place I guess and we'll only hope Shakespeare was right..."Mercy is greatest in the greatest." Still, I doubt Shakespeare hitchhiked in St. Paul in below zero weather.

When I was a kid and baseball crazy, the Chicago White Sox had the premiere double play combination in all of baseball. They were perennial All-Stars, meaning they could hit too, and in the case of shortstop Luis Aparicio, he could also steal bases. The other half of this historic combination, second baseman Nellie Fox, was also known for something else: a huge cheek full of chewing tobacco. I played second base as it turns out and came up with something from the candy counter at Joe's Drug Store on Randolph and Snelling that would allow me to be just like Nellie (Nelson) Fox when I went to school. The .25 cent Tootsie Roll stuffed into the side of one's cheek created the effect beautifully and I might add, deliciously, as well. These were short-term emulations like copying the wind-up and pitching style of a major league pitcher for example, or putting a crown in your baseball cap. I suppose talking with my old buddy Nick Tschida about the new St. Paul Saints stadium down by the old Toni building are inspiring these memories of late. He lives just off Payne Avenue these days and plans on taking in more and more Saints games. We'll see one together I'm sure when I come home in the spring. I hope so anyway. I doubt they'll be all that much to see at Target field. I hope I'm wrong but I doubt I will be.

My dad had a tough childhood but if you were born of my generation and your parents went through the Second World War, the reason I knew he did was mostly instinct. It was as if they took a whole generation of Americans born anywhere from 1910 to say, 1925 and the minute they knew and understood language, they were made to promise to never talk about their troubles and most of them, never did. I could see it in his eyes and somehow feel it in my heart as I heard him talk around things, but never about them. When I grew up with television, my Dad it seemed was seeing things for the first time with me and he was often moved to tears. Evidently he never went to the movies much. Dad was quite an athlete and of course, growing up through part of the depression, never went to the movies as a child or as a young adult. So side-by-side, he and I experienced the sound of the violins at touching moments, created in Hollywood to jerk our emotions one way or another; or felt indignation when we were led down that path and after a while, like Pavlov's dog, laughed on key and yes, shed a tear now and then, too. This must have been very hard on him in other ways as well. A few years before Dad died, he and my mom separated and I'd begin hearing people speak of him almost in the past tense. "Your Dad never had a bad word to say about anybody", was the one phrase I heard over and over and so seeing life played out on the small screen of our black and white Muntz TV, must have brought back memories of a life where he and others of his generation held in their feelings all the time and were now, away from the crowd, free to feel things as if for the first time. I'll never truly know what Dad's childhood was like but I know how he died and that was a tough way to go also. Still, and I've never been quite sure how to feel about this, watching TV with my father gave me a sense of how deeply he could feel and how tough it must have been for him and all our parents to hold all that in, all the time, when they were growing up. Tom Brokaw called them "The Greatest Generation" and maybe that is true but it was a tough road to travel and I'm glad I never had to do it.

My relationship with the Army-Navy Football Game reaches back into my considerable memory as far as it can get. It was an exercise in getting used to disappointment to begin with, because Navy nearly always won and my Dad, being an army veteran, well, you get the picture. Then one year that changed and Army had a really great team and a Heisman Trophy candidate (and eventual winner) in Pete Dawkins. After graduation he also became a Rhodes Scholar and was the only hero and role model I ever had, with blonde hair...but I digress. That year, in my memory anyway, Army also had a "lonesome end." His name was Bill Carpenter and he never went in the huddle. He just lined up and let everyone guess how he knew the ball would eventually come to him. A few years later, as a Captain and Company Commander of the 101st Airborne in Vietnam he won the Congressional Medal of Honor for ordering an airstrike on his company as they were being overrun by the enemy. The bombs happened to be napalm and many were killed on both sides, but his company of paratroopers rallied after that and while I (as a paratrooper and therefore insider) heard later, that many of his men wanted to kill him for doing so, the fact is they all would have been killed had he not acted. Back to football: while Pete Dawkins did in fact fumble the opening kick-off, Army rallied behind Dawkins and Carpenter to win, which was to me the last and most satisfying Army-Navy game I can ever remember. They're playing again tomorrow and things have changed. I wanted to go to West Point you see, but that was like "water-from-the- moon", as the Japanese say and besides, over the course of my life I'd somehow have rather found myself a teammate of Tommy Lee Jones in the most famous Harvard-Yale game ever (played a few years later), where Harvard at their homecoming scored sixteen points in less than two minutes to tie a vastly superior Yale team. Either way, I'd have received a wonderful education while being a party to a historic sporting event at one of two schools no longer associated with such things; but that's the way it goes.

Many of us, if not all, have been angry at many of the changes that we've seen over the last decades and lament over how things used to be as opposed to how they are today. This morning at least, I've decided to take another position. To begin with, having been born in 1948, I have lived through the greatest period of human advancement in the history of mankind. The human race has come farther and faster by far then anytime in the history of our own families, as well. I love the pictures of old St. Paul in general but cherish winter and Christmas pictures in particular. See all the people downtown in the snow and cold and sure, many have their game faces on as we say, but very few look miserable and why should they? There was not the slightest chance that one day we'd be able to sit back and in a half an hour or so, in our pajamas, do all our Christmas shopping online with a few movements of our fingers; no, not at all. If you had people you loved and wanted to tell them so with Christmas presents, you had to get dressed and go downtown (or at least to Wards). Something is always lost when something else is gained and that's just the way it is. Fewer of us are going to church these days but Christ is still around and for those who celebrate the holiday in other ways, that's fine too. What I'm saying is this: there's too much to be thankful for to waste much time worrying about how things used to be. We are the result and the living prototype for the future, which like all futures, is as equally frightening as it is hopeful. We are supposed to be dead from nuclear war by now...or AIDS... or TB, or of some other catastrophe. However we're not and if that's too heavy for you, turn on your flat screen television and check out the football games today and pause to remember when we got one game on Saturday, one on Sunday, no instant replay and if you saw ten passes on an entire weekend you were lucky. It took weeks to break-in new shoes and our mothers had to iron sheets. That brings me around to "Old St. Paul, Minnesota". Are you kidding me? Who, over the last year has not been thankful that we found this site and in so doing, have been able to relive moments we thought were gone forever? I have the best memory of anyone I know and I grew up in St. Paul just like you. I have increased my knowledge of where I lived, what I did and indeed who I am, tenfold in the past year and even met and had drinks with several of you on the most perfect fall day I can ever remember, and that wouldn't have happened without" Old St. Paul, Minnesota". And so sure...things have been lost but so much more has been gained, I don't know about you but I'm more thrilled than ever to still be here.

My wife is from Edina and I'm from St. Paul but in spite of that, we get along pretty well, maybe because we met in Wyoming. Now, I was still pretty good looking back then and while that never hurts, it was my sense of humor that got to her and at least in part, has kept her all these years. About three years ago now we had a bad windstorm here in L.A. and we lost a number of shingles in three different spots. Our front door faces west, our driveway is on the north side and the distance between our front place (two-on-a-lot) and our neighbor's is greater; if you approach the driveway from the north you can see the shingle difference. The repair company tried to match the new shingles with the existing ones, but you know how that goes and so for a while, it was a running battle to replace the whole roof, just so those unmatched shingles wouldn't drive her nuts. I went so far as to suggest it was a flaw <u>she</u> picked up in the suburbs of Edina and that in the REAL WORLD, a few mismatched shingles is not a big deal. If you know women at all, you of course know that argument will never fly, so I finally figured out that solving this problem was a matter of geography. The truth is, there is no good reason to approach our house from the north, where the mismatched shingles can be seen. Everything we do is south of our house so I realized if I could just keep my wife from coming in from the north, I could at least minimize the occurrence of this argument. The funny part is, and this I'll concede is rare, is that it has worked. The argument has pretty much gone away. Soon however, perhaps in two years or less, we will need that new roof and I'll act like she just wore me down, and that will be it. She doesn't go on Facebook so I can tell you this story. Besides, it's rare enough that I win any of these little stand-offs so I feel I deserve a certain amount of credit and I can assure you it's never coming from her.

Having worked in radio for more than three decades, naturally, I worked on Christmas day quite a bit. The radio is always on and somebody had to be there and there were times I even volunteered. I remember one year all those scheduled for shifts had families except for me and after morning drivetime, I took over at 9 A.M. and worked until midnight. Somebody had a pizza sent over for me and with no one else coming in that day, I put on a Percy Faith Christmas album and went out in the car and smoked a joint. When I came back in, I grabbed a piece of pizza and sort of waltzed back down the hall to the control room, where "Have Yourself a Merry Little Christmas" was playing for the ten-thousandth time since Thanksgiving and not a thing in the world was sad or lonely about my Christmas circumstance. Besides, like I said when you're in radio, it's just one of those jobs where you have to work on Christmas and you'd be surprised how many of our listeners took a moment during Christmas day to just call up and say "Merry Christmas". By that time in my life, I'd had every kind of Christmas you can think of and they were all great in their way but things change and you just play the cards you're dealt. Not long after that holiday, the station changed format and nearly everybody got laid off. Having worked so many different formats over my career, a place for me was found in the new lineup and I spent a couple of more years there and I can tell you from experience, you could do a lot worse than spending Christmas on the radio.

It's relatively easy to write about yourself and the things that happened to you (or didn't), during the Christmas holidays over the years. But while it's no longer with a heavy heart that you recall Christmas time with your own children (who are now grown themselves), it's still difficult to talk about how truly wonderful it was to see the look on their faces when it came your turn to play Santa Claus; even, as in my case, when you only played out those mornings for a few years while they were little. It's still so much more, that you must keep the memories in your head because when they reach down into your heart again, then you don't want to go there. Many things in life are like that but few land on you with a weight like the moments that slipped by while your children were growing up. There were dollhouses and bicycles and all manner of this and that. Those were fine moments and even then, you began, well... I did anyway, to step out of yourself and sort of watch it happen knowing you'd want to hold these memories fast. Later on, there were other times when you could almost see yourself in others and the stress of the season and wonder how you got through it. Now as I've said, I get the biggest kick out of finding a stranger in need and giving him twenty bucks. It's funny but I remember the first guy I gave a twenty to. He was at the bottom of the off-ramp on Venice Boulevard and he had a sign I'd never seen before...not "Hungry", or "Please Help" or one of the others you might see. His said..."Traveling." I hope he made it.

When Christmas time comes around and I think of my childhood, I remember being asked as an adult what was the one book that influenced me the most growing up? I don't like lying, but I was always very good at it and yet, I was just then making an effort to be more truthful. It was the kind of question where you were expected to say something like, Great Expectations by Dickens or at the very least some work of literature. I knew exactly which book it was but I said, "Oh, there are just so many", which seemed to suggest I was some kind of voracious reader as a child (which was also untrue) and so finally, I told an amended truth and sort of tossed it off like I was trying to be funny. I said, "Well you know, apart from the Montgomery Ward's catalog, I'd have to say The Call of the Wild by Jack London." That way, you see, I did tell the truth to go along with the lie about The Call of the Wild because I didn't read that until much, much later. I read "To Build a Fire" by Jack London like everybody else did in high school (summer school at Central in my case). Nothing compared to the Montgomery Ward's catalog and if they had all been saved from my childhood, you could chart my growth as a boy almost exactly as it was happening by the pages I was reading and visiting over and over. Toys were first of course, and then came sporting goods, young men's fashions, and finally women's lingerie which I had a little bookmark for in case my mother came upon me suddenly. I was a child and all I cared about were things and with much hope and some planning, Christmas was a great time to actually get these things and the Ward's catalog helped a lot. So that's who I was and this is what I became, a man unashamed to tell you that for me Christmas was about the procurement of things and the most influential book of my formative years was the Montgomery Ward's catalog. I changed of course, but I'm thinking that had more to do with not getting the Wards catalog anymore as much as anything else.

Whether war interests you or not, the idea of coming home from the war, even on leave, was for me a really great concept. I went to Vietnam and extended my tour twice and came back home to St. Paul two separate times. I went home after my first year but the second time, about seven months later, was a Christmas leave and after the holiday, I was dressed and ready to go to the airport to go back on duty when my mom and I each got a call from the hospital telling us my father was dying. I called the Red Cross, telling them that I needed a few more days for a family emergency. My father died the next day. We had a wake and a funeral and buried my Dad at Fort Snelling and I went back to Vietnam during the Tet Offensive. During Tet and afterwards, the war got very serious and more than once I thought I maybe had extended one time too many, and might be joining my father in the same cemetery before the year was out. Strangely, when I did get home okay six months later, I didn't visit my father's gravesite for quite some time. I can't really tell you why exactly, except to say that I knew someday I'd be going there for good and was in no hurry to see the place again, even to pay my respects to my Dad. My point, if any, is that Christmas, if you celebrate enough of them, evokes memories of such variety and all across the spectrum of the human experience, it sort of puts an extra wreath of the season around every event you experienced. Whether those memories are great or small, sad or happy, the season kind of paints a backdrop of its own that colors how you see and remember things. Now, I go to Fort Snelling every time I come home and since then, have my mother, father, an aunt and uncle and father-in-law to visit as well. I talk to them of course, but even if they could answer, I'm not sure they'd know much more than I do about the secrets of the world. One thing is sure, though, one of these days I'm certain to find out.

I slept in the same bedroom with my parents for fifteen years, three beds to jump on rather than one was the position I took. I'd like to tell you what it was like to have no siblings. I've tried before but I can say that it seemed as much of an advantage as it was a disadvantage. Being born late in life to my parents (who never thought they'd have children to begin with) they weren't exactly on the ball when it came time for this or that, and as a result I missed my first year of eligibility for little league baseball for example. There were issues with father-son and even mother-son things that got missed, but none that were that important or so I've come to believe. However, through my friends and their parents who (by having older children) knew the drill already, I managed to fit in a little better than I might have otherwise. I did in fact have it pretty good and tried to make the best of those things where I didn't. And yet, not exactly for reasons of my not having to share things, there were people who made me feel as though I was the only, only child in the world. I might have said something but I had a strong sense that anyone who would do that, did so more out of envy than for any other reason. Recently I had an exchange with a girl I went to school with who came from a large family. She told me her only goal in life growing up was just to somehow "fit in." I found that strange and yet I suppose it's the same as feeling lonely in a crowd of people. We all have felt that, but her wanting to fit in and my feeling exactly the same did give me the idea that regardless of our circumstance, we pretty much all want the same things.

I wrote a short story years ago based on a Collie dog I used to go up and visit on the corner of Brimhall and Hartford in St. Paul. I was just at that age when the "everything is possible" line of reasoning was giving way to, "No, you're never going to have a dog." We were caretakers of the apartment building on Brimhall and Randolph and there were no pets allowed. In a way, my wanting a dog as much as I did (and being spoiled and therefore getting most of the things I wanted), created that rule more than the owners of the building did. In that short story, I framed the plot around a divorced father of two who was estranged from his children. He took an interest in this little boy, who upon discovering an old dog in a yard across the street from his home, began to pour his heart out to the dog and through the father's own eyes wonder: "What weighed as heavily on the boy's mind?" In the father's mind was a medical test that he had begun to feel was perhaps an end to his own life. In finding the answer he inadvertently discovered the boy's dilemma and a resolution was at hand. All this thought sixty years later, because among the things I did have, a dog would never be one of them. Should I pass into another world, I'm hoping my wonderful parakeet Pretty Boy, who lived many years, will not be holding a copy of the story.... "The Dog Across the Street" by W. Jack Savage and says to me, in some version of the hereafter, "What's this all about?"

One of the things I like about being from St. Paul and not living there anymore is running into someone from back home. You never really know, especially out here in California, where anyone might be from originally, but with new residents always coming here chances are wherever you're from, you're bound to run into someone from home. There are exceptions of course and I was here for both the 1987 and 1991 World Series and believe me, thousands of people from the Twin Cities became proud Minnesotans again for those seven game series'. Everybody had Twins hats and some had shirts and naturally, we all thought the Twins were going to lose. It's in our genes; so when they won the first one and especially the second in '91, everybody went nuts and some starting talking about moving back to Minnesota. Now remember, the World Series is known as the October Classic meaning November and December would follow shortly. Had the World Series been played in say…March or April, a lot more of us might have moved back home. But it wasn't and very few did and yes, the weather had a lot to do with it. For many of us, our teams didn't change just because we moved out here. The Wild are different because they began while I was gone and about the Timberwolves, the less said the better. But the Gophers, the Twins and Vikings are my teams. There's nothing more to be said.

As one of the first children to sit in front of the television set, I can tell you that growing up I was no stranger to boxing. My father enjoyed my getting up out of bed (any good excuse would do) and saluting while they played the National Anthem at television boxing matches that were always on Saturday nights, but also Monday, Wednesday and Thursday during my childhood. So when Saturday's "Wide World of Sports" came around I was getting older and with hundreds of good fights behind me, I watched Nino Benvenuti of Italy try to defend his middleweight championship against Alex Rodriguez, who was managed by Angelo Dundee, Muhammad Ali's manager. Through it all and having spent many hours watching with my father, I became quite knowledgeable at an early age and I spent a good hour that day watching two things: Rodriguez winning the fight with a good left jab and his right hand defense, lowering just a little with each passing round. Championship fights were fifteen rounds in those days and sure enough, somebody in Benvenuti's camp saw it too. Around the 13th round, Benvenuti threw the wildest left hook you ever saw and knocked Rodriguez out cold. That particular fight was instructive to me and I've never forgotten it. Sometimes, you only get one shot.

I drove cab for a while after the service and on the radio they would call out certain areas and if you were near those areas and you called in first, you'd get the fare. It sounded like this: Dispatcher, "short Hill (Dale and Selby area), long Hill (toward midway)...East Side...who's driving?" Me, in cab 32, "32 at Lexington and University". Dispatcher, "32...get Samaritan Hospital, emergency entrance." Now I have to tell you that back in the early 70's some cab drivers drank on the job or at least on lunch break, especially at night. Many of the rest of us were high on marijuana and not quite sure where we were at all times...."Yeah, ah, this is 32...is that out Lexington?" There'd be a pause, then,"32, it's west of you, 1515 Charles." This was repeated over the course of my shift depending on my...condition, and apart from that, St. Paul is just different. The streets aren't laid out alphabetically or numerically. Often times you just had to know where Arundel was, or Case and in general, unless you thought you might like to drive cab forever, you just sort of hung around areas you were familiar with. It wasn't that I didn't like the east side, I just didn't know it. It was the same with the west side. In my day you got a percentage of the fare and you could take some cash in right away and of course spend it while you drove. Whereas I couldn't always find my way around, there was a time when I knew where every Arby's in town was and with the munchies upon me, would take fares that brought me in proximity to an Arby's. Back then, Arby's was very different and a real roast beef sandwich (not water injected, recombined beef) and real cheddar cheese with potato cakes and a Black Cow Shake (a root beer malt) was simply to die for. I never got rich driving cab, unless you count the stories I could tell, but while it lasted, I did have some fun...gained a bit of weight, too.

I've always found it strange that while I appeared in more plays than I ever attended as an audience member, I can't remember who I went to those plays with. The exception to that would be musicals. For some reason I remember who I was with at every musical I ever went to see. I can play drama and can make you laugh on stage, but I can't sing or dance. I suppose that's why I can remember who I was with. In a musical, I wasn't sitting there preoccupied with the notion that I could do THAT better than whoever was doing it on stage. We actors aren't all like that but I sure was. You should do yourself a favor and see a play this weekend. I'd love to come with you, but I'm having my eyebrows professionally tweezed.

In conversation the other day with a young guy, he seemed surprised that there used to be local, common products that ruled in place of the universal products of today, where you find nearly anything by name from Maine to California. Being Irish and Italian and from St. Paul, Minnesota, I was no stranger to beer growing up. Hamm's, Schmidt and Grain Belt were Twin Cities beers. There was Pabst Blue Ribbon, Budweiser and Miller I think, but they didn't dominate the market like some do today. Ice cream was another thing...from local dairies only...Kemps-Crescent was the brand we bought most often and of course there was Tastee Bread and Master Bread which were both local, and Peter's Wieners at the ballgame; and a lot of what are now universal products, simply didn't exist. It seemed the same everywhere too. When I lived in San Francisco in 1965, Burgermiester and Rainier were popular beers and instead of Old Dutch Potato Chips it was Granny Goose. Dove Bars were only a California treat and as I've said before, if you wanted lettuce and tomato on your burger, it was called a California burger. I think coffee was probably the first universal product I can remember...Hills Brothers, Maxwell House and a few others. The change was kind of gradual too and so without thinking about it, pretty soon whatever you could get somewhere else, you could find where you were. Coming back to St. Paul by car from Arizona, my parents got introduced to Coors Beer and believe me, they were impressed. Today there are lots of good beers and my favorite is Sapporo from Japan. It's available right down the street...anywhere you are.

Catalina Island is about 26 miles off the coast here in Los Angeles, and you might find it very interesting how many Angelinos have never been to Catalina: millions. It's a nice island and there are a few things to do there but once was enough for my wife and I. You know it's funny but you can hang around Hollywood for years and never see a movie star. Once we saw Kurt Russell and Goldie Hawn at the airport. The point I'm trying to make that is St. Paul has a lot of things to do and as a result many of us just never got around to doing them. Let's take Como Park for example. You may have trouble believing this but there are people who live in St. Paul who've never been to Como Park, or never been to a Saint's baseball game, no matter who they were playing, or even to the Minnesota State Fair. At the same time these same people may never miss a concert or play at a St. Paul theater or performance of the Prairie Home Companion Show. They might miss the Winter Carnival entirely but never a flea market or yard sale for miles around. During the relatively short time I drove a cab in St. Paul, I remember a mother and her three kids I picked up somewhere. She wanted to make a stop at the Lexington and University White Castle and you'd think it was Christmas morning the way those kids jumped around watching their mother come back to the cab with three sacks of White Castle hamburgers. St. Paul is so many things to so many different people that in my experience, it's the greatest "little big city" around. Great schools, great bars, great hamburgers and enough turkeys among the great people, to know there's enough of everything and it will never get too familiar. I live in Los Angeles and I haven't even owned a jacket in two decades, or gloves, or overshoes or a window scrapper for my car. I did when I lived in St. Paul and I may never own those things again, but I know what it's like to feel like you may never see or experience everything about the place you're living. I know it because I'm from St. Paul.

I very much enjoy and generally approve of posts and articles that heighten an awareness of various problems and issues. So if I ever hear gunshots or the sounds of any kind of violence to anyone or anything in the neighborhood, I'd call the police right away. Most everyone would do the same, I'm sure. You can't help but have noticed telephone numbers on TV, urging you to report all manner of other offenses should you see them. Out here in California we have a critical water situation and so we are being urged to report anyone wasting water. I don't participate in those things because like most of you, I know where that's going: that is, the idea of calling in and providing names and addresses of transgressors for wasting water, or not eating enough salad, or barbecuing the flesh of some animal in their backyards or, dare I say, someone even thinking about having an abortion. The reason I won't do these things is because it is the act of reporting these things, no matter what they are, that's getting us all ready for reporting everything. I'm often accused of being a liberal and in some respects I am, but make no mistake. Vegetarians actually believe they will create a world where animals are no longer eaten just like pro-life people actually believe they will take away a woman's right to choose. They are exactly the same and when it comes to "the end justifies the means," vegetarians and pro-lifers are on the same page. They want what they want and will do anything to see that they get it and if enlisting the public to call the authorities about every transgression under the sun will help the cause, they will encourage it. So go ahead...call 1-800 BE-A-SNITCH every time you see someone smoking within one hundred feet of a building. Just remember, your name and telephone number will go on the record...whether they find the smoker or not.

Taste is something you're not born with. If it was, I was certainly born without it. I bought a green leisure suit once. I'm pretty sure, as is our tendency to picture our exes unfavorably, if my first wife imagines me at all, it's wearing that leisure suit. So it took me many years of trial and occasionally painful error to grasp the concept that paisley and stripes not only don't go together, they shouldn't be allowed in the same time zone simultaneously. Which brings me around to Nate's on 9th and Wabasha and a young salesman who worked there. You see Nate's was never the problem or the answer, not for someone like me. I needed a role model and this kid was it. He worked there as a salesman and I remember thinking how ridiculous it was for him to say, "May I help you?" I thought..."Of course you can help me...make me look like you!" He had it down. He looked like a million bucks but he wore it with the ease of a James Bond as if he wasn't wearing clothes at all. I must tell you that just watching him move through the store waiting on people helped me, and soon I wasn't buying burgundy slacks anymore, or worse, wearing them. A few years later, I discovered Chess King out in Rosedale and relapsed into bad taste during my hippie period, but I've never forgotten this young guy at Nate's and even today, more than fifty years later, whenever I get my native urge to look stupid, I think of him and "back away" from clothing of that nature.

F. Scott Fitzgerald once called Summit Avenue "the largest collection of mediocre architecture in the world" or something like that. He was a truly great writer but I disagree. St. Paul natives get this snooty attitude about our home when they go out east in general and to New York in particular and he was no exception. I love Summit Avenue and I vow (even if I get to New York someday) to love it forever. I was interested to learn that when you look at the mansions that overlooking downtown, from say, the University Club to the Cathedral on the southeast side of Summit, you're seeing the backs of the mansions if you're on Summit Avenue. That is, the fronts of the buildings face the city. Frankly, I find that a rather snooty plan myself. What it means is, unless you're a bird or a bat or something, the only way to see the front is from way down below and from afar, without being invited I mean. F. Scott Fitzgerald lived on Summit and other streets in the area and drank to excess. I've had a few too many myself over the years, lived in a basement apartment on Summit and will probably never write as well as he did. But I am taller, better looking and have and continue to dwell on the right side of the ground in spite of my shortcomings and apart from my using my first initial as a writer (W. Jack Savage) as he did, and we continue to disagree about Summit Avenue. Sadly, I must mention that he sold millions of copies of his books and I've sold fewer than, well, I'd rather not say; but if one needs to badmouth Summit Avenue to be taken seriously as a writer, count me out.

I had such a vivid imagination as a child that I had trouble at times telling the real from the unreal. As I grew up it was easier of course but again, paintings, movies and TV and even cartoons had a way of getting to me like nothing else. So naturally when it came time to live a real adventure, in my case serving in Vietnam, I very much expected to be horrified beyond anything I'd ever experienced. When it didn't happen, I then realized how Walt Disney and his talented artists prepared me for life in ways I never imagined at the time. I fought real men trying to kill me but the truth is, not one of them ever scared me as much as Monstro the whale in "Pinocchio" or that ticking crocodile in "Peter Pan". The witch in "Snow White" terrified me as a child beyond anything I would experience in life. We all had different wars and I came home a very light sleeper for quite a while, but I've never had a nightmare about my experiences of over two and half years in Vietnam, not once. I can't say that about Walt Disney movies. They were a "right-of-passage" when I was a kid and as I slid down in my seat to escape the scary things on the screen, just waiting for it to be over, I was pretty sure the terror I was feeling was right at the limits of my endurance. I was right, thank God. Nothing in life ever scared me that much again.

When I was a little boy in the summer, I wore a T-shirt, jeans and tennis shoes. I wanted to grow up to be a man who wore a sport-coat over an open collared shirt and slacks (think James Garner in "The Rockford Files"). Since I've retired, I wear a T-shirt, jeans or shorts and tennis shoes but it's okay. I was never as cool as the men I wanted to be that I saw on TV and in the movies. I should say however, that I only wore my jeans and all, in the summer. During school we had Catholic school uniforms. I didn't exactly hate them, but I knew that when I grew up I'd prefer a climate that would at least allow me to wear a T-shirt, jeans and tennis shoes year round, if I wanted to. I live in L.A. and so that worked out okay. Besides, where you hear… "Women dress for other women" men really don't do that. I dressed for women if I dressed up at all and those days have past. If I inadvertently attracted a woman with what I'm wearing today, I'd go home and change. About a month ago I shaved off my mustache. My wife didn't notice for three days and so I grew it back. That's what it's come to and I'm just fine with that. Besides, I'm the one who bought and wore a green leisure suit once. With taste like that, wearing what I wore as a child on a daily basis might be the best of all worlds.

I was born and raised in St. Paul and I assure you the relevance of this post to the "Old St. Paul Minnesota" site shall present itself in due course. I bring it up because, well, just because. The Crocus Hill area enjoyed a longer period of those wonderful streetlights on the single post than many of our neighborhoods did and I always think of that when they started being replaced with those cold, fluorescent numbers that used to hang in intersections during the fifties. In their favor, they put out quite a bit of light and certainly more than the old style street lights. But they were a terrible harbinger of things that were to come with their severe, bluish, almost radiated light that cast shadows that seem to go on for blocks. The one at Pascal and Randolph in particular was most annoying. The St. Joseph's orphanage was gone by the time they put it up, but it was as if they wanted to light the space that it took up, just to remind you as you walked by that your fate could have been far worse than the one you were living just then. As strange as it seems, a telephone pole was changed just up the street from our home here in California with a light that looks exactly like the one at Pascal and Randolph, but with an almost orange, softness in place of the "penicillin inspired older variety" from the fifties in my St. Paul home. That's the kind of progress I can appreciate at my age. You see, over the years we lost many of our great St. Paul memories in the form of buildings in the downtown for example. While we were doing it, the lighting was being changed as well; the "mood" to accommodate what would follow. Looking back, it was almost diabolical.

Many of us, and not just we who were lucky enough to grow up in St. Paul, measure our successes with our failures and in so doing forget those wonderful first steps we took to being the people we are today. It's too bad really because I can still see that little boy walking back and forth in front of Myrtle Conroy's house just across Brimhall on Randolph. Myrtle was always nice to me and after she had a terrible stroke it was as if she had died in many ways. Her inability to talk scared me and made me very uncomfortable and it took all the courage I could find to knock on her door that day. "I want to see Myrtle," I told Jiggs, her husband. It didn't amount to much more than, "Hi Myrtle, how are you feeling?" and then I was out of there, but I had acknowledged someone who was nice to me and had a terrible thing happen to her. I never went there again and it wasn't so much that I did the right thing, as it was overcoming the fear to do the right thing. I think there's a parking lot on that corner now but I never go by there that I don't think about that day.

You know as I look back over my life, I was lucky enough from time to time to be singled out, if even just in passing, by adults when I was a boy and later by others for various things: for my art, I was a pretty good athlete, and was complimented on my voice which led

120

me into broadcasting; but you know, it doesn't really matter, does it? It was someone taking the time to say something nice about you. It seems such a small thing really, but the sum of these things can be so important to the development of a person that they really shouldn't be overlooked. I was an only child for example, which is really the same as being the youngest or the oldest or a lost middle child and so you tend to go through things alone and without instruction. When someone takes the time to address you and affirm a certain worth in your manner or something you have achieved, it becomes almost ceremonial in a way and you find yourself saying, "Well, they're friends of my parents and so...", and look to diminish the praise in some way and yet the impression has been made. I know it has because whenever I think of it and see someone either in need of a boost in some way or simply find something positive to say, I am acting upon my Dad's always saying, "If you can't find anything good to say about someone, don't say anything at all". I'm a good talker and so saying nothing at all never came naturally to me, but the power of the compliment has never been lost on me either. I only wish I started it a lot earlier in my life and more consistently overall; just a thought to begin the week.

There was a man who in good weather, would walk by our apartment building on his way to the golf course. He carried two golf clubs and wore a perpetual smile. I saw him for many years and finally one day I saw him on the golf course. He was with two other men and I heard them speaking of another golf course. There was no separating the man I saw from his smile or his golf clubs. They were the same to him and he was complete. What he did when the snows came I'll never know, but I suppose he dreamed of seeing another spring and summer walking to the golf course. I dreamed of other things, but in golf he was complete.

Dewey's Pit and Paddock Bar on Snelling and Selby in St. Paul was a hang-out of mine for many years and even after my radio career began, I always stopped by whenever I was in town. I remembered the old Pit and Paddock down by the Cathedral but never went in there. I met Dewey when he was bartending for Brian Hockenberg at Brian's Cozy Inn on Selby. Dewey was a racecar driver and a good one. Dick Nesbitt, an old Chicago Bear who was the sportscaster on KSTP ("Top of the evening to you from the world of sports") was a good friend of Dewey's and was going to sponsor him, but Dick died suddenly of a heart attack before that happened. Anyway, Dewey moved up to Selby and Snelling and my friend Jesse and I walked in on New Year's Eve for the first time, just as some guy clutching a bar towel to his broken nose and his embarrassed wife were leaving. I've got fifty stories about Dewey's including bartending there a time or two. Like I said I always stopped by whenever I came home and one time the bar was closed for good. I looked up Dewey and the miles and the drinks had taken their toll and I had the feeling I was talking to him for the last time. "Is there anything I can get you, Dew?" I asked. He said with a smile, "How about a couple of cold beers, Skip?" My plane was at noon the next day and I caught Dewey at the breakfast table that morning and put down two ice-cold Sapporo's on his table. Dewey was a great guy and he influenced a lot of local racers and carried more than a few of us on his books (including me) through some hard times. I still think of him often and the Pit and Paddock on Snelling and Selby. I looked for a picture but I couldn't find one so all I can tell you is in it's heyday, Dewey's was packed, the music was loud, the place was dark, the ladies got prettier with every passing beer and I was lucky to know Dewey Brohaugh.

I was looking at an old resume the other day and like most resumes, it makes me look pretty good. I have a Master's Degree in Communication Studies with an emphasis on Telecommunication and Film. While that is true, it doesn't begin to tell the whole story. I didn't even graduate from Holy Spirit Grade School in St. Paul. I had to go to summer school just to get into Monroe High School and it wouldn't be my last trip to summer school either. Over the next two summers I would be there, and while I had righted the ship somewhat before entering my senior year, by that time I was so sick of school I willingly chose Vietnam instead. Years would pass and after two tries at getting my GED (science got me) I managed to accumulate about oh, 12 transferable credits over say, two years of attending Normandale Junior College. After a couple of more tries I finally finished a course in Radio and Television Broadcasting at Brown Institute and during my first radio job in Thief River Falls, managed to get my Associate's Degree at Northland Community College there. As an off-campus student living in Albert Lea, I got close to graduating from Mankato State when my GI-Bill finally ran out. Nearly 18 years later, I went back and finished up at Cal State L.A. and sort of accidentally got into the Master's program when they caught me in classes pretending to be an undergraduate. By that time I was a great student and wound up teaching film studies at the university level for six years. So you see, the resume doesn't nearly tell the whole story; and this is how a lifelong underachiever like myself can wind up looking pretty damn good...at least by the time I retired.

I admire people who look good in a crew cut because I was never one of them. As a kid, my mother insisted that I have one and that was a battle I never won until somewhere around the sixth grade. In St. Paul and especially in the winter, guys with long hair looked great. They'd comb their hair with a little water, walk outside, the whole thing would freeze in seconds and it would stay frozen until you got to school. Of course, that was just this side of needing a hat and so until you did, you periodically held your hand over one ear to keep it from freezing too. Then, you moved your books to the other hand and did that other ear as well. You might think I was lucky having a crew cut and therefore not needing to worry about things like that. You would be wrong because even though Roger Maris and his crew cut hit sixty home runs, he was no match for Elvis and early Elvis at that. Long hair became a standard for looking grown up as well and in the 50's and early 60's, grown up was the only thing to be, just not the grown-ups we knew. Adults would look at you and say, "These are the best years of your lives". Really? Than why is it that I dream of nothing else but growing up, driving a car and having all the babes? Adults, most of them anyway, never quite got it. Besides, in a conversation with a kid, all adults ever did was listen to respond. They never listened to understand and for many, if not most of us, we'd look at them and simply not believe they were ever kids themselves. Even the ones we could imagine as kids, they were not the kids we wanted to hang out with. When I was growing up, an adult's vision of a perfect kid was a shorthaired snitch who never did anything wrong and promptly reported anything others were doing wrong to the nearest adult. It's therefore easy to see how Elvis and the Beatles were able to take the young world by storm. The truth is, I've never really figured out who the adults patterned themselves after, but whoever it was became the antithesis of who we wanted to be.... anything but that.

There was a period in my upbringing where I pretty much became inconsolable about going downtown. The reason for going downtown was always because my mother loved it down there. She loved to shop and didn't believe in babysitters so she hauled me along. Sometimes she'd take me to the doctor but that was a secondary thing. It was something she loved to do...going to the doctor that is, and so I went to the doctor about this or that more than a lot of kids. Finally the doctor pretty much told her to get out one day and said that she was going to make me into the hypochondriac that she was. You couldn't talk to my mother like that unless you were a doctor or unless you were right. Over time, the things I hated about going downtown grew almost into a phobia for me. First of all, I could never be comfortable...no jeans, ever. I had to wear wool slacks which were itchy, and one day, one of the little treats she'd sort of bribe me with to help me endure the process, was simply not enough. She said she'd take me to the White Castle and I said I'd rather go home. Not long after that, the trips downtown with my mother became fewer but for many years thereafter and in some respects still today, I can only shop for short periods at a time. The idea of going from store to store, even in today's mall environment is something I just won't do. God knows I loved my mother and there were few special days going downtown with her, but they were too few to make up for how often we went.

In Ken Burns' fabulous documentary on World War II titled simply "The War", he took five cities in America and focused on how the war affected each of the communities and one of the cities was Luverne, Minnesota. One of the men involved in the war recounted being taken up to the train station in Minneapolis by his father. His father extended his hand to his son and they shook hands for the first time. He remembered that as rather pivotal in their relationship. It was as if it was the end of their relationship as father and son and the beginning of their being man to man, so to speak. Many of our parents never talked about certain things. They never complained and they were grateful always for what they did have, as opposed to what they did without. My parents, my dad in particular was like that. While I find those traits commendable on the one hand, they were very sad on the other. In the St. Paul my parents grew up in, you never talked about certain things...ever. It didn't mean those things weren't going on, they were just not talked about: rape, pregnancies, child molestation's, neglect and often beatings that resulted in life long injury and even death. All those years going through all manner of unimaginable horrors and yet the watchword was, "Be silent. We don't talk about such things." I know many of you remember what I'm talking about because that's the way things were way back when. Today, in St. Paul and all over the world things are more complicated on one hand but because someone broke away from those "out of sight, out of mind" strategies for the uncomfortable, or even the tragic, things got better...much better. So while I admire the work-ethic and the idea of not complaining about whatever hardship might befall you, I think of today as a wonderful time to be alive with true opportunities for nearly everyone. I remember seeing a slight smile on the faces of my parents and my family when some of these barriers started to fall. I'd ask them about it and they'd say..."oh...nothing." They were welcoming the change but still couldn't participate in it.

I wrote a bit an hour ago or so on how, when you get older, you should travel more, not less. Something crazy happened to the computer and it was lost. Once I settled down, I chalked it up to "whatever" and I'm starting again with a thought about old friends, gone...but not forgotten. I grew up in St. Paul, Minnesota and the city has changed a great deal of course, but what can never change are those memories of the places and people that contributed to who you are and who you have always been. I had lunch at O'Gara's with a dear friend when I went home for my son's wedding last week and told her I thought there was a book in these little visits. She smiled and agreed and after I waved and left, never again thought about what I had wanted to complete that afternoon. I had sub-consciously scratched it off the list. One of my very best friends is suffering from dementia and recovering from a stroke in a home out in St. Anthony Park. He was just beginning the symptoms when I was home in October and I knew he'd be in worse shape and I just didn't want to go see him again. Naturally, it made me feel terrible but there it was and there I was. Once again, I was six years old pacing back and forth in front of Myrtle and Jigg Conroy's house on Randolph and Brimhall, trying to find enough courage to go in and say "hi" to Myrtle who was always nice to me. She had suffered a stroke and could only mumble as a result. That scared me but finally, I did knock on the door, went in and said "hi" to this dear lady who was long and terribly removed from the woman I knew. She seemed grateful and a moment later it was over. I never did that again but as I drove away from lunch last Wednesday, not wanting to see my best

126

friend in that condition, I thought of Myrtle again and realized things: no matter who you became in life somewhere else, you can't hide from who you were and who you became back home. Two days later I got up, went to the White Castle and brought hamburgers, fries and milk shakes for my friend and went to see him at the home as if nothing in the world had changed. I talked, he smiled and nodded his approval for a half hour or so, with me telling the old stories we always re-lived over the years. He sat in his wheel chair unable to shake hands, I kissed him on top of his head and left. As I drove home I cried for him but not for me. Sixty-two years later I'm still that frightened little boy in front of Myrtle's house and while I did the right thing, it still took everything I had. When I got home last night, I heard another good friend had suffered a stroke and was in a home out in Highland. Next time, unless a stroke lands on me too, I'll see him as well. I hope so anyway.

You can't blame Old St. Paul or the people who grew up in it, for there is always someone around to rain on your parade when you were growing up. We still think of those things today, in my case sixty years later. Some kids in my neighborhood in Highland and in your neighborhoods as well, were just born jerks and they picked on anybody who showed the slightest weakness in any area. It is true that we were all guilty from time to time at not always being as nice as we could have been to say, new kids, small kids, uncoordinated kids, kids with glasses and the list goes on. For myself, it was a way of learning not to do those things and I got better as I grew. However, some kids simply never did and they became an excellent deterrent to doing anything that might wind you up in jail, because quite a few of those kids were and are still there today. I felt sorry for them. It was as if they couldn't help it. We all caught our share growing up but the damage they did to real nice kids was pretty awful. Life growing up was like that sometimes and St. Paul was no different. My experiences were with kids from large families, one worse than the next from the top on down. It was as if it were expected of them. Then, I ran into one years ago. "Hey Savage", he said in that same tone of voice he used when we were kids. I looked at him and smiled. There was no fear anymore and it was a moment that reinforced my feeling that I had survived somehow. We shook hands and chatted for a while and I was so impressed. He couldn't have been more affable, more of a gentleman in every way. I wanted to ask him, "What happened to you?", but I never did and still today, thinking of him, I believe people can change. It sure never seemed so when we were twelve.

You really do need a working knowledge of what it felt like thinking you never looked right while you were growing up to understand something like this. If you imagine that sort of insecurity was mostly confined to young girls, you may be right, but I suspect by a narrower margin than you might imagine. I can't tell you how I happened to be there except to say that I was and witnessed a minor event which happened to a girl I didn't know and people I didn't know. The girl was older than I was and her boyfriend just loved her. You could see it at once and it was fun, being younger, seeing that kind of love manifested in two people around our age. Then suddenly and I never saw what happened, the girl got soaked with water somehow and her hair and makeup and all of it was ruined of course, and where she was having THE day of her life one minute, the next minute she was crushed. People including her boyfriend tried to console her but it just wasn't happening. I was as I said, outside of this group but I was a sort of invisible witness that day. I felt for her but being an outsider, I started to drift off when I heard this exchange and I never forgot it. Her friend, a girl, said something about her boyfriend and that "He loves you!"; and through tears she responded, "I don't want to be loved looking like this!!!" I seldom put myself in girl's shoes in those days but on that occasion we were as one. "If I didn't look my absolute best, I wasn't worthy". I instantly understood and in the awkwardness of my early teens, I knew as she did that we still had a bit of growing up to do.

I enjoyed all the reminiscences by the St. Columba people the other day. Their Catholic school experience in the Midway area was a little different from ours at Holy Spirit. For one thing, there seemed to be more of an emphasis on the arts there. One gal said they had a school band. We surely had nothing like that. Music was important but only where the glorification of God was concerned, you know. A few of us stopped back at Holy Spirit during our various freshman years and when the nun learned I had art every day at Monroe, she just shook her head. I shook mine too. Through it all though, there were some pretty good times at Holy Spirit. I have through the years variously blamed my experiences there on a few of my shortcomings and they were real and damaging to a point. That was long ago and if nothing else, they taught me life isn't always fair. My dad went to Cretin in the twenties but my application letter said I passed the test but there was not enough room. That was a bit of luck as I assure you I'd have failed there. I was watching Robert Redford being interviewed the other day and I was taken by how unapologetic he was talking about how boring school was. I do agree but I still should have made more of my opportunities there. I've always been a little guilty about it, but I was happy in the Army and in Vietnam, more than in any of my school years. It is funny though, in sixth grade St. Columba had the worst basketball team I ever saw. I felt sorry for them. Maybe they were bad, but they had quite a bit more going for them than we did.

This is about camping out in the back yard in beautiful St. Paul during the summer. In our day, everybody was Davy Crockett crazy and camping out was big. It was usually a pup tent from army surplus or maybe even a blanket thrown over a low clothesline in good weather. Now, let's further imagine you have a bird feeder. You know how it is when you fill the bird feeder after leaving it empty for a while? Nothing happens at first and then one or two birds show up. They leave and tell half a dozen other birds each and pretty soon the hungry birds are having a fine time. That's pretty much the way it worked with the mosquitoes. Just as it was getting dark one or two would swoop down to see what was going on in that tent, and before long mosquitoes from all over the neighborhood had heard about the "all you can eat buffet" in the tent in the back yard. If you had a blanket, you crawled under or a sleeping bag, you zipped up but it was no use. The mosquitoes were a part of sleeping out in St. Paul in the summer and that's just the way it was. The bigger and better the tent helped but by the time two people went in and two people went out, every mosquito in the neighborhood got in. I know you remember. You know how I know? Halfway through writing this I started to itch. How about you?

I offer these words this morning to other writers and artists because if you're lucky, a time will come when you can dedicate larger amounts of your time to these pursuits without worrying about getting up and going to work. It's called retirement and I've been enjoying it for seven years now. However, just prior to retiring and thinking I'd maybe work three more years or so, I found myself in a most prolific period of my life during which I wrote three novels, two short story collections, a non-fiction collection of musings and a very ill advised collection of my paintings and drawings, which if assembled today would contain less than an eighth of what passed for my best back then. Believe me when I say I am grateful for these accomplishments but at sixty-nine I feel I'm closer to death than you, with still a few things to say and with illustrations to go with it. In other words, I'm on the clock and not making the most of my opportunities. I've tried but after a bout with bronchitis a year ago, my muse flew out the window taking with her more than the bitch deserved, I assure you. For me, it's interconnected. My first book became an excuse to design its cover, which got me drawing and painting again after many years. I have three books ready to go that if I began again today, I could finish by the fourth of July, but it's just not happening. In the past if I was turning out quality paintings, I could say "Well, I'm just busier with this", but I don't have that to lean on anymore. Thank God for Facebook; and with online paying of bills, I don't have the writing of checks to crow about. I should be angrier and I'm not, which makes me more frustrated still and so I say, don't take your work habits for granted. They're more important than you know.

I had lunch today with my oldest friend. Dave lived down the block on Brimhall and was two years older but until he hit school we were best friends anyway. I told him about the camping recollection I shared the other day. He reminded me that camping out overnight was only part of it and that we were basically camping out all day long as well: starting campfires, roasting hot dogs or just getting away for the day with a sandwich to any wooded area. Once it was that big long rough on the Highland Golf Course. The rough had about three holes in play so we found a few balls as well; but deep in the middle of it was wild enough for us. If you could connect water to it somehow it was even better. There was a little creek down in the valley from where the Pavilion is now up in Highland. Of course, by the time we could venture as far as the river, that was as good as it would get. He remembered it being a little wilder the deeper you got into the area. There were deer back in there then. Dave and his wife bought some income property out here in Sherman Oaks that will bring them to California more often now, and it's still amazing to me how almost sixty-five years later you can still run into and hang out with your old best friend and have it seem as familiar as it always had been.

Growing up in St. Paul, I loved sports, I loved summer vacation, I loved Jackie Gleason on Saturday nights and in spite of everything, I loved God also. But were God here, he or she could tell you that I loved girls more than anything or anybody. It really wasn't even close. From the first time I saw one…I knew, before I really knew…I had to have one, the sooner the better. Parents, mine certainly but adults in general, were wary of these feelings and rarely approved. You could see it on their faces. "You're too young to think about such things," they might say, adding to the ever-growing preponderance of evidence that adults really didn't know anything. It may have started in the Montgomery Ward Catalog women's lingerie section or with Betty and Veronica in Archie comics; once love of women had you, that was it and the learning curve would last a lifetime. Loving girls and women taught me a great deal about life. For example, some girls liked bullies, tough guys. If you weren't one of those and had no hope or desire of growing into one, you learned two things right away: not all girls are as good as they look, and in spite of their wonderful and growing figures, their taste in boys might make them more trouble than they're worth. These were difficult lessons, especially when you were learning other lessons of life and how to throw a curve ball. Janet Shore was her name and she liked to kiss. I haven't been the same to this day. It was second grade. Mind you, I never knew she was kissing Nick Tschida as well and God knows who else. Those lessons would land like a ton of bricks later, when you were better able to absorb the blow. I remember them all and in my way, love them all still. If nothing else about growing up was worth it, the girls sure were.

In spite of righting the ship at Monroe High School in 1965, that summer I had moved to San Francisco by myself, gotten a job and rented an apartment. I moved back after some months but it still being late September, my mother was telling everyone I was going back to Monroe for my senior year. I enlisted in the Army the next day. Now I'll admit the romance of "going to war for my country" was programmed in me from an early age and so I welcomed the process. My whole family was veterans going back to the Spanish-American War and of course like everyone else, I was raised on war movies. It seemed the next step except for one thing: a girlfriend to kiss me as I went off to war. I made an effort to have one but just then no one was interested and so, at least to begin with, no girlfriend to come home to. I didn't know then there would never be one from St. Paul, which turned out to be fine as I discovered certain wonders of the Orient along the way. I met a lot of guys from St. Paul and the Twin Cities in Vietnam who did have wives and girlfriends back home. They seemed weighted down by it sometimes, making me glad I didn't. I was just a screwy teenager and stayed two and half years over there and was very, very lucky. Six weeks after getting home I was bored to death and nearly re-enlisted. I traded my senior year in high school for that experience. I've never regretted it.

I loved my mother as much or more than anyone in my life, but I don't miss her the way many of you miss your mothers. She had a stroke and went to the nursing home. After work, I'd go to see her every day; then… every other day and finally once or twice a week. My uncle visited her every day, as he had his own wife for many years before. Years went by and when I was offered a job out-of-state, I took it. When I'd come home I saw her every day but it was only a few times. When she died, I was a mess. Some would say (as I did then), deservedly so. I remember once getting off the bus after work and walking the three blocks to the nursing home. I couldn't go in. I walked back to the bus stop, got on the bus and continued on my way. I was not built for the nursing home experience and it grieves me to this day. When I visit her grave, I no longer cry. Anyway, after she died, my uncle Nick started with assisted living and gradually moved on to nursing homes. I still lived in Wyoming but visited him every time I was home. It was the same deal but I did my best. The last time I came home before he died, I went to see him at a place in Inver Grove Heights. He didn't know who I was or much care either. He was just thirsty. He was asking for a glass of water to nursing home people going by but it was as if they were deaf. I found a kid working there and he gave me the ice water I asked for and I gave it to my uncle. I stayed a while longer but when I left, I felt like my going to see him was actually worth something that time. I was able to get him some water. I got to thinking about all the other times when you just sit there and talk, trying to cheer someone a little and all the time wanting to get out of there. Finally, and after all the years of visiting members of our family every day, my other uncle, Albert, had a stroke and wound up in the nursing home, in Hastings. Naturally I saw him when I came home as well. What a cruel fate I thought, for a guy who visited everybody else, to wind up like that. The last time I went to see him he looked at me and said, "Skipper.... I've been here a year today." It had been eight years. I often wonder why I was privy to these little lessons and I'm going through another nursing home visitation issue, with a friend now. I'm not doing any better with it and wonder if some future of my own isn't being shown to me. If it is, do me a favor and don't come to see me.

I hope you don't mind but I'm basically hiding tonight. The home page is especially vile and biting with all the news of the day. So while I'm here I'd like to tell you a story. This happened last night and with the help of a dear friend here on OSP. She is acquainted with the ex-wife of an old friend who I met twice in the Randolph and Hamline area where I grew up. Well, actually I met her once and saw her another time. Anyway, my friend re-introduced to me to this lady last night on Messenger and she asked if I remembered throwing a firecracker at her while she was on a horse at Eden's Ranch in Mendota back in the day and I said no, it wasn't me. First of all, I don't particularly like firecrackers, horses scared me a bit and I was never at Eden's until after the war (Vietnam). Moreover, I did screwy things as a teenager but nothing like that at all. Now remember, this is fifty years ago and she said some kid named Gott, Rick Gott, told her it was me that did it. Never mind that I was humping the hills of Vietnam near Bon Song when the act took place. Anyway, during this conversation we caught up a bit on those people we had in common and in the end, she almost sadly conceded that I was probably not the one she hated for throwing that firecracker for nearly fifty years. This brings me around to Fred

Pizinger. One winter night he heard I was hitting on Claudette Long, a schoolmate at Monroe, and he punched out Greg Beckwith, one of our members here, thinking he was me. So with all the hate in the world and especially here in the United States, I'd like you to do me a favor. You see I've internalized what retribution I have left to incidents on or about fifty years ago and so if you know a Rick Gott of Mendota or a Fred Pizinger of St. Paul.... tell them I'm looking for them!

I played most sports growing up, for fun and in organized leagues as well. But I never got on an organized hockey team. It was no one's fault. I wasn't that strong of a skater and at Holy Spirit and at Edgcumbe playground, there were some real good young hockey players. The year I might have made it, Lindwood playground decided to not field a team, so all their players came down to Edgcumbe and anyone in the margins, like me, didn't make it. A kid at St. Paul Academy purposely shot a puck and hit me in the mouth when I first went skating and that was my first impression of some of the kids who played hockey. The Cotters who lived on Saratoga had a cool rink. It was at least 15' by 30' and I remember one day, Tom Griswold and Terry Cotter, two guys who liked playing rough, played each other alone with Tom Cotter and I watching from the relative safety of their garage. The sounds were laughing and giggling and banging the puck off the garage and when it was over they both had bloody noses they shook off like nothing happened. They were friends and another time I saw them have a wet towel fight that you'd swear would end in fists. It didn't that day anyway. I'm watching the hockey playoffs tonight and it's funny but whenever it starts getting rough, I think of these two guys. Growing up, there was one hard and fast rule about bullies. In the winter, if they played sports at all, it was either wrestling or hockey. Still, I wish I could have made that team that time.

About forty years ago and I remember it like it was yesterday, three friends and I were drinking late at an after-hours joint on Iglehart and talking about what we were all gonna do someday. The truth is, I can't remember what was on their bucket list but for myself, I said I was going out to Hollywood to try to get into films. Everyone laughed of course and one guy said, "You'll get into the movies when the Twins win the World Series". This was hilarious of course because the Twins were terrible as usual. Ten years later and with only six hundred bucks to my name, I quit my job and went to Hollywood, well, near Hollywood anyway. It was tough at first but whenever I felt down, I'd always check the sports page and the Twins were having a heck of a year and that would pick me up. It was 1987 and by August, you started seeing a lot more Twins hats here in L.A. By September with each success the Twins had, winning the Division, the playoffs and improbably the World Series, I went from telemarketing to finding a radio job, from community theater to finding an agent, from student projects to independent films, from AFTRA and SAG to several episodes on "General Hospital"; and all of it began over late night drinks in St. Paul's old neighborhood. It's 2017 now and that was thirty years ago. I bring it up because some of you I know are dreaming "outside the box" so to speak. You're from St. Paul. Don't let the world scare you. Did you check the standings this morning? The Twins are in first place.

Like childhood anywhere, growing up in St. Paul was a time when you really hadn't done anything: nothing substantial anyway. You were a kid and so you prepared for those coming accomplishments by pretending to be people who were accomplished and doing so was maybe the most fun you ever had growing up. I grew up a caretaker's son and so the whole apartment building on Randolph and Brimhall was pretty much my playground, especially in the winter. I've written before about laundry room basketball and hockey and playing "goal-line-stand", diving over pillows on the bed. But come spring and summer you could go outside and if there was no one to play with, throwing a rubber ball against a wall of some kind and then fielding it was something I never really got tired of doing. There were several variations too, so you never got bored. You could pitch a whole nine-inning game, looking for a no-hitter. If you didn't field the ball cleanly to make a good throw to first, you'd either start over or settle for a one or a two hitter. There was no cheating and just as often, you'd announce the game while you were playing it. Then while you were announcing and winning your own game, maybe somebody would walk by and see you and you'd immediately pretend you weren't doing what you were doing until they went away. If someone came to join you, you could announce out loud. By fall it was street football but you needed other kids for that. So throwing a ball against a wall and fielding it remains one of the few things I miss about growing up in St. Paul.

Last night there was nothing on TV (as is frequently the case) and I wound up watching an episode of the "West Wing". When you've seen it as much as I have, you notice things. The characters arrive in the dark, they leave in the dark, and none of them ever seems to need a nap or carry any telltale signs of taking a lot of speed. They are the brightest and the best for about eighteen of a twenty-four hour day and some even have a love life after that. Now I'm going to make a big jump here to Dewey's Pit and Paddock on Snelling and Selby. I hung around there for years and we shot a lot of pool and had some good pool shooters, too. Some other bars got together and started a pool league in St. Paul and you'd go around and have matches, sometimes at their bar, sometimes at the Pit. Nobody, including me wanted to join the team. None of us were joiners and metaphorically, Dewey's was where you un-joined the world for periods of time and being on a team meant you had to be at a certain place at a certain time every week, kind of like a job. This was not considered consistent with who we were. I was thinking last night that joiners wind up in the White House and working for various captains of industry and so forth and the rest of us seemed to be at Dewey's a lot. Now I had a lot of fun in those days and would not trade it for a job in the White House. Still, I hired a youngster in Cheyenne, Wyoming for the radio who wound up working in the George S. Bush White House. He told me a couple of years ago that I was his role model. So then I thought, what if all of us from Dewey's somehow impacted all the movers and shakers in various White Houses over the years? Actually...that would explain a lot.

In the coffers of my childhood memories there are people I never knew but for one reason or another, I still wonder about. My best friend Dave lived on my block on Brimhall and right next to his house was an empty lot. We played there a lot and then one day, someone built a house on that lot. There was the great smell of sawdust and wandering through the skeleton of two-by-fours as it went up. Finally, people moved in and there was a boy who was several years older than we were. There was also his mother but I never once saw a man there. The mother gave us chocolate cake with no frosting once. It was still warm. It was not unusual for older kids to be in their own world. I never knew what grade school he went to. I'm not sure if he ever spoke to Dave and over all the years, I never heard him speak...not once. Somehow, I got it in my mind that it was because he had no dad living there and that he was quiet because he was sad. Years passed and one day I heard he was the football quarterback at St. Thomas. I remember thinking that was somewhat strange: a sad, quiet kid rising to the level of high school quarterback. I didn't even know he was Catholic. I never saw him much. I never knew if he listened to the radio or even if he had friends. He would be about 74 now and he lived on Brimhall and he was a quarterback at St. Thomas. Maybe one of you might remember him?

I lived in the movies when I was growing up. If I couldn't replicate a situation I saw in some black and white film from the matinee movie, it seemed everything that touched me growing up was redone

138

in a movie I saw later. I remember only pieces of one really but it involved an older girl (it often did, you know) and my drawing of a palm tree. The tree was very good and of course, I had never seen one in real life, but I was anxious to show it to my mom. I had dropped it once already and had to break police lines to get it before it blew into the street, so now I had a good grip on it. Before getting home, I remembered a beautiful girl who worked at the counter at the drug store. She seemed to like me, so I went it, ordered a nickel Coke and put the drawing on the counter. She loved it and now it is a week later. I have another drawing I think is even better but it's raining hard and I try my best, but the drawing and I are soaked as I pass the drug store. Some older kid was at the counter flirting with the beautiful girl, so I went home. Not long after that, I saw this movie..."Woman in a Dressing Gown", with Anthony Quayle and Sylvia Sims. It was a melodrama about a married woman who thought things were fine, but found out her husband was about to leave her and their son for a younger woman. She took what little money she had saved, bought a new dress, had her hair done, makeup and everything, and it rained. As she walked into their apartment, she looked like a drowned rat and while I felt sorry for her, I remembered my effort with the girl at the counter. In the end her husband did the right thing and stayed but the problem was, had I been him, I thought I might have taken the younger woman. I was very young but one can't help wondering how these little events shaped me as I grew up. How very lucky I am to recall these little episodes now, in old age. I cannot imagine my life without them.

I remember wanting things very badly as a child. It started with maybe a toy or something and because I was a spoiled only child, my hopes and dreams came true much of the time. Later and many times because I did receive what I wanted most, I realized that maybe I was using up my good fortune on things that weren't that important. There were issues, incidents where I got what I wanted that resulted in bad things, things I could have done without. As the years went by, I subconsciously grieved over these issues, but that never kept me from wishing or even praying for, events to go my way. More and more of them did not, which over time I've always felt were in my own best interests. As that occurred, I began to believe that whatever or whoever was deciding things, they had a better handle on what was best for me in the long or short term, then that which I decided I wanted in the first place. There were many times and many things I wanted that I felt I deserved that never took place, and I found myself grateful that they never occurred, and after a time I began to realize that's the way it was going to be. Acceptance set in and never really set me back. That's what acceptance is, in the end.

It's hard to remember the exact details because it was all about my not wanting to stand out in any negative way and so I put some care into my appearance. I had a one sport coat: a brown herringbone job which was still in fashion, a navy blue dress shirt and a blue and red paisley tie that looked good with the rest, and some corduroy trousers and oxblood penny loafers. I looked good and the assignment was to cover what, if any progress had been made in a strike of some kind but mostly, a press conference with "Josh somebody or other" who was the darling of the strike because he was from New York and it was held at the Capital. I was a soon-to-be graduated Brown Institute Broadcasting student, spending a day working for the Viking Network, a real network from Brown giving students experience in news coverage. I gathered what information was expressed (which was nothing), went back to school, wrote the story and included a voice actuality I was able to get at the Capitol, inserting it in my story and then listened to it on the air. What you need to know is that my marriage had one foot in the grave and the other on a banana peel because I was a regular at Dewey's Pit and Paddock, and I started the day with the longest marijuana roach in the ashtray. So, I pulled off a real news assignment at Minnesota's Capital while in broadcast school and I wish I could tell you that I came from Brown that day all dressed up and told everybody at the Pit about my day. But I don't think I did. Something happened to me that day. I saw a future for myself I never imagined before. It led to a career and yet as I traveled the state over those first few years, having kept my marriage together, I always stopped back in Dewey's whenever I came home. Then some nine years later, the marriage is over and after quitting a job, I'm back in Dewey's. "What are you doing here?" my friend asked. "You're a success. You're a hero at the bar. It's not your deal anymore." He was right and while I was welcomed back, I got my job back in Wyoming and that was it. You can get anywhere in the world you want to go from St. Paul. Believe me, I know.

It's time for a word or two about Whiffle Ball. It was a sort of non-toxic game of baseball played with plastic bats and balls that wouldn't break windows and you could play it nearly anywhere. You could play it with baseball gloves but playing it without gloves developed what we called "soft hands". That is the ability to catch a ball at high speeds that offered almost no resistance. It needed to be slowed down and sort of surrounded with both hands to successfully catch it. There were two types of balls: one with holes in it and one that looked like a baseball. You could curve either ball when pitching it but the solid one curved better. You could also customize the balls such as wrapping one with black electrical tape and when the plastic bat got old or stepped on or something, a broomstick worked perfectly. Because your playing diamond was smaller, you could steal bases and playing on grass and do "head first" slides. My mom always wondered how I got grass stains on my tee shirts. All you really needed was about four guys on a team or even three if you made the hitting team catch. It had the feel of baseball too, with collisions at home plate, retaliation headhunting and home run boundaries over high fences or even buildings to simulate Fenway Park. Starting with four on a side nearly always led to others joining in and we'd play nine inning games and sometimes extra innings.

Whiffle Ball was great fun. There's something more. Whiffle Ball inspired the heroic. I saw many a player slide on asphalt, dive for balls, cross-body-block shortstops to break up double plays, also average and small kids (too small for Little League) drive in winning runs, girls too. Whiffle Ball welcomed all comers and came with no hats or uniforms or trophies in the end. It was just for the fun of playing. I loved it.

In 1966 Operation Nathan Hale took place from June 19th to July 1st north of Tuy Hoa, in Phu Yen province, Vietnam. However, in spite of the joint operation with the 101st Airborne Division and the 1st Cavalry Division ending July 1st, my 1st brigade of the 1st Cav stayed on for more than a week. I know this because I was wounded there on July 5th under somewhat strange circumstances. On July 4th, we were treated to a real meal alongside a river and actually got some sleep that night. The next day we set out again. We came upon a clearing in the jungle and two animals, a cow and a donkey came walking out of the jungle on the other side. We knew the enemy was very close because animals like that just don't hang out in the jungle unless they're being used as pack animals. Our first sergeant killed them and soon after, the butchering of the cow began. Right after that we were joined by our Long Range Patrol who had missed the party at the river and refused to go back out. So they took six of us and made us go instead, hoping to catch the enemy in between. "A" Company 1st of the 12th barbecued the cow that night, while we sat in silence a mile or two away and listened to a squad of the enemy having their dinner some fifty feet away. There are sharply differing accounts of what happened the next morning, but four of us were wounded (Sergeant Hudson lost his arm) and flown out when the rest of the Company flew in moments later. I had my bell rung pretty good in addition to my wounds so I can't honestly say what happened. In a way, the event saved my life. After I recovered from my wounds and malaria, I was allowed to transfer to a gun company where I became a door gunner on a Huey gunship. My old company caught hell a couple of months later, suffered many casualties and many guys were killed. Therefore, I'm not a big fan of the fireworks and I stay home with our animals now. We sort of comfort each other every 4th of July.

I don't act in plays anymore. I don't really miss it the way I thought I would, but I think I miss rehearsing the most. You work on scenes and try different things and do it over and over again. You try different tempos of delivering your lines, different intonations or even dialects. I worked with a guy once who just kept saying he was missing something playing this Englishman. So one night at rehearsal, he tried it as a French fellow and all he could do was this really ridiculous Maurice Chevalier impression. Then somehow, halfway through the scene, he found this tenderness, as if he was playing opposite a child or something. I swear it was so touching, I felt tears come to my eyes. We stayed late that night because he had found something in that character as a Frenchman that he couldn't find as an Englishman. It's funny how the imprint in his mind of what a Frenchman was became so moving, whereas his Englishman was not. It was a small scene but important to the play. In my memory, we never did get it quite right but what we settled for was better than what we had early on. That's what I mean about rehearsals. You have an opportunity that you don't get in life and the more you work on things, sometimes the better they become. Anyway, I met this other guy years later doing a play and over drinks afterward one night he said he'd been married four times, but his fourth had lasted nearly twenty years. I asked him how he made the last one work. He said, "I found my character."

I'm only guessing here because I rarely saw much of St. Paul's downtown south of 7th street, but when I did, I was down there with my dad. On this day, I was deeply ensconced in my sporting goods period and one day Dad and I walked into Berman's Sporting Goods on, I want to say 5th and Cedar or something like that. Try to imagine my joy! A store with all sporting goods: Louisville Slugger bats of all sizes, baseball spikes, hats, shoulder pads, shirts, helmets and the brands ran the gamut of the best that money could buy. As a child I had no problem asking for the things I wanted; even things you were never likely to get: a pony, a real child-sized car you could drive around in, etc. But I was older that day in Berman's and when I saw it, I knew it would never be mine, somehow. The Japanese call it water from the moon: something you can never have. Still, it was the most beautiful thing I ever saw. It was a Wilson "Heart of the Hide" Mickey Mantle baseball glove. It was priced at over sixty dollars and this was the fifties. I loved it and dreamed of it like you might dream about a beautiful woman, but at sixty dollars it just wasn't going to happen and it never did. Berman's moved to a sort of arcade off 7th and it was a very small place then and yet I always stopped by for years. As I think of it today, it was a time when I learned about limitations. It never kept me from wanting the things I saw, but certain parameters had been established. I remember it still sixty years later: a landmark day downtown with my Dad.

I have been known to make sweeping generalizations from time to time but St. Catherine's College on Randolph in St. Paul holds the record of any institution in Minnesota for the quickest response time for sending a nun down to tell you to get off their property. I further believe that if the police or the fire department had that kind of response time or anywhere near it, there would be no crime or fires of any consequence in the city. It is or at least it was, very beautiful at the college especially this little horseshoe pond near the southeast corner of Cleveland and Randolph. Were you to walk in through the front gate of St. Catherine's off Cleveland, there you'd be almost certainly less than one-hundred yards from that pond but I assure you, you'd never get there. She'd cut you off. Oh maybe, Usain Bolt might beat her there but you wouldn't. So I imagined (of the half a dozen times I tried to even cut through their property), that there was this nun, ever vigilant, sitting in a chair by the front door. That's all she did. Once, I was pointing at it from the front gate on Cleveland and she came out of the door and just stood there. I imagined Protestant bodies being slowly devoured by the crabs in the pond or another nun with binoculars hiding in the garden that protruded into the pond from the south end with a walkie-talkie alerting the one in the building of potential threats from passer's by. The last time I came up to the front gate on my bike. I was a little older by that time and she wanted us to go back down to Cleveland to leave the area. We ignored her and went out the entrance on Randolph. To this day, it still feels good to remember that.

Growing up in an apartment building on Brimhall and Randolph, I always wanted pets. Indeed, I brought many dogs and even cats home that I had managed to charm into following me over the years, but it was no use. Terry Brown and I found these little toads down by Crosby Lake. I loved toads and I made a little house for them in a box. I'm going to stop there for a minute because I hadn't thought of them in many years until some years ago, my wife said she was tired of the aquarium and being an adult, I knew she intended to flush our little goldfish to which I said no. So I put him and the water from the aquarium in a pitcher with a cover and drove to a small footbridge where I used to run and under which was a stream. I got down, took off the cover and slowly watched our friend swim out exactly eleven inches. He had never swum any farther in one direction and he paused to experience the moment. A few seconds later he was gone and a week later the stream dried up, but I reasoned his fate was better than being flushed. Mom and I wound up letting the toads go out on the lawn on Randolph and Brimhall. I remember crying and worrying all night about them trying to get all the way back to Crosby Lake with all those streets to cross. The day I let our fish go was the first time in many years I thought about those toads. Not long after that I quit bringing things home to be my pets.

In St. Paul and I imagine nearly everywhere in America, growing up in the fifties and sixties was a simpler time. But simpler didn't always mean better. If it was, why were so many of us in a hurry to grow up? With the exception of Saturday mornings and after school, television programmers assumed we all went to sleep at six o'clock. The lone exception was "The Wonderful World of Disney" once a week. All the rest were detectives and cowboys and if you think TV is violent now, the cowboy shows alone were killing dozens of bad guys every week. We did have numbers, though. Baby Boomers that we were, there were always plenty of kids to play with. Boomers started being born in 1945 and guys like me who came out as rookies in 1948, had to contend with a lot of older jerks along the way. And in fights, it's true we didn't have guns like today's kids. We were civilized. We'd take tire irons and beat your brains out. We didn't have West Nile Virus and so doing anything about the mosquitoes was fifty years away. And no matter what you heard, they didn't just come out at sundown either. I was a boy who always wanted to kiss the girls and in the 1950's, there was a name for guys like me…deviant… and worse. The grownups were always telling us childhood was a wonderful time and why not? Most of them grew up during the Depression followed by World War II. The truth is and today's kids don't really seem much different, childhood in St. Paul was at times, real boring and felt like "doing time" during a lot of it. If you do not believe me, ask someone my age, which was the bigger thrill: getting their first bike or getting their first car? Happy motoring!

I have written about Monroe High School where I spent three years, mostly in terms of wishing I had made more of my opportunities there and even today, I still think about it in those terms. Still, school is more than learning in terms of classwork. You take in the attitudes of your classmates and generally, Monroe was a very upbeat experience that way; school spirit and so forth I found to be at a very high level. There were pretty girls of course and the tough guys and the athletes and the very smart students and there was also student council and things like that, not to mention social organizations, dances, Homecoming, Sno-Daze and all manner of opportunities for participation in extracurricular activities. Now imagine for whatever reason, you chose to participate in nothing and sort of assumed a zombie type existence where the only interaction you experienced was walking from class to class, lunch and then class to class again. Even then, you still could not avoid seeing the movers and shakers in the school: people who were popular and usually nominated for everything. The big guy at Monroe was our quarterback in football, he played hockey too, and with his strong throwing arm, played catcher for our baseball team. His name was Len Salstrom. He was good at all of those things but for me, the thing that stood out was what a nice guy he was. I'm sure he knew who he was but of all the possible outcomes of being Lenny Salstrom, he chose the high road. He had a smile for everyone. He won a scholarship to Gustavus Adolphus and from what I heard, died suddenly in his sophomore year. I didn't know him and of course, I never achieved that kind of popularity in any endeavor; but he taught me how to act if I ever did. It's just so sad when any young person leaves us early. He was a true winner on and off the field, at least in my memory.

If you took a fairly typical kid in St. Paul in the fifties or early sixties and watched him or her from their house to wherever it was he or she was going, you could be almost certain to catch them talking to themselves. At first, maybe not, but after a block and half the minor lip movements began and soon thereafter, various gesticulations: an arm might shoot out in some direction for no apparent reason or sometimes, jumping over something that wasn't there. The "talking to themselves singers" were easy to spot. Their hands would come up to their mouth as if holding microphones. The more obvious ones acted like they didn't care but some, when you'd catch them, they'd change the subject quickly in order to move past the moment. Others.... I knew a guy who would punch you in the arm if you drew attention to his talking to himself. The funny part was, nearly everybody did it; and if you didn't talk to yourself, maybe you had theme music like "007" going on in your head. It didn't matter where you were either. Kids did it everywhere. The exception might be if you were not in your neighborhood. A kid might talk up a storm walking down Edgerton to say, Payne Avenue. But take that kid put him on St. Clair and West 7th, he wasn't quite so chatty and if he was, it was more like a ventriloquist, trying not to move his lips. The best place to see it was from a bus. Some kid would be walking down the street with a slight smile and raising one eyebrow as if he hadjust said something witty...to himself. I did it. I'm betting you did too.

So here's what happened and this story has a few parts so you might want to follow along closely. My parents went to Novena at Holy Spirit Church on Randolph. It was a Catholic service celebrating a painting really, with miraculous properties and was referred to as "Our Mother of Perpetual Help". There was a lovely song and the service was rather short but being a child, the only song I knew was "Goodnight Irene". In telling me the story, my mother always smiled to remember me singing "Goodnight Irene" while everybody else sang that lovely song. Let's call it fifty years later. I was at the Del Mar Racetrack at Oceanside on some floor covering junket my wife was involved with, and seeing Goodnight Irene (a horse) in the fourth race. Remembering the story, I bet her across the board and as she was the long shot, coming in second made me eight hundred dollars. I'm not a racetrack guy so that was a big deal for me. That was not the only time Our Mother of Perpetual Help came in for me. You see, in the middle of the fifteenth century the legend of Our Mother of Perpetual Help's miraculous powers began to form. By the time about 1962 came around, one of the resulting superstitions held that if you made the nine Novenas consecutively you would never die a violent death. It was only nine Tuesdays and it seemed an easy guarantee and I was an altar boy, and though I was pretty sick on one of the Tuesdays, I made it anyway. Now fast forward about four years; I was sharing a fox hole with a dead guy and a screaming guy in Vietnam and while never calling in the debt so to speak, I remembered the deal I thought I'd made. So when someone in passing asks me if I believe in God, I've never said no. I really don't care if the deal was with Mary or Jesus because they came through. I'm not sure about a lot of things, even that, but this I do know...it works for me.

I had a dear friend, well, more like a dear acquaintance really. We had been lovers once decades ago, even talked of moving in together. Then I'd see her now and then and finally not at all. One day, here on Facebook she barked at me for some rant or another and called me Skip. Knowing it was someone from St. Paul and confessing that I had forgotten her last name, I finally realized it was her. We recently saw each other again at the home of a friend I came to visit. I remember introducing her to what I consider one of the greatest films ever made, though it seems to be on no one's list but mine. After watching "Sorcerer", she excitedly messaged me and we chatted about the film. Within a year of that I heard she died, and yet once a year since then, Facebook sends out a notice that she's having a birthday. Maybe I was indignant once but now, thinking of her today, I'm glad for that annual reminder. I'm glad to remember her once a year now, even if I'd lost her for decades in the middle years. Everybody liked Judy.

I grew up in a one-bedroom, basement apartment on Brimhall and Randolph. We were a smoking family: Mom and Dad and me after about thirteen. That wasn't uncommon in those days. My mother wanted blond wood furniture. As a result, our often overflowing ash trays led to several burn marks wherever we had ashtrays, which was everywhere in the apartment. We had a big heating pipe that ran the length of the apartment with smaller ones leading to the radiators. Every morning, Mom would iron my shirt and hang it up on the smaller pipe under which was an overflowing ashtray. By the time I put it on, the Turkish and domestic blend of Camels along with the superior blend found in Winston had made of my shirt, a sort of walking advertisement for cigarettes in general. I complained and Mom quit hanging it there. The apartment was always warm though and when the heat wasn't on my parakeet Pretty Boy would fly up and sit on the big pipe. It was small, but I was the caretaker's son so I could play in the laundry room. I liked growing up there and in recent years have fantasized about renting that very apartment again to live out my final days and while it's true I hated my shirt's smelling like a pool hall, my friends were always welcome at my apartment. Many of them could never have friends over and very few could play laundry room basketball like I did; yup...six of one, half a dozen of the other.

I remember every kid in my neighborhood. Across Randolph, there was Jeff Weber and David Weber, but Dave got the nickname "Butterscotch" and we called him that always. Even later we called him Bud rather than David. Jeff might have been the best athlete of all of us. Down Brimhall and across from my building were Terry Brown and his sister Barb. Terry was fast, the fastest kid in the neighborhood; a nice kid at times but he could be a jerk. Dave Schrieber was two years older but he and I were best friends. Next to his house lived Dave Swanson who went on to play quarterback at St. Thomas. Just past Palace were the Peterson's. Gary played all sports but is remembered for a hole-in-one he got up at Highland. I think he got a trophy for that. He had a little brother whose first name I can't remember. He was a nice kid. On Snelling and Palace was Gary Peterson. I played golf with him. Across Randolph and up Brimhall were the Colstocks: Terry, Tim, Mike and Mary Beth who was beautiful...just gorgeous. She married Greg Poferal who went to and eventually taught at Cretin. Steve and Gaylan Funk were on Randolph. Farther up from the Colstocks were the Fahey's. Nick was the one our age. He was good at everything and even acted in high school. Further still was Gary Hitz and up to Hartford, John Lamski. John was two years older and a bit of an enigma. He was mostly okay but went through a period of picking on everybody. When I think of Saratoga I think of the Cotter's: Pots, Jim, Terry, Buck and Tom who was my age. Their mom Agnes was wonderful. Then there was Peter Latif. Poor Peter was younger and desperate to hang out with someone. He had a boxer named Butter. Poor Peter seemed to always be walking home crying. I didn't exactly pick on him but I didn't help when I could have. The Jensen twins lived on Randolph and Janie Hughes and Candy Shields across Randolph. This is too long and frankly, is making me sad. Like I said before, a great memory is a double-edged sword.

I never know why certain little memories stick in my head now, for more than sixty years. The block I'm writing about is the north side of Randolph between Pascal and Warwick. From west to east, it's the last of the short-end blocks with a house facing Warwick, an alley and an apartment building. It's much the same today except for the parking lot for the apartments, built where a slopping lawn used to be. The alley (for whatever reason) was the last to be paved in the neighborhood. The house property had a wall with a lilac bush right by the alley and one day, a kid, maybe a year younger or something wanted to take some lilac's home to his mom. He climbed the wall and was pulling on a branch; then he fell backwards right onto the sidewalk. He was out of breath and crying but still holding the lilacs when two older ladies who saw what happened came running over. The kid slowly got up. I was just standing there and one of the ladies suggested they drive him home. Through tears he told them he couldn't take rides from strangers (for which they had no answers) and as his tears sort of morphed into sniffles, he and his friend continued on their way. It was a bad fall and I felt sorry for him. I've wondered about it for years; getting hurt trying to do something nice: lilacs for his mother. It was as if it was some kind of lesson put in my way, a lesson I resisted learning, because there were times when

I spent too much on my kids at Christmas, or on my wife. The lesson was to just be there for someone and when I did, I'd sometimes think of that little event that happened on my way home from school. Maybe it was: "the intent is worth the risk". I'll never know but it's still there.

It's just age I suppose but when I order wheat toast or pick up a loaf of wheat bread at the store, if I ever felt somehow better about my choice, you know, because it's wheat, that went away years ago. If now and then, I have a craving for a nice Bloody Mary for example, I'm just as likely to order something else so I don't have to bother taking the celery out of my drink. I actually had a bartender ask me once if there was anything wrong with the celery. "No", I said, "it's just celery." Finally realizing that juice of any kind is just as bad for you as sodas, has led me to drink water almost exclusively. I don't really know why. I lived on Cokes for years and was very happy. In other words I have made changes based on the things I've read and heard. But the transference effect, you know, feeling better or smarter about myself because I'm doing these things, does not exist. I still like hamburgers better than anything and in terms of vegetable toppings, I come from St. Paul, Minnesota where a burger with lettuce and tomato on it is still called a "California Hamburger." Bacon on a burger however, is something else entirely. Even the thought of it makes me smile. There is a film called "Who is Killing the Great Chefs of Europe?" In it, Robert Morley, a food critic, is told that he is "calamitously fat and if he doesn't lose weight immediately he will die." To which Morley responds, "Deprived of the only thing that gives me pleasure, how could you imagine I should want to live?" I don't smoke anymore but I do still drink thank God, and while these other changes may or may not be good, they do satisfy my need to be seen as caring about something I really do not.

There is a hierarchy to growing up where the label you wear identifies you in a group of some kind. You start out being a little kid. When you go to school you become a student. While at school there were sub-groups: scouts, athletics, perhaps you had a paper route, making you a paperboy and so on. There were also religious sub-groups but they never liked being referred to as a sub-group so you had to watch your mouth around them. Each step on the ladder further defined you in some way. Along the way, I have been variously: a little kid, an only child, a student, a high school dropout, a soldier, a sort of hippie, a radio announcer, an actor, a college professor, a writer and an artist. In a way, I'm proudest of going from a high school dropout to earning a Master's Degree and teaching at the University level for six years. Also having started at Monroe High School and Edyth Bush Theater, the one constant in my life (apart from everything else) was my acting. In terms of my career in radio, it was similar to growing up in St. Paul. I was always trying to escape. Alas, once you're on the radio, you become more and more not qualified to do anything else for two reasons: every other job sucked, and that is how you wound up in radio in the first place. I started in Thief River Falls and ended up in Los Angeles and while I never made any serious money, I had a real good time and even got out with a pension. Now I'm retired. It's a good job but like anything else, it has its drawbacks. There are contradictions too. I always liked to sleep in and now I'm up most days at six A.M. In some ways, St. Paul prepares you for everything. The four seasons alone illustrate that the only constant in life is change. You'd think I'd be used to it by now.

I had this dream and in it, the Lord appeared to someone on the St. Catherine's College Board around 1960 or so and said,

"I want you to let the community on the campus."
The board member asked,"Why Lord?"
The Lord said, "I am He that knows all, would you agree?"
"Yes Lord", the board member said.

"About sixty years from now Skip Savage, who will be calling himself something else then,   will recall for the entire world to read, that We were too rigid in keeping out trespassers. If We start letting everybody in now, in sixty years enough neighbors will have better memories to counteract his criticisms. I call it "Obfuscation"... do you like it?"

The board member said, "Yes Lord; but do you think he'll take back what he wrote?"

"Who cares," said the Lord. "Besides, he'll have dreamed this conversation to know our plan,
 so I think that's unlikely."

Both the Lord and the board member had a good laugh...and then I woke up.

I got to know this guy from what many people called the "Old Neighborhood," Dale and Selby. He'd done time in various jails most of his life really: Red Wing, St. Cloud, a couple of bits in Stillwater and we had an interesting kind of friendship. One day he asked me, "Skip, how come you never asked me about... doin' time, you know?" I said, "Hey, you never asked me about Vietnam either. I just figured some guys have things that are private. If they wanted you to know they'd tell you." We got around to telling each other about those things a little that night, nothing very dramatic. It was mostly just about passing the time. He told me he was a thief and so finally, I asked if he had any role models that he learned from, to take other people's things? It was a bad question, I could tell and I wished right away I hadn't asked it. Sometime later, he told me they were very poor and that all his brothers and sisters did it. One year they even stole a Christmas tree so they could celebrate the holiday. It got sadder and sadder for me, hearing his stories. I wished we had never gone down that road. I moved away to another radio job and I'd run into him now and then when I'd come back, and I noticed he wasn't going to prison anymore. I wanted to ask him about it, but I never did. He'd gotten himself together somehow and had the same job for years. Still, his friends were all ex-cons and I always

154

wondered why he and I hit it off so well. I was a spoiled only child and he had to steal a Christmas tree to pretend there was a Santa Claus.

Strange isn't it, how at certain moments of our lives, those moments where we set our limits for the first time, how comfortable we are climbing to heights on a Jungle Jim for example and yet, terrified to be called on in class. Little by little, the parameters of what we were willing to do for attention (in my case female attention) were established. It's true; I was willing to put myself in extreme physical jeopardy to show off my lack of fear. I've always liked Shakespeare's "As You Like It" where young Orlando and the Princess Celia exchange over his wrestling match with an older, more experienced opponent. She fears he will be hurt. He, confident in his youth, loves her concern and will fight twice as hard because of it. It is a formula for growing up and it stayed with me for years. Being young, often may well have killed me before the real terror of life on earth presented itself: swimming across the Mississippi or crossing the great river underneath the bridge itself. We, many of us anyway, were willing to be daredevils in courting the interest and hopefully admiration of the girls. After Vietnam, it was as if I had already died once, no longer afraid of things in St. Paul, or anywhere really. More importantly, I was no longer willing to die to impress and I was only twenty when I returned; not much of a legacy of courage for a young man with my imagination. So as I faced the future of a quieter "man of action", I was forced to realize the folly of growing up at twenty, when in truth, it easily could have ended much earlier. I feel lucky, yes, but also blessed to share some of these musings, with the very people I shared those times with. You know, Savage is a fairly uncommon name and guys around town would occasionally ask if I knew Sam Savage. I said no, but they all seemed to remember him with a smile. I admired him for that and though we never met, I always wondered what it would take to achieve that: a smile associated with my name. When I quit caring about that, I achieved a certain peace.

My mom and dad were great and we had a lot of fun in our apartment on Brimhall now and then, never more than Saturday nights, when they would dance in the living room to the music of Lawrence Welk. We had a sectional couch and as they would dance, I would run and jump on one section and then, trying to judge which way they were going, I'd run to the other one and land on it. Welk had a violinist who was featured weekly. He had a pencil thin mustache and played beautifully. Sometime after that, I asked my parents for a violin and for lessons. I never got it, but in re-telling this story years later, a friend asked, "Why the violin?" I remember it was one of those moments where my answer seemed to have been waiting to be used for many years. I said, "It was the first sound that made me cry with its beauty." It no sooner passed my lips when I wondered, "Where did I ever come up with that?" What's more, it was exactly true. I can't isolate the moment, maybe John Garfield in "Humoresque" or some poignant soundtrack from a sad film, but I've always loved what the violin can do. I never felt very disappointed that I didn't get the violin. As a little boy in St. Paul I probably wanted to be ten other things the day I asked for it, but those were great times on Brimhall with Lawrence Welk and while I can't play the violin, I can tell you why I wanted to.

I never got many speeding tickets in St. Paul mostly because the cars I drove couldn't get going fast enough to break the speed limit, that is, unless I was coming down hill and caught a green light or something; but seriously, let's talk about speed traps. I can't speak about speed traps anywhere in St. Paul except the Highland-Groveland area and I know because I got caught twice in the same speed trap in one year. For some reason, going south on Fairview just after Randolph, cars begin to accelerate for no reason. You are powerless to resist and so by putting a speed trap up by Hartford, they get you every time. One theory has it that as you cross St. Clair to the north, going south, you cross over into the Twilight Zone of street lights, which stipulates that no one shall make all three lights on that stretch without speeding. So you have some work to do before making the Jefferson light (crossing at amber usually), and then it's on to making the Randolph light. If you do make it, nine times out of ten, you're in violation of the law right there. However, pumped up with making the three Twilight Zone lights in a row, slowing down seems so empty somehow. Instead, you plow on at 45MPH or faster and then they have you like they had me, twice. I can only assume there were speed traps elsewhere in St. Paul so let's have it.... did they ever get you?

Growing up in an apartment building in St. Paul came with certain advantages and one of them was boxes. At times, tenants would get new TV's or refrigerators and being the caretakers, we had to get rid of them. Before we did, they made great little forts and sometimes, connecting them with other boxes was cool too. I remember a kid, an older kid really, who took a flap of a big box and in street shoes, stood on it and rode it down the Highland Golf Course sledding area off Highland Parkway all the way to the bottom! After he left, I went and got it, dragged it back up the hill and tried it myself. I got about fifteen feet before falling. Just looking at a box filled your mind with possibilities and the potential of boxes was not lost on animals either, more cats than dogs, though. Of course, you didn't need snow. Just getting in a box and rolling down the hill until it spit you out was fun. There were dangers however. As boys grew older, the destruction of boxes became a priority. At such a time, you would not want to be in the box when older kids were around. Boxes were great for artistic endeavors as well, and because you knew your time with the box would be short lived, there were no limits: paints, crayons, mud, ink, and when it came time to tear them up in pieces to be burned, they must be murdered with knives first. Yes, boxes were wonderful and frequently more fun than the things inside them.

Now, in the autumn of my days, I can state with some certainty there are two things I never got enough of growing up: Pronto Pups and Tom Thumb Donuts, and both products are specific to the Minnesota State Fair. Indeed, Tom Thumb Donuts are a carnival-oriented confection by design, don't ask me why. When I became aware of corn dogs, I had one and knew after some time that no... this was indeed not a Pronto Pup. If I try really hard, I'll bet I can come up with at least fifty things that were never good enough to go national and so become readily available. Does Veg-a-Matic ring any bells? Still, I can't get a Pronto Pup or Tom Thumb Donut when I want one. "Now isn't that amazing!" Were we not fine with Old Dutch Potato Chips, Peters Wieners and Tastee Bread before national interests pushed them out? I'd like to think this is some oversight rather than conspiratorial in some way and yes, now that I think about it, just give me back Peter's Wieners alone and I'll shut up. Yet they won't you see, because they know it is indeed the autumn of my years and one day my voice "crying in the wilderness" as it is, will be silent. Who among you then, will take up the charge? I mean we're not talking about Reggie candy bars here...no...just Pronto Pups and Tom Thumb Donuts.

I'm certainly no expert on F. Scott Fitzgerald, nor am I qualified to categorize him as one of the greatest writers of the twentieth century, though many have, but I loved his short stories in particular and they spoke to me in certain ways in my twenties. Women and partying was what I was all about in those days. As a veteran, I wasn't burying any sorrows or anything like that. I was just having fun. Still, something must have been missing, because one day I went and auditioned for a play. I didn't get the part, but I learned things from the guy who was chosen and rather than blow it off, kept auditioning until I got a part. The point is, many people, including people who like to party, had other things about them, itches you might call them, they needed to scratch now and then and for me it was acting. F. Scott Fitzgerald went to St. Paul Academy for a while but wound up in a Catholic High School in New Jersey. He played football. He must have liked it because the next year he enrolled in Princeton and tried out for the football team. He was cut the first day, too small I'm thinking but be honest now. Did you ever think of the great F. Scott Fitzgerald playing football? I never did and yet at times, I thought of myself as full of various contradictions too. The difference of course is that he and his life have been widely scrutinized due to his fame as a writer and I doubt that you'll ever find me in Wikipedia; (I know, I've tried to get in). I said once my favorite things to do were to sit at a bar and smoke and drink and talk. I miss it because I can't afford to drink in bars anymore, don't smoke (thank God) and know very few people who do anymore. However, during the years that I did, I met some extraordinary people who had odd little bits about them that seemed to join us together, in ways that made them exceptional. It's sad that drinking held many of us back from being recognized from who we were in spite of ourselves. I still drink and like to remember them, and F. Scott Fitzgerald as well. I wonder what position he played?

By my count, over a hundred and thirty guys from St. Paul were killed in Vietnam; to put it another way, guys from Harding and Murray and every high school in the city. Maybe every grade school too. There was at least one guy from Monroe (where I went) who was killed. Larry was a good guy. I remember once there was a dance up at the old original pavilion at Highland Park. I knew Larry from school but we never hung out or anything. He saw me from the other side of the dance floor and walked all the way over just to say, "Hi." Such a small thing really and yet, Larry was like that. If seeing you put a smile on his face, you were worth going over and saying hello to. Forgive me if this seems out of left field but Ken Burns and Lynn Novick's "The Vietnam War" on PBS, took up quite a few evenings of mine during the last couple of weeks and I've been a little melancholy for a few days. It's like, I can see myself shaking hands with Larry up at Highland and all these years later, I'm here to remember it and he's not.

I think it's time we acknowledge that America's is great not because of the opportunities that are available. America is great because of the multiple opportunities that are available "in one lifetime". America is a place where you can be rich and poor twenty times. I was born in St. Paul, Minnesota during a period where all the adults who went through the depression and World War II spoke in absolutes: "If you don't study, you'll never amount to anything," "If you don't apply yourself," and so on and so forth. "The decisions you make now WILL determine the rest of your life." Such complete and utter nonsense as it turns out, was considered wisdom when I was a boy. For me, there was only summer vacation and on any given day, I wanted to be ten things before lunch. In school, I studied sometimes and if I did apply myself, whatever that meant, it was probably by accident; but by nearly any yardstick available for measuring future success, I was going nowhere and at an ever greater speed the older I got. I liked to watch TV and go to the movies. You couldn't study that in college when I was a boy. So what happened? After partying for years, I got a job in radio that paid so little I needed to go to college taking a full load just to get my G.I Bill money to support my wife and daughter and newly born son. Then what did I find? College, it seems had come around to my way of thinking and now had a Communication Studies Major: TV and Film. Now I'm not sure if this Major is available in Uzbekistan but in America it's not only never too late to be a success in something, our country will customize your path to get there! Politics doesn't really matter. Multiple opportunities are available no matter who's in office. America is like heaven on earth when you think about it. If you don't believe that ask someone who came here from somewhere else.

I was looking for a friend and when I heard he had moved back to Highland, I went for coffee at the last place I saw him: the bookstore adjacent to Starbucks on Cleveland and Ford Parkway. It was gone. I took my coffee outside and sat down. Before long, the exaggerated caffeine content in my coffee had me imagining and remembering all the good, the bad, and the ugly of my very existence, let alone my boyhood in St. Paul. Across the street and up Ford Parkway, I worked at Lee's Kitchen for about...ten days. Beyond were the ball fields where I played football in the Highland-Groveland League and overlooking that, the library where my second short story collection sits on a shelf to this day. Then for no reason in particular, I thought of the play and later the movie "Tea and Sympathy" as a sort of metaphor for growing up. In the play, it was the young student's sexuality that came into question, but it could have been a hundred things, little imperfections we became obsessed with correcting as we moved into manhood. Jacked up on Starbucks as I was, I was having a fine time reflecting on the pain and uncertainty that awaited us. Looking back in my meta-physical time travel, I was enjoying my coffee in the middle of Powers' parking lot wondering why my mother nearly always chose downtown St. Paul to shop instead of Highland Park? Tiffany's is still there, a comfort of sorts. It was a beautiful day and I concluded that home, wherever that is, is where we come back to see how we made it over those hurdles (or didn't), and what did it matter in the end? I was lucky then and I'm lucky now and thank God for a nice caffeine buzz now and then.

I can only imagine that at the very least, many of you have come home to St. Paul and driven by where you used to live. For me it's not only where I used to live but where I grew up for fifteen years of it. I'm not sure I can describe it except to say that when I stop and get out, I feel so out of place it's as if someone might call the police about a man acting strangely walking up and down Randolph at Brimhall. There is an alley in back I'd like to walk down but what excuse would there be? It would be certain to draw attention from someone. It's like wanting to be invisible like Scrooge and the Ghost of Christmas past. Now I don't stop and get out anymore. I just drive by; but it goes so fast that way, it's not enough. There's a feeling of being self-conscious and very uncomfortably so, as being seen as an outsider and unwelcome presence. In an odd way, it reminds me of Wyoming. When your reason for being in Wyoming ends, you have to go. They set it up that way. One day you're a somewhat well-known radio personality and when it ends, no one sees you anymore. Maybe that's the way it is with everywhere you've lived. If it is, than why do I keep going back? I mean, I feel comfortable enough in O'Gara's, never out of place or unwelcome; and with any of my new friends from Old St. Paul, it's as if I've known them all my life. Still, I just can't do it at 476 South Brimhall. I can't walk down to Holy Spirit and back, or traverse the streets and alleys of my youth. That ship has sailed and yet like an old girlfriend you hope still lives there and remembers you, I keep coming back.

I wanted to be a priest. A lot of Catholic-raised boys had such notions, for a while anyway. Somewhere around third or fourth grade at Holy Spirit in Highland Park, becoming an altar boy, maybe being in the choir and generally being receptive to our indoctrination, made for a rather soothing possibility to consider a life in the clergy. For most of us though, puberty put an end to such ambitions and when it did, it was as if the nuns started not liking us at least as much as they had previously. When this happened and it's kind of sad too, it became an us-versus-them relationship. There were a couple of nuns who understood what we were going through, and mostly in their eyes, we became the devils they always knew we were. At such times, I always thought it might have been nice to call upon the council of male clergy such as the Christian Brothers who taught at Cretin. I supposed the Brothers wouldn't be trusted to get the company line straight. So I for one somewhat embraced my role as a devil to the nuns, and looked forward to dealing with the Brothers at the next level. For me that would be at Cretin, where my

Dad went in 1925, or so I thought. After testing, when the letter said I passed but they didn't have room for me, it was one of the luckier things to happen in my young life, but at the time I felt betrayed and never really went to Catholic Mass with any regularity again. As with many like-minded soon-to-be ex-Catholics like me, I blamed the nuns of Holy Spirit in later life for various things, but that was nonsense. I was well educated and through rebelling, learned what I didn't want out of life, two valuable things. It would be a few unpleasant years without God in my life before finding Him or Her again. Gratefully, that part never happened again.

All this talk of Seven Corners has reminded me of imagining a high-speed conveyance once while ambling along talking to myself as a boy. The top of Randolph leading down to West 7th is Syndicate. I used to love it when the bus drivers called out the stops: "Synnnnndicate!" they'd say. In my reverie, in winter you'd get on a super, enclosed toboggan on the south side of Randolph for Seven Corners. This would an express ride with no stops. By the time it hit Chatsworth, it was going so fast a special raised tunnel needed to be built and by the time it hit West 7th it banked so hard and so fast that once it righted itself, the trip from Anchor Hospital to the Brass Rail took only seconds. Then, air brakes would be applied, and everyone would get off at Seven Corners. Sadly, I somehow couldn't work out an express toboggan going back, but today, maybe sixty years later, I still think it's cool idea.

Minneapolis is bigger than St. Paul. Its general layout of streets and avenues are more logical, making things easier to find; it's sports teams, especially high school teams are better than St. Paul most of the time; it's flat as a pancake and so is easier to negotiate your car in winter. They had the first-run movies when I was a kid and Minneapolis is generally better known than St. Paul. Yet for many others and me, one of the best things about being from St. Paul is NOT being from Minneapolis. I grew up in a sports environment and began my dislike for Minneapolis at an early age. The annual Twin Cities football game between the best high schools in Minneapolis and St. Paul was one of the first detestable imbalances I became aware of. Washburn beat one of our St. Paul teams like… 64-0 once and so when Patrick Henry one year beat our representative 14-0, it was looked upon as a victory...of sorts. The Minneapolis Millers had Carl Yastrzemski and going way back, Willie Mays. I'm pretty sure the Saints had Duke Snyder but, well, you get my drift. St. Paul streets were laid out by a drunk named Pig's Eye, so legend has it. As a result, getting around is like a secret handshake. Either you knew how to get somewhere or you didn't, and if you didn't you were probably from Minneapolis. St. Paul was built on seven hills. You could hardly walk to school seven miles "uphill both ways" in Minneapolis and St. Paul had prettier girls! I'm not going to explain it, they just were...and are. We have the State Capitol and following a train of thought, gangsters preferred St. Paul. Everybody knows that. I lived in Minneapolis in my thirties. It was okay, just not St. Paul, ya know? No, I'm from St. Paul and if you don't know where that is, you've probably been voting for the wrong party for all these years. If you don't know what that is, go ask someone from Minneapolis.

Many years ago, I reconnected with my childhood best friend Dave Schrieber. Dave and his brother Tom lived on Brimhall a few doors down from our apartment building. Dave was two years older and Tom two years younger. Yesterday, Dave brought his brother Tom to lunch in Burbank. I didn't want it to end. We recalled when Tom, while hanging on our clothesline pole, caught his wrist on the line hook and needed twenty stitches. I remember following the blood trail to their house. We played a lot of street football under the elms in front of their house. I was struck by the fact that they never looked like brothers as kids. Yesterday they could have passed for twins. We all did pretty well for ourselves in the end but nearing seventy, I never imagined I'd be around to have lunch with Dave and Tom again. They both still live in St. Paul and are great guys. I have felt and today still feel so lucky to have connected with so many of my friends and classmates from my childhood. Long before that childhood was over, I was antsy to move on but yesterday, I was so grateful to have been a part of it... I can't fully express it, I guess. My memory has been on overload lately and I can't seem to write fast enough and the more I do the better the whole things seems. Yet, I remember also that it didn't seem so then; not as much as it did yesterday.

No point in denying it, I suppose. I am the teller of stories and so my perspective colors everything else. As I think of growing up in St. Paul I kept, I don't know, waiting for something to happen. Things were happening of course but I wasn't always talking about them and not writing about them either and yet without realizing it then, they became seared into my memory. I was different, you see and once I had a Minneapolis newspaper route, only a few clients and it didn't last long. Then I attended one carrier meeting where other paperboys who did well won premiums. This one kid acted somewhat superior and why not, I suppose. He had worked hard and done well. His premium was one of those badminton sets you used to see. It came in a plastic pouch with two rackets and a few birds, but no poles. He acted like a kind of jerk but I found myself hoping he had someone to play with and some poles to stretch out the net. I didn't have to work for my badminton set because I got one for Christmas, one of probably twelve gifts I got that year. Like I said, I was different and that paperboy wasn't the only kid who resented my not having to get a job or take one seriously.

I was always a finicky eater growing up but when you said the word "pancakes," I was there. One day, my mom was going to make pancakes but realized we had no syrup, so she sent me upstairs to Aunt Ruth and Uncle Andy's apartment to borrow some. Neither were real relations but they were both great and Andy liked pancakes too. Mom used Karo Syrup, of which the less said, the better. Andy used Log Cabin so when he offered to make me pancakes, I said yes. I figured how bad could you screw up a pancake? I was almost wrong as he made me buckwheat pancakes, which I had never had. They were as big as the plate and somewhat crunchy, but with butter, Log Cabin syrup and bacon, they were great and to this day (and believe me I've tried), I've never been able to recreate them. He also put apple jelly on them, and with cold milk to drink, I thought I would die! Years went by and I never refused Uncle Andy's buckwheat pancakes except once. It was the same deal: we were out of syrup and I knocked on the door and asked to borrow some. Andy sort of winked at me and smiled, and motioned to his kitchen as if to say, how about his pancakes? Mom had already made batter and as I tried to explain that, he got real disappointed and kind of angry and I was sorry I even asked. I felt so bad I never had pancakes with Uncle Andy again. He died of a heart attack not long after that. Last week I thought about making buckwheat pancakes but the store didn't have any apple jelly. When I asked, the store manager told me that he couldn't remember them ever stocking apple jelly. The truth is, I never forgave Uncle Andy for laying that guilt trip on me and that's too bad because he was a good guy.

When I think of growing up and I wish I could pinpoint the time frame, there came a general malaise among the Catholics I grew up with in the late fifties; but it didn't begin with us. It began with our parents. We all went to church on Sunday, for a while at least. That is my mom, dad, and I. After Dad was laid off from his job at Union Brass and Metal, his drinking got worse just staying home to take care of me and our apartment building, of which we were caretakers. I went to church with Mom for a while and was finally just sent off to church by myself. What happened to my other friends' parents I can't remember (if I ever knew), but left to our own devices we simply quit going to church. The joke on Randolph and Hamline where we hung out went like this on Saturday night, "What Mass are you going to skip tomorrow?" So you see, that would never have been possible if we'd continued going as a family. My family troubles were one thing but with the others? I guess I never asked but there must have been something because over time, issues in their family life seemed to be maintained, while mine got gradually worse. Even when Kennedy became President, there was no going back to church. I don't know why except, the truth is, I didn't really like it. So much of it was forced on us over eight years of grade school, we all had become resentful at a certain level. That was our deal. I still wonder about everybody else's parents.

I was at a stop light in Pasadena some years ago and I was checking out this cute woman walking across the street. I liked the view until she turned to cross the street I was waiting at, and I saw she had a cigarette in her hand. I stopped looking. She became disqualified from even my imagination, because she smoked and I no longer did. I loved a girl at Holy Spirit in St. Paul until Lent of a year. We all went to Mass and took Communion and brought our breakfast; then after Mass, at our desks we opened our bags and usually took out a sandwich. She took out an egg salad sandwich and it was over. I remember everything but can't remember her name to a certainty because she was disqualified. I'd rather not go into why because I'm embarrassed, but I had an issue with yellow food (which I thought was gross) but let's just think about that for a minute. Suppose I never had a problem with egg salad. I might have been married to that girl for fifty years and had many grandchildren and all that. I also would have certainly been more social and not in fear of the yellow food being served at some function or other that I was expected to attend. Moreover, I would have been somebody else. Now let's go back to the beginning. It was fine to disqualify a smoking woman in many of your minds, wasn't it? Also admirable at a certain level, isn't that true? However, this little girl had my undivided attention for probably several weeks and when she ate an egg salad sandwich, she became invisible the moment she took one bite. It was fourth grade or thereabouts and I was saddled with this, this issue and I knew it would plague me for years to come because of my overly sensitive nose. Lent prepares us for Easter and lasts forty days. Thirty-five point seven of those days, this girl's conscientious mother packed an egg salad sandwich for this girl, who sat three seats away from me, every day. She was not alone. It got so bad, I'd pretend to come down with the flu every Lent for at least two years. All this, and I wonder why I didn't make more of myself as a child. Am I glad I'm turning seventy this coming February? Yes, I am.

I've said before that growing up in St. Paul I always imagined myself as an adult being somewhere else. Still, there was nothing constrictive about St. Paul at all. In fact, St. Paul was as big or as small as you wanted it to be. My world from Brimhall and Randolph had fairly rigid parameters that were set by me. Some others were set by the people I knew and hung out with but I was never looking to expand them at all really. The boundaries set by Highland, Midway, and Monroe High School life (excepting maybe the State Fair and going downtown or being with a girl that I met somewhere), were my world for the most part. In size, this mirrored many of the smaller towns I started my radio career in; and here's the punch line: I now live in one of the largest metropolitan areas in the world and my life today is exactly that small. From my home in Monrovia, it's a ten mile round trip to the gym and back. I go to the Veterans Hospital and that's a little farther out, and now and then go to see friends in L.A. My world has contracted to a size I've always known. By that criterion, I never had to leave home at all and yet, it was never about size. It was about me; me in war, me in Hollywood or New York, me living and working with others who visualized more for themselves wherever they were. Old St. Paul for me has been a doorway to look back at the kid who imagined these things. I was among the first generation to watch TV and every week there was somewhere knew and exciting and it became a catalog of places I

168

wanted to go and people I wanted to be. In so doing, I lost track of my immediate surroundings I guess. Then all these years later, it's fun to go back and remember.

From Hamline and Randolph to Snelling and Randolph, the rectangular shaped blocks ran length wise from Hamline to Pascal and going north, continued that way to Jefferson and partially beyond. At Pascal, the north side blocks featured the short end of the block all the way to Snelling and all the way to St. Clair. I lived one long block and three short-end blocks from Holy Spirit School. You began to know where people lived by the school lines they took to get home. School was on Randolph at Albert and the school lines were the Hamline, the Jefferson, the Randolph and the Hartford. I can only speak for the Randolph line but at Pascal, you could cross and go north that way. The Tempkes lived on Pascal as did my friend Jeff Cormier and the twins, Paul and Paulette Mullner; continuing north, Judy Plumbo, Liz Spahn, Molly O'Connell, Steve Popelka Jim Dubois, Jack Laukimeyer and Warren (Maynard) Shob. This included the Warwick people, of course. However, there was a girl named Patty something or other, very attractive in a blonde sort of way, who lived south on Warwick. After flying my kite one day, I saw her through her kitchen window, wearing only her nightgown and while it's sixty years ago, I still remember it. Now continue to Saratoga, Tom Cotter and I, though I lived on Brimhall, as did Dave and Tom Schrieber. Going south on Brimhall were the Colstocks, Jeff Fahey, John Lamski, and Jeff Weber. I'll bet most of you remember as much about your neighborhood and the people who lived there as I do mine. That's only a Holy Spirit list. A lot of kids went to Maddocks and I remember a lot of them too.

In every neighborhood in St. Paul, there were organized sports for kids. For baseball in Highland, there were two little leagues: Highland and Hilltop. Highland had a real baseball diamond for baseball only, with a wooden fence painted green, and real dugouts.

Their teams were named for the Scottish tradition of highlands: The Laddies, The Scots, The Hootmons, The Highlanders and the last two I can't remember. I played for the Hilltop baseball league in the shadow of the Highland Tower where the indoor hockey rink is now. Our teams were named for major league baseball: The Cubs, The Dodgers and the Yankees who had home or white uniforms. The Giants, The Braves and The Tigers had gray or away uniforms. There were three fields: two for the minor league games and one for the majors. I didn't make the majors initially and was sent to the Millers. Then, the Giant's coach came around looking for someone to move up to the majors and his team before the first game and I was picked. Though I rarely played that first year, we won the Championship and I got a trophy. That was a big deal for me and it would be several more years before a team I was on, won a Championship. There is one thing to know about organized sports in St. Paul or anywhere really. If your parents came to every game and were involved, you played more than some other kids unless you were pretty good. By the time my parents quit going, I was too good to keep out of the lineup. I batted in the 440's and played second base. I'm an actor (or hot dog I suppose you'd call it), so when my two biggest fans: Mom and Dad quit caring enough to go, I kind of lost interest too. I learned a lot…much of it painful, but a lot nevertheless. Of the field I played on, I had a certain history before I ever played. My father Walt Savage played semi-pro football on that field in the 30's. My cousin Roger Miller coached the Yankees in the 50's and I was his batboy. I even got a uniform. By the time my kids were that age their mother and I had divorced, but had I been there I wouldn't have let them play Little League Baseball.

I painted a picture some years ago. I had a title in mind but after showing it to a horse-woman friend of mine in Alabama, I realized I had the horse's ears wrong for what I was trying to portray. I gave it the title I intended but that was all wrong, so the other day I just changed the title. All of a sudden, the painting worked and yesterday

I put it up for maybe the second time ever. I usually change profile pictures with a different painting four or five times a day, and then again overnight when I go to bed. I had too much to drink last night and left the horse picture up. This morning, the daughter of a fellow I served with, both in the same brigade in the infantry and as a door gunner on Huey gunships, mentioned her dad; how he loved horses, and how the painting reminded her of him. Jackson Gibson, "Chief", was a real good man and along with Bill Simpson and me, were the last of the infantry door gunners who went over. I dug out the original under its old title and had some prints made. I'll send one off to her tomorrow. I never knew Chief as well as some of the other guys and didn't know he had horses. We lost Bill Simpson a few years ago and Chief just this last year after a terrible time with cancer. Our platoon gets together once a year in North Carolina, at the home of our platoon commander and his wife in the Outer Banks and I've sure felt grateful for that. Strangely enough, I renamed the painting the other day as I said I would. I call it "Let's Go Home" and I may not have intended it, but I'll always see Jackson Gibson and his horse in this painting from now on.

When I was a little boy, before even starting school, I think, we had a fellow in our apartment building on Brimhall who was involved with the Edyth Bush Theater. There was a rec room in the basement where I lived and the actors would rehearse there. Somehow, I was invited in one day. To me, they were just playing. That's what I did everyday: pretending to be someone doing something or other. One of the actors and I were sitting next to each other and I said acting must be a good profession. He said, "It's not, really." I somehow knew what he meant and said, "But it's fun isn't it?" He agreed. For me, to still be playing pretend when you were all grown up would be the best of all worlds. I did a little acting during my three years at Monroe and after Vietnam, I auditioned for a couple of plays around town. I was finally cast in a play at…you guessed it…the Edyth Bush Theater. For nearly all of the rest of my life I acted in plays. It was very much like a part-time job that didn't pay anything, but I loved doing it. Eventually I came out here to L.A. to see if I could make a living at it. I did okay for starting in my late thirties: made a few bucks, joined the unions and lived in a world of headshots and resume's and auditions. I continued to do plays and by then, I had grown to an age where I was finally getting the great parts I always wanted to play. It was a fine time in my life. If I had to say why I didn't enjoy the success I might have, it would be that I was trying to create a certain, specific look. When you do that, you reduce your chances for being considered for other roles. Anyway, I got a great featured role for a play in North Hollywood that got good reviews and created a little buzz. Some managers came out to see me at my invitation, but nothing developed. Then I discovered writing where I could play all the roles. Oddly enough, I haven't looked back and all of it began at 476 South Brimhall in the rec room.

My memories of the elm trees in St. Paul are very dear to me. They have to be because while the city I knew growing up has come to seem more and more the same every time I come home for a visit, it will never be the same without the elm trees. I was thinking the other day, what if some filmmaker wanted to recreate the burning of the leaves in the fall for a movie? Where would he go? There must be elm trees somewhere with streets beneath them. Maybe there's even someplace where they still burn them in the streets like we did. With the exception of Warwick, the north side of Randolph was a highpoint with Brimhall, Saratoga and Pascal going downhill before leveling off. I can see it now without even closing my eyes. The elm leaves' smoke wafting over the side streets with parents raking and tending those fires that glowed softly into the night. There was something about that yearly ritual that warmed my heart. The only thing I can think of close to it was the annual paper sales. Hundreds of kids and sometimes their parents would be hauling gigantic piles of tied up newspapers, coming from every direction. There were more of us kids in those days and for me, that's the Americana I grew up with. By our sheer numbers, we were a part of nearly everything in one way or another. I'm better than I've ever been at keeping negativity out of my life (as I should be by now); but there have always been those comforting snapshots of life along Randolph as a boy. They have always lightened the darkness.

When I was growing up, I always thought a tornado would finally come and destroy lots of homes in Highland where I lived. There were some pretty big thunderstorms I remember, and lots of tree branches and even trees blown over. What I mean is weather was rather exciting when I was a kid, be it flooding or blizzards or even record cold, and we had them all in St. Paul. I always thought Jack London would like St. Paul. His "Call of the Wild" was so beautifully written I was sure I would never be able to write like he did. I was right too, but I got to thinking about novels and stories that combined dramatic weather with say, a mystery. That's exactly what I did in my novel about St. Paul, The Children Shall Be Blameless. Of course the tornadoes were in Nebraska, but there were lots of other "goings on" in the midst of the bad weather: embezzlement, overcrowded hospitals (where treated patients were simply given out to anyone waiting), communities bonding together to help one another, a death count and one case of a mysterious stranger looking for his long lost sister, still missing many months later. They say write about what you know. Well, I'm from St. Paul. That qualifies me to write about any weather I so choose, and while orphans and long lost siblings and murders and illegal interstate traffic are beyond my experience, they still are not in a way. Jack London wasn't a dog, but wrote a great book from a dog's point of view. I wrote about my tornadoes with no research at all and the words flowed out from my fingertips as if they were happening just then. What I learned writing the book was that St. Paul is as great a platform for storytelling as anywhere on earth. You should try it sometime.

The example I usually give when telling someone why I no longer live in St. Paul is that I can never remember having snow tires on when the first snow fell. The truth is, my sense of denial about living in Minnesota weather began long before that. As a child, I was dressed warmly with overshoes, gloves, a hat and sometimes even a scarf. As a child, I also had a crew cut and so it didn't matter. As I got older none of my heroes on television had crew cuts you see, and so I wanted to grow my hair longer. As I did, my common sense seemed to fly out the window because it wasn't long before I was no longer wearing overshoes, never a hat and I assure you, I wasn't alone. It didn't matter who we were trying to look like because none of "them" wore hats, overshoes, parkas, gloves and scarfs. They all kind of looked like Edd "Kookie" Byrnes on 77 Sunset Strip. You wanted your hair to look like it did when you combed it before school. It never did of course. That's why you carried a comb. The simple truth of the matter was this. Me and lots of other guys like me decided we would rather freeze than look like "Nanook of the North." For us spring was fine, so was summer, and fall was great but winter did nothing to enhance our vision of self, imaginary or otherwise, and so we simply decided to ignore it. Over time, I began to feel that I was just never meant to live anywhere that had winter.

I love it when people say to me, "Oh, St. Paul huh? You must like the cold!" "Why no," I say, "if I did why would I be talking to an idiot like you in Pasadena?" I never say the last part of course, but I sure have wanted to once or twice. It was on Blair. We had rented a lower duplex and it was the best Christmas I can ever remember. If I had to choose, this is the one. I don't recall what I was doing for a living at that time but I remember having money to spend. The marriage wasn't two years old and we had separated twice, but it was Christmas and my wife had gotten me a dog. The dog kept me home and out of trouble and the world seemed right. My daughter wanted a dollhouse. I found one for sixty dollars, good money in the seventies, but it didn't matter. I could only afford to furnish a room and a half with dollhouse furniture. For what that cost I could have put her up in a suite of rooms at the Hilton. Again, it didn't matter. Having done that, I went looking for something for my wife. I saw a beautiful fur jacket. It was expensive but I had just spent a hundred on my daughter and my only concern was if she would like it. I gave it to her a few days early. I remember, she put on makeup and wore it over to her sister's to see what she thought. I could tell I had done well. I can't exactly say why that was my favorite except to say that I sure hadn't been much of a husband and father to that point. It was the beginning of my getting it turned around. I also felt I needed that for my own confidence. My daughter had more fun making little furniture for her dollhouse and my wife wore that fur jacket for years to come. Somehow, that Christmas gave us a chance and with some big career decisions coming up in the weeks ahead, I doubt the marriage would have gone on without it. Some good years followed. I drove down Blair the last time I was home and tried to find which house it was. I couldn't really remember.

The thing about a White Christmas is the secular nature of the term. Oh sure, I've seen depictions of Joseph leading Mary on a donkey through the snow dotted landscape of the suburbs of Bethlehem, and while they do get a bit of snow from time to time, there's nothing in scripture that I know of to suggest a White Christmas. Still, Christmas just seems well suited to that Currier & Ives design and let's face it, a St. Paul Christmas is quite often the most beautiful Christmas you can imagine. I loved those wonderful pictures of a downtown St. Paul Christmas with so many people on the sidewalks, shopping from store to store. It was different back then but the weather is not. It's still the home of the Winter Carnival, and Christmas in St. Paul denotes a holiday to be celebrated as much because of its weather, rather than in spite of it. People saying Merry Christmas to one another and all the decorations somehow warms the time of year if not the weather. I was doing a play at the University of Redlands here in Southern California many years ago, and I remember a young Asian student in the cast that I got talking to during a break and the subject of snow came up. It turns out she was from St. Paul and being a November production, talk of Christmas came up. I never met anyone so certain of the importance of snow and a White Christmas as we talked under the palm trees. I was content to be in Redlands but in her eyes, I could see that homesick look so common in people from our place in the world. You can't beat Christmas in St. Paul...if only in our dreams.

It's funny how one Christmas memory triggers off four or five more. My mom and dad liked to drink and both were funny but in different ways. Most of the time, Dad was hilarious when he didn't know he was being funny at all. One Christmas Eve he wanted to call his little sister Ethyl and her family in Detroit to wish them a Merry Christmas. Now you younger members may not recall the big deal making a long distance call was back in the fifties. There was not direct dialing or anything resembling that at all. You had to get an operator and then sometimes wait for a long distance operator. Dad couldn't remember the number, which was no surprise because being Christmas Eve he'd had a few drinks, so now you had to involve directory assistance...in Detroit. From our one-bedroom apartment on Brimhall in St. Paul and remembering that it was Christmas Eve, operators were frequently busy and so what Mom and I heard for a good ten minutes was, "Yes, operator...Clyde Hardwick on Rutherford Street...in Detroit." Two minutes later, it was another operator and we heard the same thing. Later, we guessed Dad said, "Clyde Hardwick on Rutherford Street" maybe four or five more times and by that time, we had gone on to other things. Finally, and with Dad slurring his words a little more each time, maybe fifteen minutes had gone by and we heard Dad say, "Yes operator, Clyde Rutherford on Hardwick Street". Mom and I cracked up while Dad looked at us like we were crazy. We never did get to wish Merry Christmas to the Hardwicks that year but I've remembered that attempt for at least sixty years.

Holy Spirit Church is celebrating its 75th Anniversary. Originally, it was in the basement of the building that's there now and the new one was being built on top of it while I was going to Holy Spirit Grade School across the street. Services continued in the basement for at least two years when I was in school. I remember because I made my First Confession in the church downstairs in second grade, but First Communion was upstairs in the brand new church the following year. All this time, we who lived in the Highland area were treated to the wonderful church bells from the Gloria Dei Lutheran Church on Snelling and Highland Parkway. A year or two later, Holy Spirit got its bell and there was the "blessing of the bell" and all that and finally it was raised up and went...gong, gong, gong. It turns out that what we had heard (and continued to hear) from the Lutheran Church was a recording of the "greatest hits of church bells" and the contrast was very stark. It was my first religious lesson in the adage that the studio version of anything is frequently superior to "live", in many ways.

I don't really have a relationship with California food like I used to have with St. Paul food. Naturally I'm glad I do not, because overweight as I am, I don't need anything like that in the shadow of my 70th Birthday. People tend to like salads out here and if I never saw a salad again I could do just fine. I came to love many things growing up in St. Paul: Geno's spaghetti and meatballs, Weber's glazed donuts, and White Castles of course. However, there was a moment in time when I might well have turned into an "Arby's Beef and Cheddar, potato cakes and Black Cow Shake (basically, a root beer shake)" man. Now this order is still available but it's not even close to being the same. You see when they first came out, they served real roast beef sandwiches. There was no cheddar cheese "sauce". Instead, there was actual cheddar cheese melted on top of actual thinly sliced roast beef with Arby's sauce and those flat, triangular potato cakes (two of them back then); and with the shake, I realized for the first time why I fought in the war. I was driving

Yellow Cab then and could tell you, within a half mile, where every Arby's in the Twin Cities was, in case a fare took me near one. Now I won't deny that during the period of which I speak, the marijuana munchies didn't play a role in this obsession, because I'm sure it did. Then, in keeping with the downfall of Capitalism in general, Arby's hired an MBA. Soon, water-injected-roast-beef came along and with it, cheddar-cheese-sauce (flavored Velveeta and half-and-half) and the world would never again know the joy of a real Beef and Cheddar. I should be grateful because at its height, my obsession had become scary.

I remember one year when we had more rain than usual and very high winds. The result was that we sort of missed the beautiful colors that fall. All the leaves it seems were on the ground and being raked up before Halloween. Not long after we had an early frost and the tree branches were very cool. It rained last night out here in Monrovia. Either that or the city came around getting all the driveways wet just for laughs. It rains so seldom here it seems like that sometimes. With the elm trees gone, you just can't know what it was like in St. Paul back in the fifties and early sixties; you can't know either because there were so many kids. I often wish I could have enjoyed being a kid more than I did. Seems like I always wanted to be a grown up. All downtown seemed like a grownup place. I went to many movies though. I remember the last movie I saw at the Paramount, "Journey to the 7th Planet." It was an awful movie but us kids seemed to flock to bad movies when we were young. Even Disney traumatized the hell out of me with their animated features. Still there was Candyland, Bridgeman's, and Musicland and pretty girls from all over the city; than a ride on the bus, 14A or 14B, Randolph-Payne and back to Randolph and Hamline. Even doing nothing on your corner was doing something.

After a modest success or two at Monroe High School in the sixties, one might feel that acting in plays may well have been forgotten, after more than two years in Vietnam. Yet one of the first things I did when I got home was to audition for a play at the Edyth Bush Theater. I didn't get the part but I continued trying until I did, and acted for many years in various theater productions from St. Paul to Los Angeles. Some actors also attend plays but others do not, feeling they'd rather be in a production than watch others do it. That was me I'm afraid, but by doing a couple of plays in Long Beach when I first came out to California, I had an experience where a Hollywood star came to see us almost entirely incognito. Buddy Ebsen was a member of the Long Beach Community Theater, and somewhere in the first week of the run, he'd come five or ten minutes into a play, lean back, close his eyes and for all the world to see, appear to be asleep. Five or ten minutes from the end of the play, as if on cue, he'd get up and leave. From almost playing the Tin Man in the "Wizard of Oz," to "The Beverly Hillbillies," to playing Barnaby Jones on TV, here was a guy who began in vaudeville in the 20's. Then, near the end of his life, he sat supporting his local theater, play after play with no fanfare whatsoever. St. Paul has always been a great theater town with stories of that kind of support from our local performers: Dave Moore, Peter Goetz and others. In fact, it seemed wherever I went there were actors like that. The theater was one of the great blessings of my life. There's nothing like it.

I walked into Dewey's Pit and paddock one day and several of these people I had come to know and been hanging out with were there, and it was like I was having a cute hair day. You know or at least I hope you know how some days you just seem to shine to other people. My mother used to say, "Are your ears ringing?" meaning people had just been talking about you in some flattering way. It's kind of hard to know how to act when something like that happens except to maybe smile and try and discern what it was so it could happen more often. Turns out it was nothing more than helping one of their little brothers one time and that was nothing really, but it was something to him. Anyway, I was talking to my good friend Nick about a musician in a local band who had fallen victim to the drugs lifestyle and had wound up taking his own life. Nick was quiet for a moment and then recounted an event at the Highland Pool when he was being bullied. This musician was a couple of years older and had broken up the abuse and afterwards, had winked at Nick as he walked off. I hadn't talked disparagingly about this guy at all, and you could tell that nothing I or anyone could say about him would ever dim the memory of that kindness he did for my friend...not ever. As I get older and for some time now, if I find myself wishing for a different "me" during times of my life, it's never tougher or better looking or anything like that. It's always kinder, nicer when I had the chance. Saying to yourself, "I tried" doesn't seem enough somehow and yet, I'm so grateful for those moments I did.

There are those of us who equate God's love for us (or not), with our favorite team's performance on the football field. I have seen the Gophers win a Rose Bowl in my lifetime and even a National Championship; two World Championships for my Twins, and while I cherish those memories, there has always lingered the pain of four losses by the Vikings in the Super Bowl. I no longer blame nor laud the Almighty for anything that happens on the playing field. I've had plenty of thrills and disappointments over a lifetime of being a sports fan, but I suppose with age, my priorities no longer depend on things I can't control. I love my teams. That's just the way it is and if it looks like they will lose, as it certainly did today, I remember my dad shaking his head and saying, "That's a part of the game, Skip." In my mind, Dad and I faced the end with ten seconds left in today's divisional playoff against the New Orleans Saints. Anything can happen of course, but when you've been a Vikings fan as long as we have, that's so much nonsense. Even if it can, it won't and so, when it did today we were dumb struck. After the fifth of sixth replays we knew it had happened...the impossible and in our favor! No, God has always loved me and I'm betting He loved that game as well. So, the

Vikings live to play again next week. Even if it ends then, we had today, my dad and I. There is just nothing like football.

Change, (I mean, you can't do anything about it to begin with, but depending on your mood,) it can be good or bad. I grew up in St. Paul in the 50's. I'm not sure how much World War II had to do with it, but the further we got away from that, the more casual everything became. Oscar Wilde was asked what he thought about sports once. He said, "I approve of any activity that requires the wearing of special clothing." I would say at least in the St. Paul I grew up in, there was a sense of occasion with certain things back then. You dressed up to go to church, for example, certainly more back then than we do today. Nearly all men wore hats. My mother made me dress up in my "itchy pants" to go downtown and I can't tell you the last time I saw boys and girls wearing Cub Scout, or Girl Scout shirts or dresses. As a boy I always assumed I'd wear a shirt and tie when I grew up and here I sit, weeks from turning seventy, wearing exactly what I wore as a kid: a T-shirt, jeans and tennis shoes. I don't attend church regularly anymore but when I do, I always put on a shirt with buttons; but since the only pants that fit me anymore are jeans, that's what I wear. Imagine that outfit at a service at Holy Spirit with Monsignor Keefe presiding! You'd have to flee for your life. He'd call the police or kick you out himself; and women...don't get me started! There's a saying that: "Ginger Rogers did everything Fred Astaire did, only backwards and in high heels." I love a woman in high heels, but never envied them having to wear them. No, some things are better but in terms of what we wear and why we wear them, it seems to me we've lost something.

When you were a kid, it was fun to break things sometimes. Terry Brown lived across the street from me on Brimhall. He was a year older and we hung out now and then. Terry was very fast and had a flair for the dramatic. There was this broken window up against the trashcan down his alley once. We broke it even more and in the shards of glass that remained was a shape of a perfect glass knife. Terry claimed it as his own "homemade knife." Back at his house, he took a rag and wrapped it around the bottom to make a handle. The rest of the morning, we wandered around with him holding his homemade knife and showing it to anyone we might meet. Once I looked behind us for some reason and saw a spotted trail of blood. Terry had been holding it so tight, it cut through the rags and into his hand. Then before running home to get it taken care of, he carefully handed it to me. I took the bloody homemade knife home, hid it under some leaves by the back door, and then went looking for someone else to hang out with; but the knife stayed on my mind. I went over to Terry's in time to see him and his mom on the way to Anchor Hospital where Terry took a few stitches. I can't remember whatever happened to the homemade knife but it was a morning of breaking glass, finding something cool, leaving a blood trail; not a bad day's work for a morning in the neighborhood.

When you hear the expression: "getting out of your own way," what follows is: if you could do that, you'd really be great or something similar. Growing up in St. Paul I never actually heard that applied to me but I always knew it was true. Even a left handed compliment like that is still a compliment and for those of us who lived for adulation more than anything else, I feel we were willing to find something good to say about others, in particular those who seemed to be lacking in applause in their lives. Actually, the genesis of it was something my dad always said, "If you can't find anything good to say about someone, don't say anything at all". Truth is, if you can't find something good to say you're not trying hard enough. When I was coming up, I'd see General Tom Schwartz when he was at Cretin and Lenny Salstrom at Monroe, and you knew it was possible. You knew that if you could get out of your own way, anything was. As I think of it now, I started running away (in my imagination) from an early age. It was as if I wanted to start again with a clean slate and that is probably why I became an actor. Come what may, pretending to be someone else was almost necessary. Today because of Facebook and Old St. Paul, MN. I get together with classmates from Holy Spirit twice a year. My old flight platoon in Vietnam meets every year, as well. It seems less important to me now, but I must have somehow learned how to get out of my own way or accepted myself as someone who never would, because I've accomplished things I never imagined I could. Maybe vanity saved me. As I think about turning seventy, high on the list of things I'm most grateful for is having all my hair. Strange I suppose but there it is.

Some days it feels like I am in my thirties and the next day I am about to turn seventy. When I was in my mid-thirties, I was working for KFBC Radio in Cheyenne, Wyoming. I did AM mornings including a talk show, and rock afternoons for our FM KFBQ and play-by-play of basketball for the local high schools. I was also acting in a play at Cheyenne Little Theater. Scottsbluff, Nebraska was in town to play Cheyenne East and Central with their two high schools on Saturday and Sunday afternoon. I got up Saturday, smoked the longest roach in the ash tray, got dressed, worked my abbreviated Saturday morning show, got a burger, had another puff on a joint, went to the gym and did two basketball games in the afternoon. After that, I had just enough time for dinner and on to Cheyenne Little Theater to play Simon Able in Sly Fox. Afterwards, I had a few drinks with the cast, smoked the rest of the joint on the way home where I slept and then did the other two ball games on Sunday. My boss, who had a newspaper column, dedicated his whole column to wondering how I could talk professionally for more than twelve hours and still have a voice left for Sunday's two basketball games. I loved it there but when your reason for being in Cheyenne goes away, the rule is, you have to go away too. Those were good years in Wyoming and they led me out here to California where I've been ever since. The last thirty-five years have seemed to go by like that Saturday in Cheyenne: full, fun, fast and more than half without a joint or a cigarette. So when I say I'm lucky, believe it.

"We shall not cease from exploration and the end of all our exploring we will be to arrive where we started and know the place for the first time." It is pretentious I'm sure, to begin with a quote from a man I never really read, but T.S. Eliot is widely quoted and here, nailed how I felt about growing up in St. Paul, Minnesota like no one else. Since I continue my explorations, I do feel that each time I come home I know it for the first time. A part of it has to do with how much I have learned about being a part of Old St. Paul, MN, all the things I didn't do or even know about. I never expected to come back as often as I have in recent years but I never planned on staying gone forever, either. I always knew I'd come back and see the old neighborhood. As I've said before I feel so conspicuous doing so, and I can never hang around for long. The change doesn't bother me and besides, not much has changed in the Randolph and Brimhall area.

One of the other things that's no longer around in St. Paul is burning things. Everyone burned leaves in the fall of course but when I was a kid, it wasn't unusual for people to burn things in their trash cans all year around. During the fifties if you said "trash cans" you were talking about a fifty-five gallon drum, basically in a sort of rusted brown color and unless you lived in an apartment building like I did, nearly every house had one, and burning things in it, like garbage, was very common. Businesses had these gray brick square ones and say you had a bunch of cardboard boxes, they made some very big fires. I came out of 476 South Brimhall one day and saw a huge fire in the back of Terry Brown's house across the street. I ran across the street and realized it wasn't their house, but a huge fire in the gray brick thing behind Jerry's Liquor Store on Snelling and you could see it reflected off the Brown's back windows. I remember it like it was yesterday. What did I think I was going to do? Break in and rescue somebody? Probably.

Now that we've talked a little about the great candy bars we grew up with in Old St. Paul, let's revisit the sugar champion of all of our lives: cereal. Sugar Corn Pops don't forget: "They're shot with sugar through and through by Sugar Pops Pete." The Sugar Bear would sing it like Bing Crosby, "Can't get enough of that Sugar Crisp, Sugar Crisp, Sugar Crisp, can't get enough of that Sugar Crisp it keeps me goin' strong." The list is endless and if you thought you were eating healthier with Wheaties, think again. Even today, sugar is the second ingredient behind whole wheat in Wheaties and nearly every other current cereal formula. Many years ago, the food and drug administration took note of this and one researcher compared a bowl of corn flakes with a bowl of flaked cardboard from the box it came in. It was learned that the box, served with milk and sugar was better for you than the corn flakes. This created a false advertising issue for the cereal industry and that's when you started hearing the phrase in all cereal advertising..."A part of this complete breakfast", with a picture of toast, juice and milk to go with the cereal.... AND "eight essential vitamins" that were not present before the FDA got involved. That was all well and good I suppose, but once I trained my mother to leave the Wheaties box on the table where I could look at it (like the commercials), I knew I was eating the "Breakfast of Champions" and very little mattered beyond that. No, like kids all over the world, we kids of St. Paul were sugar receptacles from first thing in the morning to a bowl of ice cream at night. The truth is, sugar might be bad for you but I'm turning seventy this month and it hasn't killed me yet.

When my friend Bill and I were living on Grand near Victoria, we went shopping once and he noticed that while he bought the lowest price in everything, I bought everything I saw in the commercials on TV. I knew it was true and it didn't end there. I did a lot of things exactly as I saw them on TV or in the movies. I wanted hair like this or that guy, clothes too and it didn't end there. I wanted their lives: where they lived, what they did, and of course their girlfriends or wives. I wrote a sort of poem about a Saturday night coming back from confession at Holy Spirit once. In it, I picked up a little stick and started throwing up little rocks and hitting them with the stick like a baseball bat. It was getting dark and I couldn't see the little rocks, but in spite of their different sizes and different weights, I could judge their fall so perfectly, I'd never miss hitting them...never. The stick broke and I continued on, now using it as a tennis racket. Still, I hit every time and finally threw it away, like it was nothing. I like that memory because some of the things we had as kids, unbelievable eye-hand coordination and other gift, were often taken for granted. I wanted the gifts I didn't have: a car, a woman, an adventurous nature and the means to pursue it. Sometimes it extended to other kids, if they looked good for some reason, I wanted to as well. There was a programmed yearning for more, different, and I'm sure I was getting most of it from TV. It was something to do, something to think about. I doubt that it did me any harm.

As a boy, growing up Catholic, I knew I could never live up to the standards of the church, that is, being worthy of the love of God. I had masturbated and then tried not to sometime later, and failed. That was it. My faith became more personal in some ways after that. I never "threw the baby out with the bath water" entirely, but I did know I could never do without that rush of feeling again. If I had to find an average, I would say that from that moment on and over the course of my life, I have probably thought about sex every eleven minutes after that first time. I know, at least I think I know, that it got in the way over a lifetime, but that really can't be helped. Taking the longer view and acknowledging that I did go back to church for a time, I'm glad the rigid standards of the Catholic Church drove me away earlier rather than later. While God never let me down, the platform that is organized worship nearly always did. Out of the ashes of moral disappointment, I find I did my best and my best has gotten better over the years. Those deals I made with God seemed bigger than they were and nine times out of ten, (assuming God does take a hand in these things), his or her unwillingness to grant my wishes became as important as those they did. Indeed, I'm still trying to reconcile these issues. I'm still unwilling to chalk up my failure in spiritual matters to my inability to control my erections, but in the end that may be true as well.

When I was a kid, I used to watch the older kids walk by with great interest. I mean, how would you know how to walk when you were older if you didn't see how they did it? Among the older kids of St. Paul in the fifties, there was one over-riding characteristic they all seemed to have: a serious expression on their faces. After all, they were older. You can't walk like a goofy kid forever. Some took up the whole sidewalk when they walked… best to avoid those guys. Another was (whether it was true or not), they all walked like they were going someplace. This sounds elementary but in boys and men, I assure you it is not. If you amble along aimlessly, you're more likely to identify yourself as someone to be picked on. We learned that early. An exception would be if you're hanging around a game of some kind waiting to see if someone would ask you to play. One other thing: the older the kid, the more comfortable he usually looked when he walked. A kid one year older than you might not walk like a big shot but once he saw you, he did. We had several of these in my neighborhood. Now remember, this is the fifties and the sheer density of kids was incredible. We were everywhere. Some guys walked side to side, some guys up and down and the gravity walk (very popular with athletes), was when you simply leaned forward in the direction you were going and your feet followed along behind. Jeff Weber, who lived across Randolph from me, was a gravity walker. I'm not sure about Jeff but guys who walked like that usually had back trouble in later life. The "paper boy" walk is obvious. It was a sort of waddle from carrying a lot of papers on your left side while rolling them and throwing them with your right. I noticed all these things as a child but could master none so I did what a lot of others like me did. We almost never walked alone. In a group, any walking blemish you might have could be obfuscated. It wasn't easy being a kid. I often wonder how I made it through.

I like metaphors. I can't remember if I came up with this by myself or heard something similar once, but its origins go back pretty far, I think. "When you think of life as a football game, I'm not at the two minute warning, but in my case the marching band has been off the field for some time." It must be pretty old because except for college, you don't think of marching bands and football as automatically as you used to. Anyway, in turning seventy in a few weeks, I'm certainly closer to that two-minute warning than I was when I started that joke. The other day, I got to thinking about it and would like to make a couple more fourth quarter drives to sort of finish up strong. After all, I have accomplished a lot more in my last thirty-five years than I did in my first. I had just turned thirty-seven actually and I do give myself credit for finally growing a pair big enough to do something really stupid, and have it turn out pretty good. From my perspective, if you've always wanted to do something, you might be dead before I finish typing this thing, so you might as well do it today! It was hard...damn hard at times but after the first year, I felt strong enough for anything. I made mistakes but I kept on going and even today, I'm still proud of that effort. You know, things morph into other things and while it feels like a new life for a while, it becomes a lot like your first life in that things change, and more often than not, so do your goals. So without saying what my original goal was, when it changed, I got my Master's and taught Film Studies at my university for six years, wrote seven books, produced paintings and drawings of which over a thousand have been published (including nearly fifty covers) and retired from a radio network with a pension. So while I still hope for a big finish, you may reach seventy one day, and whatever <u>it</u> is in your life, go for it now. The energy created by that one act will see you through.

I think of a shower as a "fast clean" as opposed to a bath, which is slower. I can't take a shower in my house so I take baths. We have a shower, but my wife insists that whoever takes one, must wipe down the walls afterward. If I wanted to wipe down shower walls, I'd get a job at a gym somewhere. I will not do it. Therefore, I take baths. At the gym I'll take a shower, but not here at home. I also like and used to insist on carpet under my feet; but we have pets and after a "laborsome petition", I give in to vinyl tile. I'm glad I did because the design we chose allows me to revisit memories of seeing things in various designs: people, animals, houses with windows, etc. I did a lot of that as a boy in our apartment on Brimhall, going so far as to paint a leaf or two on the wallpaper with my mother's fingernail polish. One panel of our new floor immediately gave up this Dickensonian character with a slightly misshapen head, mustache, almost Scrooge like leaning back in his chair. It's reminded me of the figures I used to see in the grain of wood or the shape of clouds. So while I continue to lose battles to my wife in the style of our home (she's originally from Edina, you know), it's only natural I look for the silver lining. After all, she is usually right but I'll be dammed if I'll let her know that.

It's a rather gloomy morning here in southern California. The marine layer they call it, and it moves up from the south bay and Long Beach and usually burns off by noon. I spent many a gloomy day in St. Paul growing up and while I'm sure my home had more cloudy days a year than in California, it was not nearly as many as it did seem then. Was it months and months of cloudy days? Of course not, and yet it felt like that at times...to me at least. I remember being socked in with fog at LZ Hammond in Vietnam. We flew up near Bon Song to cover a Medevac helicopter that was picking up a guy who had gotten bit by a snake. Anyway, the fog was only about fifty feet high but spread out thick as far as you could see, like whipped cream really. Otherwise, it was a clear beautiful day. As a kid, I loved going camping, if only in the back yard. In Vietnam, I lived outside and in tents for more than two years. I don't think I've spent more than three nights out of doors in all the years since then. Enough was enough, I guess. I was running up to Mount Wilson, not far from my house, years ago on a cloudy day. I decided to go higher that I usually did with the last marker being Manzanita Ridge. Just before getting there, it felt like the fog had burned off. I looked out and realized I had run up through the clouds and below me, it was still cloudy all the way to the ocean. It never did clear up that day so I felt like I was the only one who saw the sun. That was a cool feeling.

Both Phalen and Highland Golf Courses, the two St. Paul Golf Courses of my life, underwent remodels years ago. As a boy, I knew the old ones well, especially Highland. Now this is not about golf, but I have to set this up along the confines of the first nine holes of the old Highland configuration and it went like this: holes one, two, and three ran generally along Montreal up to just about Snelling. The fourth and fifth holes wound their way north around the old tennis courts, Highland field (the hockey facility now), then past the Highland Tower to the reservoir and Highland Parkway. That's where we skied and took our sleds in winter. Holes six and seven went to Hamline and eight and nine back to the clubhouse. My friend Dave and I got up real early and the plan was to get up get up there and ski but there was an overnight frost and lousy skiing; so we sort of went cross country skiing on the course and were wandering inland among the back nine when a deep fog descended on the course. These were the days of "Land of the Lost" and other stories like that, so in this cool dense fog we sort of got lost. As I recall, there were some strange sounds while we were in this fog and our imaginations led us into time passages and electrical doorways into new worlds, or even ancient worlds with dinosaurs and stuff. For at least an hour and maybe two, we wandered around in it before the sun came out and burned off the fog. By this time, we were at one end of a big long rough that ran parallel to two holes on the back nine. It stands as one of the coolest winter days I ever spent growing up.

Old Visitation Convent as it was then called, was sort of at the end of Fairmont. I always figured it was the female equivalent of Nazareth Hall for boys, that is, people heading into the clergy in some capacity. For whatever reason, it had the biggest smoke stack you ever saw. In the circumference of the bottom of it would be enough room for an efficiency apartment and in fog you couldn't see the top. Anyway, years went by and my friend Randy rented a garage on the convent grounds where he worked on his Volkswagen bus on weekends. Sometimes I'd go with him, drink beers, and talk non-stop all the while. On a real nice day, Randy loved working on his vehicles; it was one of the things that defined him, really. One winter he went down to Texas to see an old girlfriend and came back with a badly broken ankle. With not much mobility, the drugs got a real good hold of him and come spring, when he didn't even put his motorcycle back together, we all knew things had changed. The rest of the story isn't any more hopeful and my friend died some years later, down in Florida, Key West maybe, of a spider bite. Last night I got thinking about that day at the garage at Visitation. Whatever happened down in Texas that winter was a watershed of sorts and my friend was never really the same. Along with Jesse, who passed a few months ago now, Randy and I had more fun together then I knew I'd ever have again. I like to think I might see them again across the Great Divide, but if I don't, those guys and that time live on with me until I get there.

As my world began to expand growing up in St. Paul, there was really only one place that I felt comfortable going to alone, and that was Midway Center. Living on Randolph and Brimhall I could have gone down to Highland Park but I never felt very comfortable there. I can't say why. Just taking the bus to Midway center, walking around and winding up in Wards always made me feel good. There was no more to do there than anywhere else, but for me there was nothing threatening either. It felt more familiar. I was an only child and had friends I hung out with but sometimes nobody was around. I remember asking this one girl I was interested in if she wanted to go to Midway Center with me. She just couldn't see the point...to just go to Midway Center. Or maybe it was just me. It's funny how some places just seemed to feel better than others. This was during grade school but in high school as well, whereas there was "comfort food" there was also "comfort places." For me it was Midway Center.

You may not have realized it, but think about those times when you started going to another barber or stylist, dry cleaner or druggist; or when you couldn't afford to shop at the little grocery store anymore and went to the big one, or the dentist or the doctor, or even your church for whatever reason. The list goes on and on and even if as a kid you kept going there with your nickels and dimes, soon it wasn't enough and the store finally went away. To a large extent, this is what happened to our neighborhoods in St, Paul. One minute we were self-contained; just a short walk away from everything we needed and then the world changed. Supermarkets took over and it was no problem because everyone had a car and some of the merchants didn't help either. Say you wanted sideburns like Edd "Kookie" Byrnes or Elvis. Some barbers wouldn't do it and hairdressers refused to change; or just like their bigger competitors, some drug stores quit buying your favorite candy because they weren't selling enough to make a profit. While what we wanted drove the market, advertisers on TV especially took advantage. We watched it all happen and yet, in some ways, I still rebel by finding myself loyal to one shop or another, one merchant who remembers my name or smiles to see me coming. At the same time, think of how lucky we are to still have the Nook and O'Gara's, Tin Cups and the White Castle. Har-Mar is still there I think, and the Original Coney Island is back open and Mickey's diner of course. I am nostalgic but I come home often enough now to have found some terrific new places everywhere, and these little memories keep one foot in the past. One night my dad walked up to Joe's Drug Store on Snelling and Randolph. I was sick and he was getting me a malt. Joe gave him a little toy train to take along at no cost to make me feel better. What a great neighborhood we had.

I could tell that kids from all over St. Paul went to the Highland Pool. I never knew how far they'd come until I joined Old St. Paul. Anyway, one day I was taking a break up by the tree there and catching some sun and all of a sudden, I started hearing someone calling my name from outside the fence, yelling it really. I looked around and finally saw an older guy in a straw hat. It was Ed Marhoon, a friend of my mom and dad. After a while, he quit yelling on the north side of the pool and then a few minutes later, he's yelling on the south side. I was embarrassed, so finally I went up to see what he wanted and he said he wanted to take me to the Twins game. I didn't want to go but I got my stuff. He took me home where I changed and we went to see the Twins play the Washington Senators. I'd been to Metropolitan Stadium when the Millers played the Saints but was never to a Twins game. I'll admit I wasn't enjoying myself but what could I do? Ed was a good guy and why he wanted to take me to the game I'll never know. We were down the left field line where all the seats faced deep center field so you had to crimp your neck trying to see the infield. He bought me a Coke, which was two inches of Coke packed with ice. By the eighth inning on day-games, the sun was right in your eyes as you looked home. The Twins lost and it would be many years before they ever won when I was there, including taking my kids half a dozen times. Harmon Killebrew did homer to center that day and I saw one of my heroes, Herb Score warming up in the bullpen, but it was no use. Naturally I thanked him, but whereas many kids I'm sure would have been thrilled, I was happier at the Highland Pool. I've never felt guilty exactly, though I'm no stranger to that. I would have kept quiet but you just can't have a guy in a straw hat screaming your name at the pool.

While I do have a considerable memory, February 25th, 1948 is simply not there. Not long after though, little snapshots begin to appear. On this date in 1950, my mother decorated my crib with balloons. I sure remember that. My world for fifteen years was a basement apartment at 476 South Brimhall in St. Paul, Minnesota, and I loved every inch of it. I could rattle off the names of my parakeets and the dogs I brought home hoping to keep. No disappointment I ever knew could compete with the advantages of being a spoiled, only child to Walter and Barbara Savage and while there was great sadness in my teens as our family broke up, I was always loved. By age twenty, I was already home with my service and Vietnam behind me. After that, you could call me aimless but I prefer "contemplative." I had a lot of fun, though. The family years were just too wonderful and painful to revisit, so I rarely do; and then one day I was fifty, still somewhat "contemplative" but managing a strong showing for twelve more years before retiring. I go back to St. Paul and write about those days all the time now, but my eight years of retirement seem more like eight weeks, as is common with the contemplative. There's no explanation for reaching seventy in relatively good shape, although there are signs of the doddering old fool I'll wind up as...if I'm lucky. Would I do it all again? Of course not. A lot of it was hard and painful and I was never built for either. I am grateful though and I have been for many years. Believe me when I tell you, I damn well should be. Thanks for the wonderful birthday wishes!

In the last day or so, I've had a certain anxiety. It reminds me of wanting a favorable outcome so much that it almost sabotages any chance of the thing being successful. You try in every way to gain that assurance, all the while knowing it will not happen. When I was growing up in Highland Park, I had enough of these episodes that I began to wonder if maybe they were still good for the excitement and enthusiasm that came along with them. It felt like I had somehow found a way to marshal all my forces to achieve the desired end; and it didn't stop with physical planning either. "Dear God, just give me this one thing and I'll...do thus and such, and never do this or that again." God, or not, in His infinite wisdom, came through sometimes but not very often; and sometimes came through only to see the whole thing was wrong and it was like He or She was whispering in my ear, "See, I told you." God could be aggravating that way but I'm sure He or She always knew best. The truth is, and in spite of attaining a Master's in graduate school in my fifties, I'm not all that well read. However, I do remember everything I did read. If I read a line or two that I thought was particularly good, going even as far back as Monroe High School, I would specifically commit that to memory. In my mind, I figured I could dazzle guests at a cocktail party someday by supporting my argument with sentences that began, " It was T.S. Eliot who said...". I have no trouble admitting that now. Some of the finest writers and thinkers on earth have been as shallow as me or at least my intentions. The big thing about expectations and walking home from Holy Spirit after school (and I thought of this often), was how to call upon that enthusiasm in other things whenever we wanted to use it. I never did. I learned a few tricks and my memory bails me out from time to time, but of my current anxiety and how it will turn out? Who knows?

My grandpa, Pete Goodman, whose real last name was Bosco, worked on the railroad all his life. Grandma (who I never knew) got a call one late afternoon in about 1917. It was Grandpa saying a railroad car had overturned with a shipment of watermelons down near West 7th and for her to come down with the girls (all in pigtails): my mother Barb (known as 'Bay' to her sisters), Dorothy (or 'Duddy' to everybody) and young Alice, to get some watermelons and bring them back home to Frog Town. They get on the streetcar, transfer downtown and get to the site as the sun is going down. Each girl and my grandma take a watermelon and they go home. By the time they get there, Grandpa is calling saying the railroad detective had watched all these going's on and to bring the watermelons back or he'll lose his job. So that night they went back down with the four watermelons and Grandpa was suspended for a week...true story (I heard it fifty times.) Years later, my aunt Alice married Al Loken from Long Prairie who owned two bars on University in the 50's and 60's: one on University and Arundel and the other on Farrington and University. For years, he was known as "Big Al." By the time he retired, they were living on Edmund and one day my friend and I are short of money, nursing our drinks at the round bar in the Woodshed on Dale, when the bartender puts two new drinks in front of us; "These are on Big Al", he says. I look down the bar and there's my Uncle Albert..."Big Al" on University Avenue for two decades; one of the best guys I ever knew. In a way, that story is St. Paul to me...one big neighborhood.

It's natural to think back on this or that occurrence in your life and think, "Gee, if only this had happened (or hadn't happened) my life could have been different." I think back on my three years at Monroe High School in the 60's certainly more than I ever thought I would. It was a good school with excellent, involved teachers and counselors and a student body full of very optimistic, 'up' kids and I can't help but wish I had done more with my opportunity there. There were many problems at home and I wasn't prepared to deal with them. The funny thing was that by the time I was facing my senior year, I had righted the ship a great deal. However, that summer things just got too much and I knew I couldn't balance my life at home and another school year too, so I struck out on my own for a while, then wound up joining the army when that didn't work out. Monroe lives in my memory as an opportunity lost. Strangely, the same might be said for my life in St. Paul. I had a lot of fun but could never quite get it together there. Still, I seemed uniquely prepared for whatever came my way when I went somewhere else. In a lot of ways, all the moving around I did in radio for all those years was a sort of mirror of my high school experience...starting from scratch and then leaving again just as I was becoming fully established. The difference was I never looked back after leaving a radio job. I still think about Monroe High School, though.

I hung around Dewey's Pit and Paddock for years as did this young fellow. He was a little slow, but he was a good kid and he drank with us and we included him in our conversation and so forth. One Halloween night he came in as Darth Vader with a mask and cape and as the night went along, some of the people who also dressed up came out onto the sidewalk and sort of showed off for the cars passing by. This kid, Chris was his name, came out one time but forgot his mask. Thinking he was Darth Vader, especially after a few beers, he had assumed a Darth Vader manner...real actor's studio stuff, and you could see that world domination was on his mind as the cars passed. So I grabbed him and said with a laugh, "Come on, Chris...you forgot your mask." Instead of showing terror at having done something stupid (for which he probably had some experience resulting in ridicule), he looked at my smiling face and smiled back at me. It was about acceptance and the kind of drinkers we were; if you were okay with us, you were okay. Chris had found that at our bar and possibly nowhere else. I still think of Chris and what a terrible thing it must be to find acceptance of who you are, difficult to obtain. Sure, some of us were drunks...I know I was, but impaired in our own way and by choice, we were still more accepting of one another at face value than a lot of other groups of which I was a part.

There is a vanity in wondering how people reacted to some news about you and there's no getting around that. I suppose I'm embarrassed at a certain level, because I've never written about this and yet wondered what it must have been like for my mom and dad ever since 'it' happened. My mother and father were separated when I went in the army, so I had to get them to sign consent forms separately, for me to enlist at 17. Dad had more misgivings about signing the consent than Mom. I pretty much gave her no choice. Less than ten months later I had been wounded and my mother had to go and tell my dad and to say that I would be all right. I've supposed he would ask if I was coming home and she would say no. I asked her about it, several times actually. She never said very much, just that she told him and he was upset, of course. I don't know why I've always wondered about that. I mean, suppose something happened to you and the most important people in your life didn't react the way you thought they might or even should. Suppose they didn't react at all. Now further imagine that you are far away when this takes place so you have no way of knowing. You just have to imagine until you get home and ask, "When you heard the news, what was that like?" and then maybe..."When you told so and so about it, how did he react?" These questions are fair because your life is your movie after all and you want to know what scenes wound up on the cutting room floor while you were away. I finally concluded that Mom just called him. There were guys, even guys from big families who didn't have that. The day-to-day grind of dealing with seven or eight kids was just too much to "stop the presses" over one of them getting hurt, even in the war. Of course, part of it was that it was not a time of immediate communication like it is now. It was weeks between letters and if someone from the army showed up at your house, it wasn't to tell your folks you'd been wounded.

When I was a boy, there was no park down by Crosby Lake and I think Montreal ended near where the little dirt road down there began. There was a farm though and on that farm, there was what seemed like a mean dog: a German Shepard I think and he barked and barked. We'd hide our bikes just over this little fence and head down to the river and the lake through the woods. There were a few backwashes, little canals from the lake and we'd fool around down there for a while. One day we went down to the river and as I was just sitting there, this huge thing floated quietly by. It was a barge and it was real close to our side of the river. It was like a "Mark Twain" moment if I ever had one because that's what I wanted to do...work on a barge and go up and down the river. Years went by and my friend and I ran into a guy who actually did that. He told us we would have to go to Joliet, Illinois, join the union, then sit around this union hall, and wait for jobs. We thought about it for...oh, a day or so and then blew it off. Needless to say, I never worked on a barge but it was a great, romantic idea that never turned into reality; not the first and it wouldn't be the last but it was fun thinking about it. Besides, I turned into a writer anyway and like most writers, what I made up in my stories was a lot more fun than the life I led. I could get my head around that when I was a kid.

There used to be a Phillip's 66 station, across from our apartment on Brimhall. Various guys worked there over the years and there was this one Sunday when it was hot and humid and nothing much was going on, when the two guys at the station decided to amuse themselves by wetting rags and whipping each other with them. They were having a great time but there was no getting around it being a little weird because wet towels hurt when you snapped someone with one. I knew the two guys from my neighborhood and as I watched them beat the hell out of each other, I mean welt-raising whipping of each other, I remembered another time when I saw these two go at it in such a way. It was winter and the one guy had many brothers, two of which were my friends and they had a big hockey rink. It ran from the end of the house to the alley and had blue lines and everything. It was a two-man hockey game they were at: checking each other and giggling just like they did at the gas station years later, shooting pucks at each other, going for each other's heads. It was like they were having fun seeing how much they could hurt each other before someone didn't laugh and believe me it was dangerous just watching them. It was confusing for the boy I was, although rough football or just screwing around could be fun and I enjoyed it with my friends growing up as well. Yet, we were just kids...they were teenagers by this time with jobs and I sort of wondered why that phase hadn't ended with those two. I can't tell you about the other guy, but my friend's brother went on to have trouble all through his adult life: drinking problems of course but other things, concealed guns, resisting arrest, DUI. It was almost as if in growing up, he didn't have that friend who liked to mix it up that way anymore, and he started to get in trouble; or maybe he was just headed that way all along. In St. Paul, like nearly every place else, we learned that the world wasn't quite right and that there were people who weren't either. I did anyway.

Many of us, if not all, have been angry at many of the changes that we've seen over the last decades and lamented over how things used to be as opposed to how they are today. This morning, I've decided to take another position. To begin with, having been born in 1948, I have lived through the greatest period of human advancement in the history of mankind. The human race has come farther, faster by far then anytime in the history of our families, as well. I love the pictures of old St. Paul in general but winter and Christmas pictures in particular. All the people downtown, in the snow and cold and sure, many have their game faces on as we say but very few look miserable, and why should they? There was not the slightest chance that one day we'd be able to sit back and in a half an hour or so, in our pajamas, do all our Christmas shopping online with a few movements of our fingers; no, not at all. If you had people you loved and wanted to tell them so with Christmas presents, you had to get dressed and go downtown (or at least to Wards.) Something is always lost when something else is gained and that's just the way it is. Fewer of us are going to church these days, but Christ is still around and for those who celebrate in other ways for the holiday, that's fine too. What I'm saying is this. There's too much to be thankful for to waste much time worrying about how things used to be. We are the result and the living prototype of the future which, like all futures, is as equally frightening as it is hopeful. We were supposed to be dead from nuclear war by now...or AIDS...or TB, or some other catastrophe. Now we're not and if that's too heavy for you, turn on your flat screen television and check out the football games today and pause to remember a time when we got one game on Saturday, one on Sunday, no instant replay and if you saw ten passes on an entire weekend you were lucky. It took weeks to break in new shoes and our mothers had to iron sheets. That brings me around to Old St. Paul, MN. Are you kidding me? Who, over the last year has not been thankful that we found this site and in so doing, have been able to relive moments we thought were gone forever? I have the best memory of anyone I know and I grew up in St. Paul just like you. I have increased my knowledge of where I lived, what I did and indeed, who I am, ten-fold in the past year and even met and had drinks with several of you on the most perfect fall day I can ever remember; and that wouldn't have happened without Old St. Paul, MN. So sure...things have been lost but so much more has been gained; I don't know about you but I'm more thrilled than ever to still be here.

Many St. Paul drivers, and I was one of them, are in nearly complete denial about where they live. I'll give you some examples. In all the years I drove in St. Paul, the only time I had snow tires on when the first snowfall came, was when I hadn't bothered to take them off after the previous spring thaw. I often had both gloves and an ice scrapper, but there were always half a dozen times a winter when I was missing one or the other, and the memory of either trying to scrap with gloves or scrap with the scrapper wearing no gloves, lives in my memory still. These are nothing compared to driving on black ice or the general lack of driving co-ordination by the entire population of the city for the first few times each winter. You'd think we were all from Palm Springs. One other thing: bars in St. Paul are much friendlier than those here in California. One of the reasons for this is that they can often stay rather crowded once winter sets in where drinking and driving in St. Paul is an event not unlike something from the Winter X-Games. Those events are not as much for the drinkers, as they are for the rest of us just trying to deal with the slippery conditions...and the drinkers. Last February my wife and I came home together and had to deal with winter for the first time in many years. That pretty much ended any talk of selling our home out here and moving back to St. Paul. However, during our visit I had to get from Eden Prairie to the Nook on Randolph and Hamline and get gas on the way. I managed to do it and along the way, noticed that all the vehicles that had spun out into snowdrifts, waiting for tow trucks, were four-wheel drive SUV's. Winter wins again.

When I compare my love of games as a child to the organized pursuit of playing those games at a higher level, it's not as though I missed the boat entirely, and I was certainly not alone, but the essence, the payoff, if you will, got lost almost at once. "If you want to win," they'd tell our young, hopeful faces, "you have to work and work hard." Now remember, in the 50's these were coaches from either the depression era or peripheral to it and so everything was equated with pain, discipline and hard work. We were seven years old and the only thing fun about it was getting either a uniform or a jersey, like all the other kids on your team. That didn't mean you were going to play. It just meant you were a member of the team. If that was fun to you, you probably became what they called "a joiner" in later years, but if you wanted to have real fun you played in the street or behind some business and you played with whatever was available. That was called "playing." Playing was fun. Calisthenics wasn't fun, nor was drill at any level and blocking, in tag football for example, amounted to getting in someone's way more than "opening holes." While it is true that we were emulating what we saw on television with the pros, we wanted that feeling then... and not at some future time after years of discipline and hard work. I would wonder where I was missing the boat but I would wonder more at those kids who just wanted to have fun for fun's sake. No discipline and sacrifice for them...just fun. Okay they were right and I was wrong, but dreams of playing on the big stage came with the activity I suppose. Being the littlest kid who rarely played on the best team should have taught me more than it did.

On the last day of 2014, as many of us in our 60's do, I look back over my whole life as a sort of platform for assessing the previous year. I was just thinking about the serendipity of how my radio career began. Back then, "career" was such a foreign word to describe any of my endeavors, that it held no real meaning to me. Just finding a decent job and going to it every day was my immediate goal. Anyway, I had inadvertently finished a Radio & Television Broadcasting course at Brown Institute and accepted a radio job in Thief River Falls, Minnesota. That's when the phone rang and a voice told me I had just been hired for a position in waste treatment that paid real good money. I had applied there six months earlier and forgotten all about it. My marriage at the time was as shaky as you can get and I was asking my wife and daughter to leave St. Paul and follow me way up north to work for very little money in the middle of winter. The other job would have made us secure in this little two-bedroom duplex on Blair in which we had become rather happy. Finishing school and feeling I might have found my niche in life changed me. I told the voice 'no' and accepted the radio job and it would be many years before I made the money the other job was paying. We can never know what would have happened had we gone another way in life. Like most people, I wish I had done a little better at this or that along the way; and that wasn't the last time I turned down "more money" to do something I wanted to otherwise do. The tally of these decisions and their results seems less important now in my retirement; but they were a big deal back then, the only deal really. When faced with those pivotal choices, you can't help but wonder what might have been, never thinking you probably had no choice at all and were going to wind up exactly where you are in any case. So, 2014? It was another pretty good year and I'm happy to say that as the years go by, I'm more happy about it than resigned to the way things went. With fewer ahead than those behind, I'm willing to call that a good deal.

I never partied much in San Diego during the times I spent there. My wife lived there when she first moved out here and we had many dinners and drinks when I'd come to visit, but the first drinks I enjoyed in San Diego, somewhere in the early 70's, resulted in a very important conversation with a fellow who was managing prostitutes. He was a very personable fellow and funny too, and being funny myself, I understood perfectly when he bought my friends and I a round of drinks after I had been laughing at his act. The man had style and we got to talking about this and that, life in general, and he said something to me that changed my life and my luck with women. "The problem with you white guys," he said, "...is that you never ask. You take women out, open the door for them, spend all your money and never ask for what you wanted when you asked them out in the first place. You never ask for ...IT." I thought about that conversation for a while and began to develop an approach I was comfortable with which included something like, "Oh by the way...I'm available for sex tonight. Do you think that might be something that would interest you?" I know you think that sounds stupid but if you only knew how often those words, almost verbatim, worked, you wouldn't think so. Naturally, I heard "no" almost as a matter of course, but it did in fact offer a purpose for our date; and it opened lines of discussion, where there likely would not have been any, before I met this guy...in San Diego. One word of caution...yes, I became more successful than I had been before, but I must tell you I didn't use my new powers in a responsible manner. If you're considering actually asking for what you want in this life, consider that before you begin.

When I think of downtown St. Paul, I can almost smell the caramel corn from that little place next to the Riviera Theater. On the left side of Wabasha and down 7th Street on the same block was an establishment that shall (in my mind at least) live in infamy: Newman's. My mother was a shopper and took me along with her every time and there were landmarks that charted our progression in her trying on dresses and so forth. As a small child, I don't remember it being so bad, but soon it took on the proportions of an endurance, that no promise of lunch at Eddie Weber's or even the White Castle could assuage. So, let's go down the final stretch: the Emporium, the Golden Rule (Donaldson's), and then the final block before getting on the bus for home at 7th and Wabasha was where you would find Newman's. Their display windows and the storefront were different. It had a horseshoe configuration with a little display island in the middle and I came to know it well because just as my mother never wanted shopping to end, by the time we hit Newman's, I was beginning to learn there may be worse things than death. Invariably she had to stop in, and trying on those last few dresses became almost unendurable for me. If you look down the left side of Wabasha now sixty years later, imagine an extremely overwrought little boy, waiting with his mother for the Randolph-Payne bus, while he imagined getting some dynamite and blowing Newman's off the face of the earth!

I remember a boy in my neighborhood that was being teased one day to explain why he was not a little girl. He said simply, "Because I don't wear a bonnet." The idea that we wake up each day and sort of put on our sexuality as we put on clothes is interesting to me because let's face it, there's a lot of ambiguity out there. I'm pretty sure you don't have to think too hard to remember someone who was gay when you were growing up. In high school in particular, I wouldn't have changed places with those people for anything. I can't say I saw any of the cruelty I'm sure some of them endured, I'm glad I did not. I knew of a few at Monroe. Just rumors really, in those days.

The two I knew of for sure were nice guys. One was murdered later in life and one, like so many others, took his own life. Wherever you were, there was always somebody who needed more understanding and even protection than most of us were willing to provide. Things are better for gays today I am happy to say and comparing the St. Paul experiences I know of, with other places I've lived, we were no better or no worse than anywhere else, especially back then. I've always thought how ironic it is that Anita Bryant became such a pivotal figure in the gay movement, and while her intent was to destroy them, instead she empowered gays everywhere to stand up for their rights. God works in mysterious ways.

When I was a kid, we all wore tennis shoes: black top tennis shoes. We called them "Bozo Boots" because Bozo the clown was around and …well, you know. Anyway, there was really no other choice, so we'd watch basketball where some teams had white tennis shoes and of course, that's what we wanted. I finally got my pair when my mom picked them up downtown. Back then you had to measure your shoe size every time you went in a store, but tennis shoes seemed to get around that rule. They were white low-cut Jets and I mean really white, and for a kid basketball player in the fifties, I looked pretty cool.

I've never liked the 4th of July fireworks since my time in the army, but as a child I loved them more than anything. We always went up to the Highland Golf Course. The best part was, I could stay in my pajamas. I'd never been outside in my pajamas. It was the fireworks and the 4th of July yes, but something about being up at the golf course in my pajamas…and it was somehow okay, that was the coolest thing. So we went and the grass was wet; now I was in my pajamas with the legs pulled up because it was wet and when I ran, I could skate across the wet grass. Mom put a blanket out for us to sit on and hugged me. Mom and Dad always hugged you more when you were in your pajamas. So there I was on the blanket with Mom and Dad, all before the first of the fireworks even started. Actually, I can't remember the fireworks that year, just the three of us together on that blanket.

Dale and Selby was always an interesting corner, in St. Paul. My friend Randy worked at Crea Brothers Liquor store on the corner and told me a story about a white woman who made a left turn and hit a Pontiac driven by a black fella. It wasn't much, but the guy jumped out of his car and went on a rant. His buddy on the other corner kept yelling and beckoning him to come over. When he did, his buddy whispered in the guy's ear. After another sixty seconds or so the guy walks back to the accident scene and starts to faint as if injured, but realizes he has on a good sport coat so he takes it off and hands it to another guy and THEN he faints. You can't make this stuff up. There was another guy who had turned state's evidence against some friends of his in a mugging case, sending several of them to prison, while avoiding it himself. Naturally, he got out of town fast and stayed gone for a couple of years. He came back driving a powder blue Thunderbird convertible and decided it was okay to drive up to Dale and Selby. He was wrong and he took a brick to the forehead and just managed to keep control of the car long enough to get away. He took some stitches at Anchor Hospital, just ahead of those fellas who were still looking for him, sold the T-Bird at a loss and this time, got on a plane at Wold-Chamberlain Airport and headed back to where he came from. I know. As a little boy, I waved goodbye to him as he walked to that plane. To read his obituary yesterday, you'd never know it began and nearly ended on Dale and Selby.

As kids, there were warning signs that something might not be right with someone we knew. For example, early on in our weekend drinking experiments, this one kid just went crazier than everybody else did. We thought he was hilarious of course, but before long, we could see that he just couldn't pull back on the throttle, so to speak. Sure enough, he just slowly died over the next 35 years or so. Then there was this other kid I played with up at Little League in baseball. Joe could catch anything, anytime, anywhere. I remember people used to throw things his way and say, "watch this", and Joe would somehow make the catch. Within a year, he couldn't catch anything...nothing; and guys started doing the same thing and again said, "watch this" just to watch him fail miserably at catching the least little thing. It took one year and I've always wondered what happened there. He went from the best fielder ever to a joke, in one year. Joe wound up having drinking problems later in life too and died young, but that "catching the ball' thing has always made me wonder what happened with that. All of us drank and some handled it better than others did and of course, we noticed that some of us seemed...thirstier than the rest of us. I'll never know what the answer to my question was because Joe seemed to take the inability to catch anything in stride and it was a few years later that his drinking took over. Still I wonder.

Like most American males of my generation, the only overseas traveling I would ever do was with the Military. For me it was Vietnam and several Asian cities on leave over nearly two and one half years. Strange as it might seem (being that I sort of always considered myself a New Yorker even though I would never go there), I always compared nearly every place I lived to my home in St. Paul. I had a sales job that took me all over once where I found Sioux City, Iowa the most St. Paul like. It was the hills I suppose but I felt very much at home there and my memories are very specific. For example, I had to kill a few hours waiting for a client one afternoon and went to the library where I read <u>Marathon Man</u> by William Goldman: half the first day and the other half on a second. Oh, and the morning of the second day I stopped for breakfast at a local pancake house. The cook or somebody, had added yellow dye to the pancake batter, I assume to make them appear egg rich. The result was mostly green pancakes. The overall strange thing though was thinking I could be happy there, while I never seemed to be happy in St. Paul. Today, having lived for several years in Wyoming and in Oklahoma, in addition to thirty years in California, I feel in the comfort of Old St. Paul and the friends I've made here; that I come home under a white flag of peace, so to speak. The best of the old, the best of the new and I never seem to have enough time. It wasn't always that way and so it's a sort of blessing in a way, now that I'm old. A week from Tuesday I'll come home again. The last time I never got in a stop to the White Castle. That has never happened before. We'll see how it goes but it has started to feel more and more familiar every time.

Naturally, the Macalister Bike Shop was gone...loved that place. When I got up to Palace, I decided go right and maybe run by Mattock's where I went to kindergarten. It was gone and as I ran by a kid, I asked when they tore it down. He laughed and said, "Before I was born." Back up to Randolph and Snelling, at least the geography hadn't changed: up the hill to Niles, down, leveling off at Hartford and back up by Eleanor. At Ford Parkway, I turned left at Highland Tower and down into the parking lot of what used to be Highland Field. To my left, the old warming house was still there, but now there were two big blue water towers and the golf course was all plowed up for remodeling. The Field itself was now an indoor hockey rink. At Montreal and Hamline, I decided to run up by the Pavilion and over the footbridge, across Montreal and back to Hamline. At Hartford again, I ran around Cretin and north on Albert to Holy Spirit. Up Randolph and back to my car. I looked at my watch and it was practically nothing...maybe forty minutes. I remember when a route like that would wear me out walking. I paused for a second at the south side lawn of the building I grew up in. I played a lot of football on that lawn...mowed it a few times too. It's a nice neighborhood still, as it was when I was a boy. It's changed of course but really, not so much. Growing up wasn't all that easy for me in spite of my advantages but I sure loved playing football on that lawn.

Usually, people who are dreamers have been dreamers all their lives. That's one reason why so many of them, including me I suppose, leave our hometowns. There's nothing nefarious about it really but as dreamers refine their intentions over a period of growing up, they sort of become invisible after a while. Their friends and sometimes their families have just heard it for so long they long ago quit listening. St. Paul is no different in this respect, and while all that is necessary to achieve the dreamer's goals is available in St. Paul (certainly more than most cities), when the dreamer is ready to actually do something, he or she would like to be taken seriously; and it's not going to happen among those people who've heard it all your life. So you leave St. Paul, maybe several times before you get it right and finally chase your dreams in earnest. You may succeed albeit not right away, or you may wind up doing something else but at least you're finally doing it. After a time though, it's remarkable how many dreamers I run into back in St. Paul, here on OSP or even back home when I come for a visit. Whether you had success or not, we're all from St. Paul, and the measure of that almost demands we come home whether to stay or not, just to remember the journey we finally made. What's even funnier is that the feeling of..."I'll show them!" doesn't resonate anymore, if it ever did. What does resonate is that you tried; and whether or not anyone is particularly impressed or even cares, there's always the White Castle.

Lent, to me, meant several things I'm pretty sure the Catholic Church never intended and it began right after our First Communion. For those of you who are not Catholic, there was a certain fasting tradition if you were to receive the Communion wafer. Most of us were at least encouraged to attend Mass and receive Communion every day during Lent. That meant no breakfast before church and so the students would then eat their breakfast in the form of a sandwich of some kind at their desks, at least at Holy Spirit; and they were never finished by the time class started. Now this meant that the classroom smelled like sandwiches all morning, every morning at least until lunch. There was a lunchroom in the basement and I've always wondered why it was never used for breakfast during Lent, but it never was. For some of us with sensitive noses, whatever we were taught during Lent never landed during the morning hours because we were too busy trying to think of something, anything really, to keep from being nauseous. We were also encouraged to give up something for Lent to the glory of our Lord. For me, the choice was simple. After that first Lent and for the five more I would endure at Holy Spirit I gave up sandwiches and to make it extra special, I gave up sandwiches period until sometime after joining the army. I'm pretty sure I was not the only student who was affected that way but I have always wondered if it was only Holy Spirit that did this, or were other Catholic schools in St. Paul more considerate of those of us who didn't always go to Mass during Lent?

Among the many things that I loved growing up, root beer floats have a special place in my heart. In the fifties and early sixties there were several root beer brands around, but the most prominent in my memory were Hires, Dad's and Barq's. Put a couple of scoops of vanilla ice cream in a glass half full of root beer and you were in business with a delicious float. Before you start, let me just remind you that A&W hadn't gotten into canning their terrific root beer yet and so comparisons to a frosty mug root beer float, do not apply. I preferred Hires because it was more carbonated than Dad's for sure, and even Barq's. This seemed to keep the bubble aspect of the float going for just a little longer and when the whole thing finally melted together, well, there just wasn't anything better than sitting in front of the TV watching Richard Diamond talk to his assistant "Sam" (Mary Tyler Moore's legs) and then drinking that last little bit of a root beer float before bed. It was also great because a whole bottle of pop couldn't fit in a glass so you'd keep filling it up, making it like a gift that kept on giving. Thinking about it now, I can't tell you the last time I had a root beer float; sad, really. It's one of the simple joys that got lost along the way.

I'm afraid I can't think about growing up in St. Paul in the fifties and sixties without thinking about hair; not girls hair, but boy's hair. It was a time of great hair role models: Dion, George Chakiris (in "West Side Story"), Jimmy Clanton, James Darren and Elvis of course. The truth is, crewcuts were great but only looked good on less than ten percent of those wearing them. They were great for accenting everything wrong with your face: big or small ears, the same with noses and pimples of course. There was a version called a "Hollywood" which was a crewcut on top with long hair on the sides; again, great for some, not so great for others. So... you'd sit home and watch commercials about how to look better: Top Brass, Brylcreem, Vitalis, and many, many others featuring male models you'd never be as good looking as, no matter how hard you tried and nobody tried any harder than I did. I had and still do have very fine textured hair and used to drown it daily in Wildroot Hair Tonic trying to get it just right and rarely succeeding. It became an obsession because no matter where I went, nearly everyone had cooler hair than I did. Add the TV ads to that, and it was hopeless. Even Perry Mason had better hair than me. My best friend in those days had thick, wavy hair and theorized once that he got it by eating a lot of peanut butter. I binged on peanut butter for days; nothing happened. My life would have been a lot simpler without several of my...let's just call them problems, and hair was one of them. Then one day (and I remember it like it was yesterday), I woke up and combed my hair and it was great! I got on the bus and made a "grand tour" of St. Paul so that everyone could see my hair: downtown, University and Snelling, the Highland Pool and finally, Randolph and Hamline where I hung out. When I say it was great growing up in St. Paul, I conveniently leave my neurotic episodes behind. I do so because there are people on this site who knew me back then and can attest to my eccentricities and I'd rather not get them riled up. If you're a guy and never cared about how your hair looked growing up, more power to you. Sadly, I can't say that.

It's only right that I concede that it's easier to wax philosophical about St. Paul winters from the rarefied air of Monrovia, California, than from a bar stool at the Badger Lounge on University, especially in February. There's a wonderful song, several actually, from "Mr. Magoo's Christmas Carol" which I love and watch every year (because I own it), and it's called "Winter was Warm". Scrooge is just being shown the door by the one love of his life for being too interested in money, when she recalls how he used to be in this lovely song. I really can't take winter anymore and didn't do well with it when I had to, but there were some fun times and more of them in St. Paul than any I can think of living out here. There we were, all five of us, standing up on a toboggan going over the cow path on Highland golf course and daring the gods to inflict great bodily harm on us as we flew off in all directions. There was going downtown which seemed magical in the winter and forgive me saying so, but I was an all season admirer of the ladies; and frankly, all bundled up in the winter waiting for a bus for example, women looked as good as they ever did in summer. There were a few good snowball fights and tackling each other in the snow was good for a laugh now and then, and that's not even mentioning stopping by the Oak Room for a night cap when we had grown up. It's true I may go to hell for the thoughts I had when hitchhiking at below zero and seeing a driver reach over as if to open the door, and watch them lock their passenger side door. If I do, I feel that quite a few of those drivers will be there before me and we'll talk about that then.

I was listening to "What I Did For Love" from "A Chorus Line" the other day and the old Holy Spirit playground came to mind. It was a fenced in playground with lots of playground equipment: Teeter-Totters, a merry-go- round type thing that the big kids would get going so fast nobody could get on and if you were little you couldn't get off; monkey bars, a maypole and three sets of swings. Then there was one swing better than all the rest. It had a big thick chain and you could get going real high so it was just great. When you were lucky enough to get that swing, you just stayed on it until the bell to go in rang. I'm sure it was no more than second grade and I fell in love with a little blond girl named Janet Shore. She lived down on Randolph near Chatsworth and we used to kiss between the garages across the alley from her house (ask Nick Tschida). One day, I was on the treasured swing on the playground and I saw her pass by. I slowed down with my feet but still jumped off higher than I ever had and somehow kept my balance. Just then and for days later, I realized I was in love. Janet moved away before third grade but I never forgot her. I gave up the best swing on the playground for her, no small thing in those days. That's what I did for love, the first time anyway.

When I was kid in the fifties and if there was any kind of dispute as to who did what and what year it happened and so forth, we had our own version of Google. It was called the *St. Paul Dispatch.* "Call the *Dispatch*", someone would say and someone would and presumably someone would answer and the dialogue went like this, "Hi... listen, didn't Del Flannigan win the Welterweight title from Honeybear Akins? I was there… I know he did." Then it would be, "Yeah, yeah... oh, I see... yeah... well okay, thanks." So he'd come back and shake his head and say, "Awww… he didn't know". Upon further questioning, he would concede that the guy (at the *Dispatch*) said it was a non-title fight. In all the years, I never knew the *Dispatch* to fail to answer a question and so I got the impression they just knew everything and were standing by 24/7 to answer one. Does anyone remember doing that?

In 1959, I was eleven, crazy about baseball and a student at Holy Spirit grade school. I wanted my dad to take me to opening day of the St. Paul Saints that year and made the mistake of telling my mother that Dad promised me he would. It wasn't true, and Dad refused and we never did go to a baseball game together. Still I wanted to go and asked permission to go by myself if my teacher at Holy Spirit, probably Sister Demerice, said I could. She agreed and that was it. I may have had two dollars but I think it was more like a buck and half. I went from Snelling and Randolph to Midway Stadium (when it was on the east side of Snelling). The Saints played the Charleston Colonels of the American Association and it was a beautiful spring day. I got a Peter's Wiener's hot dog and a Coke first and sat down the left field line. It wasn't full but there was enough of a crowd for an eleven year old at his first baseball game, so I settled in and watched the Colonels take the early lead and hold it until the ninth inning. By that time using my money judiciously, I had had Tom Thumb Donuts and a Walnut Hill candy bar and was thinking we'd probably lose by the one run we were trailing by, when Bobby Dolan the Saints shortstop stepped in with a man on base and two out. Even at eleven, I knew the implications. If Bobby were to hit a home run with a man on, the Saints would win. However, I also knew the realities and as I sat there, summing up my day, I knew it had been great fun, even if I was by myself. Even though I was feeling bad about lying to Mom about Dad, a new door of independence had been opened and just then the slight hitting Bobby Dolan hit a home run that just sneaked over the fence and the Saints won. I didn't need anyone to share that moment with. I was a part of the greater whole, cheering like mad for our St. Paul Saints. Before writing this, I checked and Bobby Dolan hit one more home run that year and then never again. Dad and I carried on but I never asked him to take me anywhere again; I was eleven, after all.

I was not above bringing a comic book or two to Holy Spirit school when I was growing up. If your class book was big enough, you could lay down the comic between the pages and check it out for a while. Naturally, I got caught one day and was told, along with my punishment, that comic books would "ruin my mind". That was nowhere near some of the other screwy things they told me at Holy

Spirit; which brings me around to Turok, Son of Stone. It was a cool comic with a cool concept. Turok and Andar were two Indians who wandered into a sort of valley that time forgot, where there were dinosaurs and cave men and like that and they got trapped in there. They adapted and weekly their adventures held my attention. I quit reading the series after my comic book years but picked up a copy of Turok near the end of its run because I'd heard Turok got out of the valley. Here's the deal and I never forgot it. Turok got out but Andar, his friend, got hurt and couldn't make it. Turok went back. He couldn't leave his friend behind and as he went back, an earthquake happened or something and his way out was lost, maybe forever. There was a lot to learn growing up in St. Paul back then but some of the biggest lessons were learned outside of the classroom: "Never leave your friend behind". Holy Spirit educated me but in eight years, they never taught me that lesson.

I'm not as well read as you might imagine but I have read enough to give the appearance of someone who is well read. The reading I have done was in fits and starts and when fully engaged in the subject matter, I retained a great deal more than the average bear, making me slightly more of a substantial "would-be intellectual" at least into my thirties. At such a time and during the Carter administration, when nobody had jobs and I didn't even have a car, I found myself applying for jobs and getting there by bus. I was living in Minneapolis near Lake of the Isles and took a bus somewhere and transferred in an effort to get to Hewlett-Packard out on Larpenter near Snelling. On the bus sitting next to me, was a fellow who appeared to be not quite all there. He struck up a conversation with me and began by saying public television was the only outlet showing interpretations of American classic adaptations to which I agreed, and he immediately referenced the "Big Blond" by Dorothy Parker of the Algonquin Round Table which played on Channel 2 the night before, featuring Sally Kellerman. Slowly I turned and said, "Yes, I saw that too. It was very good I thought." He sort of shrugged and said, "Robert Benchley's influence, wouldn't you say?" I started the day without a car and taken by surprise as I was, nodded slowly, looked at him and said, "perhaps" and wondered all day and for years and even decades now, if this fellow had bated me into revealing that I really didn't know what I was talking about. Because I didn't...not then anyway; or if perhaps, given to his appearance, he just went around revealing phonies all day of which I was one. I was at Minnehaha and Snelling with no car and no forthcoming job at Hewlett-Packard either. That was quite literally thirty-one years ago and I can recall it like it was last week. I always wonder at the random encounters that seemed put there for a reason that linger in my memory.

St. Paul is a great sports town and never restricted to local sports only. It's basketball season once again and in 1974, UCLA had an 88-game winning streak (imagine that kind of domination today). Ironically, the last time they had lost was to Notre Dame 88-games earlier, and that day I was sitting in Fabian's Bar on St. Clair, just off Fairview and a block from my mother's apartment. I'm almost certain I was not alone and I cannot remember who I was with. Whoever it was never had my sense of sports history, which is probably why I have blocked him out in my memory. Fabian's was like any number of beloved local neighborhood bars in St. Paul: 3.2 beers, a grill with burgers and fries, a watering hole for the locals and on that day, a sports heaven whose witnesses became immortal in my mind. Notre Dame was at home and trailing by eleven, as they should be, to the best team in college history. So there I am, an ex-Catholic (if not agnostic) and I feel this kind of intuition I'd learned through a lifetime of impossible comebacks. It kind of blacks out everything else, and I looked down at my half-eaten hamburger. When I looked up it became magical and soon, an eleven point lead became only one and with under a minute, from deep in the corner, Dwight Clay of Notre Dame (who hadn't made a shot all day), put up a shot I swear I never had one doubt about. I knew it was in. As if to reaffirm the impossibility of it all, the ball rattled in the basket before falling in. Never mind that UCLA had four good chances to win the game after that, you just knew other forces were at work. They missed and the Fighting Irish were back in the national spotlight. There were so many wonderful neighborhood bars in St. Paul and yet on that day, one patron saw the impossible at Fabian's on St. Clair and Fairview. Not fertile ground to witness sports miracles, you say? Nonsense!

There is a poem by Thomas Ford called, "There Was a Lady Sweet and Kind" and while I never read all of it until five minutes ago, I came to it at an early age growing up in St. Paul beginning with its third and fourth lines: "I did but see her passing bye, and yet I'll love her 'til I die." The Christmas season: the department stores, the crowds downtown, the marquees of the Riviera and Strand, Paramount and Orpheum, and the light snow falling and all of it punctuated with "Merry Christmas!", made fertile ground for falling in love. For me, it was a time when women were never more beautiful and if not love in reality, a falling in love with love itself and hoping to know one day, a partner for the season. I remember as a boy one Christmas following a girl into Musicland on 7th and Wabasha. How gorgeous she was, and I took great care not to be seen staring at her over the 45's. Oh, the memories of meeting her, loving her and spending a lifetime doing so, only to watch her pay for her records, say Merry Christmas with a smile I'll never forget and walk out of my life forever. It was okay to do that because I wished those wonderful things for her as well. I was in love with the season and all that went with it. There are those who would pigeonhole Christmas in any number of ways but the romance of the season lives on, year after year. Yes, I often hide from Christmas as many of you of my age do; but as long as I can remember when I didn't, love in all its forms will always be a part of it. I've thought about that girl in Musicland, for nearly sixty years and while she never knew me, the memory of it still warms me all these years later. Merry Christmas!

Weather extremes in Minnesota and Minneapolis and St. Paul are noteworthy but neither of the Twin Cities holds the statewide record in hot or cold. Tower, Minnesota, (near Virginia) has the cold record at -60 in 1996, and Moorhead (tying Beardsley of 1917) with +114 in 1936. Compared with the Twin Cities, our records are about half as cold at -30 in 1888 and +108 in 1936. Of course, there was no mention of the wind or humidity in these particular records but I'm sure you can just imagine. I've been to Tower on Lake Vermilion and my son and I caught +115 on our way to Las Vegas once. Again, we seem to take a certain pride in growing up and living in extreme weather. I began my radio career in Thief River Falls and started in January when a scandal rocked the region. It seems that Bemidji, perennial competitor with International Falls for coldest spot in the nation, was actually under reporting their overnight low temperature to appear colder than International Falls. Records notwithstanding, the stretch of the Mississippi River at Randolph to the Mississippi River at Shepard Road (where winter winds run unobstructed and straight as an arrow up and down across peninsular St. Paul), is the coldest stretch on earth. Go ahead, ask someone who went to St. Catherine's, St. Paul Academy, Cretin, Mattock's, Holy Spirit, St. James or Monroe. It's true, even now I sit here pontificating in relatively ideal weather in California, but those who never left can tell you, winter on Randolph in St. Paul was as severe a test as you'll ever face.

Sometime around 1962 I was with my friend downtown on Wabasha where there was a Hardy's shoe store. While there, a little disappointment drama played out that I could have gotten turned around. I didn't and while it's stayed with me for nearly sixty years, I was thinking today that how it affected me, almost certainly made a positive difference in some of the lives of people I've dealt with along the way. A boy a few years younger than I was came into the store and asked if nine dollars was enough to by a new pair of Flamenco boots. The pair he had was wearing out. The sales clerk said nine-ninety nine. The kid was visibly crestfallen and a moment later, he was gone. I had more than a dollar and could have made up the difference because he looked like maybe he never had the advantages I did. He left so fast I was just paralyzed with inaction and the moment was lost. I still feel bad about it and it's funny because I know the memory of that day made me more charitable throughout my life because of it. I seldom dwell on the right things I did and allow the wrong things to haunt me, so I need to back up and give myself the credit that that little scene inspired in me. This is perhaps more of the neurotic Skip Savage, who grew up in St. Paul, but I do wonder why doing a nice or thoughtful thing flies right under the radar and maybe the lesson that inspires it hangs on like a scar of some kind. Everything I learned growing up, I learned in St. Paul. I often feel as though I'm still learning.

Because my parents were caretakers, I had a lot of advantages and in the dead of winter, playing in the laundry room just across the hallway was a big one. This one game I devised was my favorite ever. The laundry room had metal clotheslines and when they rattled it was terrible so you couldn't play under those, but the area between the nearest clothes line and the coin operated washer and dryer was fine. There was a space between the washer and dryer and that was usable too. All of the apartments had meters that were on one end and extended into the playable area plus there was a low ceiling. I fashioned a basket out of the a clothespin bag with a cardboard back board and played my version of basketball nearly every night one year. For a ball I used this small rubber ball and the other basket was a coffee can nailed to a board hung on the outside of the clothes lines. My imaginary games were intense and I announced the play by play under my breath along with the cheers of the crowd. I shot left and right handed and gave each guy a different name. There were running hook shots, fall away shots, free throws and extremely animated goofy shots. Shooting the ball into the clothespin bag was not easy but there's one night I never will forget. It was a high scoring affair between me and the other me, and the me shooting into the clothespin bag became unstoppable: I couldn't miss. There were long shots and with the low ceiling, nearly impossible to make falling-down-left-handed shots. I'll bet I made fifteen in a row. It almost scared me. By the next winter I had grown too tall and I couldn't play there anymore. However that last winter, I was as great as anyone who ever played laundry room basketball; and since all the other players were me as well, that was saying something.

If you told this little boy and especially the little girl that they were going to Disneyland, they couldn't have been more excited than they were that day going with their mother to Newell Park. They told the driver and everyone on the bus that that's where they were going. I don't know why I've always remembered the episode or why I was on the Snelling bus out that far past Minnehaha, because I never usually was. I had never heard of Newell Park. The only park I knew of that could generate that kind of excitement in the area was Como Park. Frankly, this mother didn't look like she could afford the price of rides and so forth at Como. The children had bag lunches and were so thrilled with their excursion, I remember admiring their mother for instilling in her kids the sense of a special outing that she could afford, and smiling and laughing with them. Years later, I discovered Newell Park, surrounded on three sides by Hewlett, Fairview and Pierce Butler Road. It was indeed a beautiful little 30-acre public park and I knew as I stood there it would be beautiful to me because of the young mother and her kids that day years ago. Sometime after that, we moved up on Blair and my daughter Lisa started first grade at Hancock Elementary. After dropping her off the first day and meeting her teacher and watching her take a seat in the classroom, I felt a little emotional and drove the few blocks to Newell Park again. I may not have known where I was going that day on the Snelling bus, but I've remembered that mother and her two kids for more than fifty years.

Growing up in St. Paul in the fifties, I had many role models but most of them were on TV or in comic books. I've always said my two main models were Tarzan and Jack Paar and I kind of broke it down to two things, really. Tarzan had mastery over everything I feared as a child and Jack Paar, because he showed me that even if I never mastered my fears, with wit and self-effacing humor it would somehow be all right. However, there was a guy in my neighborhood in St. Paul who you just couldn't help but admire. He was three years older than I was and seemed more mature, sharper and just headed for bigger things more than everyone else. His name was Tom Schwartz and he went to Cretin. I never knew him, but I saw him play basketball a few times at Holy Spirit. After that, he went to the U.S Military Academy at West Point, received his commission and began what would become a distinguished military career, retiring as a four-star General. When I looked him up and found that out, I wasn't surprised. He just seemed like a winner through and through and indeed, he was. We would cross paths in Vietnam years later as he was arriving in August of 1968, while I was going home. Local role models were important to me growing up. They held the bar a little higher and to an underachiever like me, they sort of showed what was possible. I needed that.

I remember hearing one story about the Clover Club that came out of the 60's that was somewhat interesting and inventive in terms of dealing with a problem they had. Without mentioning any names, there was a wide cross section of tough guys who frequented the bar and as a result, there were some altercations and soon, regular people were getting scared away. So this is how they solved the problem: they made all the tough guys bouncers, all of them and yes, there were times of an evening when there were more bouncers in the place than patrons, but the idea was like the old wild west. There, they'd take the toughest bad guy and make him Sheriff and if he had cronies, they'd make them deputies. University Avenue was changing during this period and the Clover never did return to the popularity it once enjoyed but I always liked that story.

This, at least in part, is about a guy I knew who became popular with women after he got married. As a result, he began looking at his marriage as an impediment to this newfound popularity and split from his wife. After that, he couldn't get arrested. None of the women who found him so cute while he was married wanted anything to do with him; more on him later. Each year in St. Paul is held something called "Grand Ole Days". Grand Avenue is shut off for about three miles and there are events and it's a fun time. My friend had a dog that had puppies and he thought it would be a good idea to bring the puppies and find them homes. He cut a box in half, put a towel and the puppies in it and made a sign that said, "Free Puppies." Hours passed and many people stopped to see the puppies but none of them took one. By this time, my friends and I had had a few beers and weren't paying much attention so when his daughter came along and asked if she could take charge of the puppy concession, he said fine. Twenty minutes later, all the puppies were gone. His daughter turned over the sign that said "Free Puppies" and wrote, "Puppies…$5.00" and made herself twenty-five dollars. It finally occurred to me why my friend couldn't get laid after leaving his wife. People like things better if they have a perceived value. Free puppies are fine but $5.00 puppies are a wonderful bargain. As a married man, my friend had a perceived value and the women in his office found that little bump provided him with just a little more sex appeal than he had without it. Actually, he was lucky. His wife took him back and whether he learned the same lesson or not, as far as I know they stayed together. Perceived value…it seems a small thing but I've seen it time and again. Price anything right and it flies off the shelves. Offer to give it away and watch them yawn.

Because it is St. Patrick's Day, I decided to look up St. Walter this morning and I found three: St. Walter of Pontoise, just St. Walter of the eleventh century and another just St. Walter of the thirteenth. The first two were abbots in the Benedictine order and one was Augustinian. They didn't do very much at all and nothing that would get them a sainthood by today's standards. There were no miracles connected with these three and somewhere in my memory there was a book that told of another St. Walter when I was a student at Holy Spirit school in St. Paul. This person was a jouster with a horse and a lance and he participated in Tournaments. One day he was on his way to a tournament and someone needed help. I can't remember what kind of help, just help of some kind. Anyway, knowing he would miss the tournament and maybe some prize money along the way, he stayed and provided the...help. Having done that, he went on to the tournament only to find that he was a big hero. He had arrived he was told and had won every test a jouster participated in. His kindness you see, inspired a replacement in his name from on high and while there was no mention of prize money, this certainly qualified as a miracle and according to this book, that's how he became St. Walter. St. Patrick is said to have driven the snakes out of Ireland but lost his sainthood in a purge of the twentieth century where suspect saints lost their titles. I'm guessing St. Walter the jouster probably lost his too, while the three other St. Walters did not. They were judged by a higher standard I guess.

84544018R00125

Made in the USA
Lexington, KY
22 March 2018